T0064035

Transition, Infinity, and Ecstasy

Transition, Infinity, and Ecstasy

SURESH HARIRAMSAIT

PARTRIDGE
A Penguin Random House Company

Copyright © 2016 by Suresh Hariramsait.

ISBN:	Hardcover	978-1-4828-6946-0
	Softcover	978-1-4828-6945-3
	eBook	978-1-4828-6944-6

All rights reserved. No part of this book may be used or reproduced by any means, graphic, electronic, or mechanical, including photocopying, recording, taping or by any information storage retrieval system without the written permission of the author except in the case of brief quotations embodied in critical articles and reviews.

Because of the dynamic nature of the Internet, any web addresses or links contained in this book may have changed since publication and may no longer be valid. The views expressed in this work are solely those of the author and do not necessarily reflect the views of the publisher, and the publisher hereby disclaims any responsibility for them.

Print information available on the last page.

To order additional copies of this book, contact
Partridge India
000 800 10062 62
orders.india@partridgepublishing.com

www.partridgepublishing.com/india

SYNOPSIS

"World (s) in thier entirety though expanded, permeated into, *experienced* and realized would still be insufficient to Hail and realize the infinite and rare One ..."(*"Ullagellam unarndhu odharkku ariaven"*), says the 12th century Tamil Saivaite saint Sekkizhar in his Periapuranam, but is that state of cosmic-expansiveness our true nature?

It is indeed, for often it is mentioned in ancient Indian texts like the Srimad Bhagavata that those like Kardama and Kapila who attained 'Superconsciousness' and thus Perfection, led normal lives and, *"went about the world with an expanded state of consciousness"*.

Lord Krishna in the Bhagavad Gita explains that the human body as a field (*Kshetram*) at the microcosmic-level but the 'knower' of the field (*Kshetrajnan*) the Soul at the macrocosmic-level can cover the entire universe. Thirumoolar another Perfected Being explains even more elaborately when he says that the 'Chakras' which are vortexes, energy and 'Wisdom'- Centres in man's subtle bodies contain the 'tattvas' or principle-elements of the *"seven upper and seven lower worlds"*(in various dimensions) that contain the entire cosmos and hence the *full-blown Yogi* in an expanded state of consciousness can be anywhere at a given moment for he is *everywhere* in omnipresence! Moreover apart from the physical body, man possesses the ethereal and spiritual bodies which are all ultra-subtle in nature and built of atoms of higher worlds, so in reality he *exists*, reacts and always moves in multi-dimensional space but is not *aware* of it.

J.Krishnamurti had said:" *It is all about space...*" And man by *becoming* space transcends time whereby like many a Perfected being becomes Master of the 'three times' (Trikalajnani), the past, the present and the future. To become space Lord Shiva himself in the 'Vijnana Bhairava Tantra' gives simple techniques to realize His omnipresent-state and among 112 of them, the first nine techniques deals on how to attain that exalted state by involving and delving into the science of the breath – if we take one end of the bridge (the breath) that connects ourselves (which is *our* universe, the body), the other end connects us to *infinite-universes* or infinity, which is available here and *now*.

One needs to realize that the air that we inhale is only the gross part (the vehicle) while Prana which is the *sum total* of all energies is the subtle part. When one through pranayama (the yogic-breathing technique and art of control and regulation of prana) is able to control prana within the body, the infinite prana existing in the cosmos comes under his control! So all of nature comes under the control of the master of the breath, all normal laws of physics and chemistry does not apply to him, he could like Jesus Christ, Moses, Lord Krishna, saint Anthony, saint Kumaraguruparar, Eknath, saint Vaikuntar, Sri Aurobindo, the Mother of Pondicherry among others control all forces of nature and thus part ocean-waters, change the course of rivers, control storms, bring and stop rains etcetra; he can levitate and float on air, walk on water, lift enormous weights (like the rhinoceros beetle that lifts a hundred times its own weight while at the same time inhaling four times more air than it normally does, swami Chinmoy the Spiritual Guru of the Olympian Carl Lewis lifted a small plane weighing more than seven tons and Lord Krishna did the same effortlessly with the govardhana mountain), teleport to distant places and be back in a jiffy (like Guru Nanak, Saint Ramalingam and Sadasiva Brahmendra had done) and deadly poisons would not affect him and all weapons (including nuclear radiation) would harmlessly pass through him! Normal breathing through the nose is not performed and he can draw in prana under the earth, under water and even in vacuum for prana exists everwhere.

Moreover the Lord says in the 'Shri Shiva Gita' that the one who meditates with the 'feel', belief and faith (bhava) that he *is* the Lord who spans all of space is the person most dear to him.

Could man 'connect' with other life-forms and of his own kind with distance being of no consequence?

Lord Krishna in the Bhagavad Gita explains that the one with perfect equilibrium (*samadharshini*) and whose twin hemispheres of the brain functions in totality (*cittaprajnan*) is the master of the universe.

Carl Sagan in 'Cosmos' and 'Broca's Brain' claims that there are a *hundred billion* stars in our galaxy *alone* and estimates that there could be a *billion black holes* in each galaxy ...) and the late Dr.Ramamurthi a neurosurgeon of Chennai who has said that there are more than 100 billion neurons in the human brain which could telephathically connect with the equal number of people on earth with distance being of no consequence and Michael Crichton in 'Andromeda Strain' who says that in an average human-gut which is equal in size to a normal thermos flask there are more bacteria than the global human population ... And Dr.Abigail (microbiologist at the University of Illinois also an expert on human-microbial interactions): "Microbes *converse* with human cells according to microbiologists;" *they function like our mother.... We should love them... we are in equilibrium...*", so interaction between all life-forms is taking place.

World-wide and from time immemorial man has been in the quest of his roots as well of his *true* nature whether it is the Soul or the Self as addressed by the ancient Sages of India. Had man descended from stars and planets from perhaps other planes and dimensions as many ancient cultures presume and even claim, an alien? Where does he *return* to after death?

Is interstellar travel possible and were there alien visits to earth for many skeptics like the astro-phycisist Stephen Hawking have their doubts? But recently Hawking who knows the number of stars and planets (with over seven septillion (22 zeroes) stars in the 'discernible' universe alone and varying number of planets around each star) that could be in the so-called 'habitable zone' (explained vastly by the late Carl Sagan the former Director of NASA and SETI and others) believes that "thinking about aliens perfectly rational." Modern astronomers also know that there are innumerable 'parallel universes' that our future spaceships could traverse by taking shortcuts (for even travelling at the speed of light which is 300,000 kilometres per second, it would still take 12 billion years to cover the distance seen by our most powerful telescopes!) through 'wormholes'(blackholes?) and tunnels that are portals that connect them.

Many ancient scripts like the Srimad Bhagavata and the 'Kandha Puranam' clearly state that there are countless universes in many planes and dimensions and 'Vimanas' or ariel-crafts flew at 'thought-speed'(*mano veha*) and *tunneled* through the universes. There were the 'rotating firebrand'; three huge vimanas that were practically 'floating cities' that had gardens, pools and waterfalls within them that had stealth technology; King Sooran ruled over a "thousand and eight universes"(1008 andam), was Lord of the *Asuras* or Titans and battled the *Devas* or Angels on earth in southern India and his vimana could fly over land, water, underwater, hover in space, could disappear and reappear in another place which was eventually destroyed by Lord Muruga's 'Vel' – "the missile with the lengthy flame" (*nedunchudar Vel*); the *'Peacock Craft'* that could traverse the 14 planes and fly beyond within a micro-second!; the 'Agni ratha'(fiery chariot) of the four 'mind born' sons of the Creator that landed on the 'Lemuria continent' millions of years ago; Priavarta's craft *"the fellies of which dug up the depths of our seven oceans ..."*!

Does the transition of the soul through multiple planes and dimensions and countless births over billions of years from the lowest form of life, right from the single-sense and to man of six-senses and does the evolution from the animal-like man to god-like or divine-man end there for enlightenment or realization of his true divine-nature alone triggers his blossoming and realization of infinity?

Does infinity mean man is immortal as claimed by the Vedas and the Siddhars who say that immortality is already *programmed* within him as the *'Kala tattva'* or 'Time concept' and does does man possess infinite knowledge (for man is not just a 'Super Computer' but the *'Supreme Computer'* who contains *all* Knowledge) as the *'Kalai tattva'* or 'Art Principle' (the *"64 branches of Knowledge"* that includes astronomy, astrology, medicine, engineering, dance, drama, music, painting, sculpting, prose, grammar, archery, wrestling, fencing, mathematics, ...) *and* 'Divine Wisdom' (which also includes knowledge of *all* known and unknown languages, even the languages of the beasts and birds ... as King Solomon and Sage Narada did) as the *'Para Vidya'*? Worldly and Divine Wisdom is revealed which is *True Total Recall!*

Adi Sankara in his Viveka Chudamani says that just as it is a fallacy to think that the space within a pot (*gada akasa*) and without it are different, similarly the individual mind and the Cosmic mind are no different. When Total Knowledge of the Soul (*suddha chaitanya*) is realized, which is nothing but Pure Consciousness, there is absolutely no difference between the Creator and the created.

Was man programmed to grow to be even 100 feet tall in an earlier era as many religions and cultures claim that there were giants on earth in those days just as there were gigantic animals and birds?

Does transition which is the endless cycle of birth and death end only when man attains the golden radiant-form of the Lord which unlike the physical body is not constructed of atoms of our plane?

Can man conquer death by realizing the "science of breath" and attain immortallity and transit through the various planes and dimensions (transition or death to the fully evolved being is performed with *total awareness* and is pre-determined and he either leaves his physical body willingly (known as *iccha mrityu* in Sanskrit) or de-materializes, that is disappear) and finally transcend to the highest plane by evolving into various bodies and tattvas (principles) of the relative planes which he already posseses as claimed by the Perfected persons the *Siddhars* (Siddhas in Sanskrit) like Thiruvalluvar?

Can the ageing process be *reversed* and can one *turn young* (for eternity) as claimed by Siddhars like Sivavakkiar and proved by Perfected Beings like Lord Chaitanya and Saint Ramalingam whose transfiguration were witnessed by many? Though the glorification of the physical body is spurned by most, Siddhars like Thirumoolar and Sri Aurobindo in 'The Supramental Manifestation' and 'The Synthesis of Yoga' emphatically state that for Perfection to be complete the physical body too has to become Perfect. How many years does it take for one to turn perfect? When this question was put to the Mother of Pondicherry, she replied:" *300 years, or even a 1000 years!*" When questioned again a thousand years from when, replied:" *A Thousand years from when one realizes and starts the process!*" So one can understand that Perfection takes place over thousands of births!

Could the Siddhars who were masters of alchemy (*rasavadham*) turn base metal into gold and did they possess herbal-potions by utilizing which they could teleport to distant places?

Does man attain the 'Eight Great Supernatural Powers' (*Ashtanga Siddhis*) while on the verge of Perfection and is levitation of the physical body only a sign of it for in Sanskrit '*Uthapena*' or levitation is explained as just as the string acquires the fragrance of the flowers strung on it, man's physical body too gradually attains the qualities of the subtle or spiritual body?

Does everything have 'life' within it as many ancient Indian texts like the 'Sri Shiva Rahasya' say that life is said to be in the '*sleep-state*' in stones, in the '*dream-state*' in plants and trees, in the '*woken-state*' in animals, in the '*reasoning-state*' in man and in the '*Blissfull or Eternally happy-state*' in Enlightened man? Do all the rivers, lakes, mountains, planets, stars have an individual Soul as claimed by Siddhars (Perfected Beings) and is the claim of a Japanese Scientist who says that the earth itself is a gigantic living-organism and the claim of the *System Theorists* of the Western countries who say that like innumerable cells constitute an organ and many organs constitute a body, countless life-forms constitute the earth, true? Thirumoolar a Tamil Siddhar or Perfected Being claims emphatically:"*One alone creates the worlds seven; One alone sustains the world seven, One alone destroys the worlds seven; One alone is the worlds seven along with* **all lives** *too.*"("…*Oruvanumae ullagodu uierthanae.*")

Does the Soul extend to infinity as the Vedas claim and do they have eyes, ears, arms and legs in all directions (transcend space and thus time) for 'Kshatriya' or warrior-clan of ancient India, the 'Ninjas' and 'Samurai' of Japan and 'Tanjian Monks' of China could *telescope* their hearing to incredible distances, *sense* opponents hidden beyond walls and *see* persons and events of the past *and* future? Could the Ninjas in a deep meditative-state send endorphins coursing through their blood-stream to calm and cure massive injuries within a few minutes and the Siddhars of India making even cancerous-growths and severe body-mutilations regain their former normal-state within 'no-time'?

Is the Siddhars claim that by *becoming* space (for the Soul is said to be nothing but Pure Consciousness that totally *encompasses* space) one can not only teleport to distant places and be back in a jiffy but can be present at two or more places at the same time as Jesus Christ, saint Anthony (of Padua), Guru Nanak (the founder of Sikhism), Sadasiva Brahmendra, Saint Ramalingam and many others had done, true?

Like Albert Einstein had utilized the magnetic field created around the U.S. Naval ship 'Eldridge' (by placing a huge copper rod measuring 400 feet which was the length of the ship, which was again wound in copper wire and passing electricity like it is done within electric-generators) to propel and teleport the ship from Philadelphia to Norfolk a distance of about 400 miles within no-time, could man also teleport to distant places and be back in a jiffy by utilizing his magnetic-field or bio plasmic body that he as well as the earth and all heavenly-bodies possess (astronomers have recently discovered huge rotating magnetic-fields that could be portals to other dimensions and other 'parallel universes') caused by their spin and the molten-iron at the core causing the alternate flow of northern and southern poles, could man also who possesses the same fiery-form being the Creative-Power or Energy of the Lord (the *Kundalini Shakti*) at the base Chakra (whirling vortexes of energy and wisdom centre) to teleport?

Can one attain the strength of an elephant or a tiger by performing *Samyama* (meditative-state of coalescing 'dharana','dhyana' and 'samadhi' into one) as claimed by Saint Patanjali in his 'Yoga Sutras'?

Can one become immune to all diseases and immune to all natural and man-made toxins and poisons just by practicing yogic-breathing, yogic-meditation, chanting mantras or prayers combined with faith as claimed by the Siddhars of India, Jesus Christ and modern research which says that even hereditary genetic-diseases could be rectified by mere continuous positive-thinking? Can the Siddhars who have the sight of the 'third-eye' perceive diseases manifesting in the *Causal-body* (being an ultra-subtle body that we possess; *kaarana udal* in Tamil) itself and cleanse them even months or years before taking root in the physical body thus even negating 'karmaic' diseases which in modern terminology is known as genetic-diseases? Can these manifestations which can be termed as 'magnetic-impurities' that resemble miniscule bats, spiders, crabs and scorpions that latch on to the subtle bodies of man in hordes (drunkards, drug-addicts, rapists and serial-murderers are often their target and induce them to indulge in their hineous-crimes)be flushed away by pranic-breathing, sound-vibrations and bathing in salt-water etc., as claimed by the Siddhars for it has now been found that wild-cats purr at a certain frequency to help cure cuts and wounds and make their bones denser which are now being utilized in humans too? (Scientists from the 'Fauna Communications Research Institute' in Carolina, U.S.A., have found that the sound frequency of a house-cat is between 27 and 44 kilohertz and 20 to 50 for all wildcats. Exposure to frequencies of 20-50 HZ strengthens human bones ...)

Does the hindrance of the flow of any form of energy bring about sickness and ultimately lead to death? According to Ayurveda, Siddha and Chinese medicine, the hindrance in *flow* of energy – 'Prana' or 'Chi' results in ill-health in the human body and similarly it is with blood-flow, flow of money and blocking the flow of river-waters (which is also energy), that slowly but surely chokes the river as well as hosts of life-forms to death and ultimately the earth itself is grieveously harmed.

'Phantom limbs' are felt or sensations are *experienced* by amputees according to Dr.Ramachandra of the U.S.A. but according to the Saiva Siddhanta Philosophy of the Tamils these are true to the fullest poible sense for the Siddhars have proved through experiments that the extension of the amputated portion lives on in the dream or subtle-body (and so it is with any part of the body being removed and problems exist for hormones and others like the endocrine glands keep on secreting chemicals irrespective whether certain organs are removed or not) but it is not so in a person *born* with a deformity. The Mother of Pondicherry mentions that a person dreamt of going blind in her left eye, and a few months later it happened likewise. Similarly when the bridge between the physical and subtle bodies are severed, the person turns insane. On the verge of death, a veil between the physical and subtle bodies lift and hence man is able to have glimpses and experiences of the 'other worlds' and 'after-death experiences' and so

Thomas Alva Edison like many others, was able to claim on the verge of death:" *It is very beautiful over there…!*"

Is it possible to disable and even kill other life-forms by power of sight alone? Though killing any life is never allowed under normal circumstances, there are very secretive techniques that makes it possible to do so and in Tamil it is known as '*Varma Kalai*'. There are various types of varmas, one is '*Thodu varma*' where one has to touch certain vital spots on the body to eiher cure or disable a person; there is the 'Soll Varma' where by chanting specific mantras the result is attained like Saint Ramalingam made robbers immobile by chanting the '*Pitchh*' mantra; then there is the '*Nokku varma*' where by power of sight alone persons are made immobile or even killed like the Sufi Saint the celebrated Shaikh, Muhyi-ud-Din al-Arabi was able to arrest three extremely tall persons (giants) circumambulating the Holy Kaaba in Mecca by mere power of sight alone known in Arabic as '*Habs-i-nazir*' and Swami Vivekananda was able to kill a charging mad bull on the streets of Chicago in 1893. The Ninjas of Japan would shatter walls and squeeze the heart of person all from a distance by suddenly expanding their '*Kokoro*' or "secret inner-heart" or by chanting '*Akshara*' (Sanskrit mantras sourced from the ancient Vedas) and making it bounce off the 'membrane' or the Spirit within.

Were there huge birds and animals that had become extinct for the Tamil Siddhars say that there was a huge bird that could snatch and carry away animals that were ten times the weight of elephants known as the '*andabahirandam*'; the 'Kamba Ramayana' among other texts mentions a huge snake the 'anaicondran' (which seems very much like the 'anaconda') that literally means 'elephant-killer' which could *swallow* an elephant; and there are stone-carvings found in ancient temples depicting an extinct enormous gigantic dragon-like creature known as the '*Yazhi*' (pronounced as 'yallhi' in Tamil) holding in their tails elephants which seem puny in size in comparison?

Do exotic plants, trees, insects and other alien-creatures exist in the higher and lower planes as it is mentioned in Indian texts like the Srimad Bhagavad Purana and Periapuranam and in the the Holy Quran and Hadith another Holy book of Islam that there exists huge bird-like creatures with human heads; human-headed serpents (known as nagas); serpent-headed persons like Saint Patanjali and three-legged persons like Saint Brighu; single-tusked white elephant of Lord Indra the Lord of the Angels known as 'Iravatham' that carried the Chera Dynasty Emperor 'Cheraman Peruman' to Kailash the Ultimate heaven with Sundarar accompanying him on 'Pancha kalyani' a five-hued horse; single-legged deer; 'Parijatha' a sweet-smelling flower bearing plant brought down from heaven to earth by Lord Krishna with heavenly-bees following...; the heavenly wish-fulfilling cow (*Kamadhenu*) and wish-fulfilling tree (*Karpagavrksha*); 'Ul-Burraq' a heavenly-horse that had the body of a steed, face of a woman and tail of a peacock that carried the Holy Prophet Mohammed beyond the seven heavens and to Ultimate Heaven...?

What is really evolution, is ours the *only* evolutionary-cycle taking place and if man takes only a single birth what is the pinnacle that is to be attained and how is that only a handfull or so have evolved to that degree of Perfection? If the yeast (The yeast which is a single-celled living organism itself contains 6000 genes and its 'full' DNA or genome contains 12 million units of DNA. The DNA carry the code for 6000 genes, each of varying coding sequences and fewer than half of these genes are known to biologists and their functions remain yet to be determined...), bacteria, grass, shrub, creeper, plant, neem-tree, bristle-cone pine, worm, ant, termite, spider, beetle, fruit-fly, butterfly, mantis, bat, parrot, pigeon, hawk, eagle, humming-bird, artic-tern, weaver, penguin, frog, tortoise, shark, dolphin, crocodile and hosts of life-forms attained Perfection,(even the honey-bee and its hive is perfect according to Charles Darwin:" *Beyond this stage of perfection in architecture, natural selection could not lead; for the comb of the hive-bee, as far as we can see, is absolutely perfect in economizing labour and wax.*") Why hasn't man attained the exalted-state of Perfection?

Are there many cycles of creation and if so is Adam only the father of *modern man*?

Are dreams and visions meaningless and merely *wishfull-thinking* and *wish-fulfillments* as many like Sigmund Freud the father of modern psychiatry and psycho-analysis say they are, or are they channels through which messages are being received right from ancient luminaries, Prophets and more relatively modern ones like Michelangelo, Leonardo Davinci, Mozart, Beethoven, Shakespeare, Milton, Keats, Wordsworth, Neils Bohr, Francis Harry Crick, Bill Lear, Fritjof Capra (who *saw* the 'Cosmic Dance' of Lord Shiva – 'Tao Of Physics') and Walt Disney among a host of others?

Is 'Total Recall' possible and are there "*blocked-off memories*" and a "*collective unconsciousness*" and is man born a '*tabula rasa*' (born with a 'clean slate', pure mind) as claimed by Carl Jung the pupil of Sigmund Freud?

And does the 50 letters (being the alphabets of the Sanskrit language, Tamil, Chinese and Japanese vowel-consonants) contain the entire gamut of sounds and thus contain all languages of the world, the languages of the beast and bird and even of alien origin and all their texts including the ancient Vedas as claimed by Thirumoolar and therefore utilized by Carl Sagan (the astronomer and director of NASA and SETI – Search For Extraterrestrial Intelligence) in 'Voyager' a spacecraft sent by NASA and SETI for a chance encounter with alien-intelligence?

Latent extraordinary powers and talents of man have been all of a sudden and in mysterious ways unravelled of late through 'Acquired Savant Syndrome','Acquired Foreign Accent Syndrome' and other such syndromes worldwide like becoming in a jiffy a genius in mathematics, music etc., and recalling unlearnt languages by receiving unexpected blows to the head, but does Yogic-techniques like knocking the frontal cortex-area of the head and breathing-techniques like '*Kabbala bheti*' activate unused portions of the brain to trigger *complete* 'Total Recall' whereby the person like a Super-Computer that contains infinite reams of knowledge, becomes the *Source* of knowledge, all languages of man, beast and bird, even alien languages and their texts are revealed to him, the "*64 arts*"or "*branches of knowledge*" unfold and even 'Divine Wisdom' unfolds!

Does the 'Full-Blown Yogi' (*Purna Yogi*) attain the 'Eight Great Supernatural Powers' (*Ashtanga* or *Attamaha Siddhis*) and attain 'eternal youth'?

Are ancient places of worship,'Yagas'(sacrificial fire-pits), the Pyramids, Yantras (consecrated metal sheets containing conical, triangular, swastikas and pyramid-shaped figures which could be activated) and the *'Chakras'* (whirling energy-vortexes and psychic-spots in the subtle bodies of man) and the human body itself portals to other dimensions, planes and their worlds?

Are there fairies, angels, demons, titans, many gods and a hierarchy and is there an Ultimate One?

Does the world have frequent alien visits and is interstellar travel possible?

Are the 'after-death worlds' and 'after-death experiences' true as claimed by Thomas Alva Edison, on the verge of death:" *It is very beautiful over there…!"* and also Norman Vincent Peale, Dr.Kubler Ross and to counter this Carl Sagan's "Life after-death Experiences" in 'Broca's Brain'.

What are the Ultimate building blocks of nature if not 'Quarks' which according to the world reknown astro-physicist Stephen Hawking *could* be? Are *'Nada Bindu'* (*'Nada Vindhu'* in Tamil) – 'The Eternal Sound-Light Vibrations', or *'The Eternal Continuum'* the Basic Building block of nature as Vedanta and the Saiva Siddhanta Philosophy of the Tamils claim them to be? Are they the Formless aspect of the Lord that remain firmly entrenched as the *'Holy-Feet'* of the Lord above the crown of the head of man? And does Whole-hearted surrender of oneself at the *Holy-Feet* that exists above the 'Thousand-petalled Lotus' (*Sahasra Chakra*) at the crown of the head absolve one of *all* sins and both physical and Spiritual Liberation (*mukti*) is attained as claimed by Thirukural, true?

Is a 'Guru' a Master (in the physical) absolutely necessary or can a Divine personality of the astral planes like the exalted Agasthya, Narada or Thirumoolar provide illumination as the Lord Himself says in the Sri Shiva Rahasya?

Can man become the mirror-image, an exact *replica* of the Lord as claimed by Hinduism and Christianity for The Holy Bible; Rom.8.29 tells of the eternal purpose and plan is to make believers conformed to the image of his son, who is himself the perfect image of his father? When this question was put to Lord Rama, he directed Hanuman his devotee to provide the answer for he had *experienced* the three states - Hanuman replied:" *As long as Iam bound by the body and traces of cravings and limitations remain, You are the Lord and Iam a loyal servant; when Knowledge of the Soul (jivatmabodha) dawns in me, You are the Perfect-One (Purna) and Iam an exact- replica, an aspect (amsa)of You; when the Soul's Wisdom in its entirety which is Pure Consciousness (shuddha chaitanya bodha) shines in me, there is absolutely no difference between You and me, You are Me and Iam You.*"

Is the Lord housed only in places of worship or can He be realized within the body itself as claimed by many like Thirumoolar:"*The heart is a vast Temple; the body of flesh being its enclosure ...*"; the Lord Jesus who claims that the Lord is not housed in a place built of stones but in human hearts; Maulanna Jallaludin Rumi: "*If you conquer your heart, it would be like performing a great haj; one pious pulsating-heart is better than a thousand Kaabas*".

Are there relatively easy and simple ways and techniques (known as *Tantra*) of attaining the various states of the Lord and can that state be attained *here and now* instead of only in Ultimate Heaven?

And is the Tamil Siddhars'claim that like when 'verdigris' the green-rust present in copper is removed it turns into gold, in a likewise manner the body gets transformed into the golden radiant-form of the Lord (and therefore transcends space and time and not affected by the *'pancha boothas'* the five basic elements in nature or any weapon) when three 'mayas' (stains) of ego, residues of innumerable past lives and illusion are removed, true?

Man according to the Vedas was *programmed* to live for 100,000 (hundred thousand) years in a previous era known as the 'Kreta yuga', grow a 100 (hundred) feet tall and his *average* height was 32 feet!(The Srimad Bhagavata and Garuda Purana also say that at the end of this present era known as the 'Kali yuga'(which lasts for 432,000 years of which only 5500 years or so have passed) man would be just a foot tall and would live upto 12 years! And there is this mummy of a fully-grown 1 foot tall man that was excavated in 1932 in the Pedro mountains 60 miles west of Casper, Wyoming in the

U.S.. The 'Hadith' a Holy book of Islam containing anecdotes of the Holy Prophets also says that Adam was 60 cubits or a hundred feet tall when he first landed on earth on mount Sarandip in Sri Lanka after being banished from heaven. To substantiate this claim, the tombs of Caine and Abel the sons of Adam and Eve still exist in a coastal-town (Rameshwaram) in Southern India lying at the other end of 'Adam's bridge' (for he walked across the 'Adam's bridge to India) that connects India to Sri Lanka. The tombs are housed in a Moslem Dargah near the railway tracks and each measure 50 to 60 feet long. Tamil Siddhars (Perfected Beings) like Bogar too have in their texts said that *"man was as tall as a fully-grown palmyra tree"* which even now in ideal conditions grows fifty to sixty feet tall. Though the Holy Bible in genesis claims (genesis also says that there were giants on earth in those days and that Adam lived for 930 years, ancient Indian texts like the 'Ramayana' and the 'Tripura Rahasya' of a previous era say that Lord Rama's father Emperor Dasaratha lived for 60,000 years and in even earlier eras man and many a king lived for 80,000 and 100,000 years and even for *hundreds of thousands* of years!

Could man be *re-programmed* to live as many years as he did in those early eras, remain youthfull, be immune to all diseases and could he grow to the height and stature of his choice? A recent global study on AIDS conducted by the World Health Organisation found that prostitutes of a particular country in Africa were immune to the HIV virus for their DNA was found to be *programmed* to resist the deadly aforesaid virus just as the DNA of the mongoose is *naturally* programmed to be immune to snake's venom. And there is research going on to identify and isolate specific genes that cause particular diseases and scientists speculate that in future man could be genetically engineered to be immune to the 3000 diseases so far known. Issac Asimov in 'Change' says that the human body is constructed of 50 trillion (fifty followed by 12 zeros) cells of dozens of types and each again has 50 trillion atoms and that they within a life-time 'double' themselves seven times and then stop, could they be controlled to go on multiplying till we order them to stop?

The 'control' gene that causes the ageing-process as well as the growth-process has already been identified and probably in a few decades man's life-expectancy would be greatly enhanced and his stature too could be controlled. But could the elixir the elusive "*fountain of youth*" ever be found that would let man remain forever in his youth?

'Eternity' or immortallity (*Chiranjivitva* in Sanskrit, *amarathvam* in Tamil) is already programmed in man for among the 36 '*tattvas*' which are the 'Principles' or instruments that make up the subtle bodies of man, there is the '*Kala tattva*' or 'Time concept' which when yogically transcended (through 'Yogic breathing') and conquered, time becomes meaningless and he attains everlasting youth. Moreover the '*Siddhars*' or '*Purna Yogis*' (*full-blown Yogi*) who are Perfected-Beings partake the 'ambrosia' that secretes from the '*Chandra mandala*' or 'Moon's Sphere'(being the upper regions of the head) the exact spot some claim to be the pineal-gland. The ambrosia (which is said to leave a permanent twinge of sweetness lingering in the throat) is said to be sweeter than honey-laced sugarcane-juice which drives off hunger and thirst permanently and causes the body to *regain* youth!

Like the shark and the crocodile which according to modern science attained perfection hundreds of millions of years ago, almost all life-forms like the fruit-fly, the dragon-fly and the humming-bird to name a few fly midflight maneouvres that amaze and stun aeronautical-engineers and stunt-pilots; the rhinoceros beetle is able to lift a hundred times its own weight and what is amazing is (like the Yogi) that at the time of exertion, it draws in four times *more* air than it normally does; Emperor Penguins are able to dive to a depth of nearly 2000 feet into the ocean-waters at the same time slow down their heart-beat and utilization of oxygen; the artic tern is able to migrate over 14000 kilometers over harsh-terrain and (like the wild geese) *above* the Himalayas; the polar and brown bear during the harsh winter conditions go into a sort of suspended state of animation by barely letting its heart pump and drastically slowing down its respiration and sleep off for months at a time and more amazing is the frog which scientists say go into that state for millions and even *billions* of years embedded in stone and *remain* alive!

Man too is said to be born Perfect for the new born baby's breath is according to Yogic philosophy said to be 12 inches long while ours measures 8 inches. We have a *tenth* opening at the crown of our head when we are born known as the '*brahmarandra*' in Sanskrit and '*brahma pugzai*' in Tamil (known to modern science as the 'anterior fontanelle') which literally means the doorway or portal of the Lord. The opening gets obliterated when we are around nine months old, until then it is soft and feels spongy to the touch. The tenth opening leads from a secret passage starting from the upper-palate of the mouth known as *'annakku'* or *'unnakku'* or 'inner-tounge' in Tamil, through which flows 'Prana' (air being only the outer manifestation that we breathe in while prana is the dynamic sum total of all forces in nature) flows. Prana flows through the secret chamber only in new born babies and in the Yogi (the Yogi also *leaves* his body through the tenth opening having predicted the exact moment of death many months or even years earlier) and hence the breath is twelve inches long, while ours is only eight inches long. so we lose four inches of breath for every normal breath we inhale in, which again increases as we take on more strenuous work. When we breathe in prana through the mystical passage, we once again *turn* Perfect, we are no more bound by space or time, ambrosia or the elixir of youth flows which turns the person *eternally young* as the following song of Thirumoolar who was a Siddhar or Perfected-Being of the Tamil Land (who lived for 3000 years) says in his Thirumandiram 805:

> *"If you can send the breath twain*
> *into the internal-tounge's upper-cavity*
> *You shall not be bound by time;*
> *And the gates of nectar will open be;*
> *Graying and wrinkling will disappear*
> *For all to see;*
> *Youthfull will the person be*
> *This is the Word of the Lord Nandhi."*

Modern research too confirms that the idea or *feel* of space-limitation is realized by the human baby only when it is eight or nine months old, until then its feeling is of *universal pervasiveness!* The scope and possiblilities that are to be attained by man is limiltless, for though the animal too has a the mind in an undeveloped state, that of the lower or animal-mind, and yet - a pet elephant of the Chinese Emperor 'Gia-Long', one of the makers of modern Indo-China of the early 19th century ran off into the jungles of the Annamite Mountains after its master's demise but returned to his tomb for *every* death-anniversary!(from 'Just Elephants' by William Baze, 1950); and Bobby man's best friend, a faithfull dog in Glasgow, Scotland, lay guarding his not so caring master's grave for *14 years* without fail braving rain, skeet and snowfall! – Man with his discriminatory powers (man's mind has four divisions – mind (manas), intelligence (buddhi), will (citta) and ego (ahankara) is *programmed* to realize his divinity.

Sri Aurobindo in 'The Synthesis Of Yoga':" *Nothing can be taught to the mind which is not already concealed as potential knowledge in the unfolding soul of the creature, so also all perfection of which the outer man is capable, is only a realizing of the eternal perfection of his spirit within him. We know the Divine and become the Divine, because we are That already in our secret nature. All teaching is a revealing, all becoming is an unfolding. Self-attainment is the secret; self-knowledge and an increasing consciousness are the means and process.*"

That creation, evolution and destruction happens in never-ending cycles is acknowledged by the Vedas which says that the Creator created the worlds and multitude of living beings as they were in the *previous cycle.* Many Siddhars like Thirumoolar who were '*Trikala Jnanis*' or Masters of the 'three-times' – the past, present and future, claim that they visioned the creation, sustenance and destruction of the worlds in rotating-cycles like boiling rice revolve ceaselessly within a pot.

A Sufi Saint the celebrated Shaikh, Muhyi-ud-Din al-Arabi who possessed the power to arrest a person by mere power of sight alone known in Arabic as '*Habs-i-nazir*' ('*nokku varmam*' in Tamil)once when contemplating in the vicinity of the Holy Ka'ba in Mecca *saw* three extremely tall persons circumnavigating the Holy place. The Shaikh who arrested the persons who were as tall as the Holy Ka'ba which stands about 38 feet tall asked them who they were after they pleaded for their release, told him that they too were of human origin. When they answered that they were thirty to forty thousand years old and when questioned again on how that could be for it was only 6000 years since the advent of Adam, they replied that Adam that he spoke of was only the father of *modern man* and that Allah had created *30 such worlds* earlier and over a hundred thousand others, and that they were of an earlier era!

The four 'mind-born' sons (*manasa puthra*) of the Creator flew down to Earth from the 'fifth-heaven' (the Holy Bible too mentions of the apostle Paul having a vision of the fifth-heaven) after receiving direct initiation from the Primal Lord in 'fiery chariots' (*Agni ratha*) millions of years ago landed on a great mass of land that lay below India, extended in the south all the way to Australia and New Zealand, Africa in the east and America in the west which later came to be known as the '*Gondwana land*' and/or the '*Lemuria continent*' (The news agency 'NASA'(from Washington) in its May 27, 1984 edition on "India – the oldest country on earth":" *About 180 million years ago, there was only one continent,(that is, one vast expanse of land) in the whole world, and that was called 'PANGEEYA', which began to break up as years rolled on. The land that is India, about 60 million years ago was a very big island by the side of Africa. Later that island too, moved slowly towards Asia, and, removing China from its place further eastwards, joined itself with Asia. That island is the India of the present day. About 120 million years ago, another expanse of land which had been joined to India by name 'GONDHWANA', separated itself, and from it South America, Africa, Australia and Antartica were born. So the present expeditions to Antartica are, so much as to say, only to a part of India. Only from India, all other continents and countries moved away and formed themselves into separate countries as at present."*) And 'fast-forwarded' the evolutionary-process. The four holy men stayed on earth for more than 400,000 years and among them Lord Sanarkumara is said to be a youth of 18 years for eternity. The Prophet Ezekiel's vision of God mentioned in the Holy Bible seems remarkably similar for it clearly mentions the landing of a flying-craft which has four beings within and it mentions too that they had 'four-faces' and in all ancient Indian texts the Creator is mentioned as '*Nanmukan*' or the 'Four-faced One'.

Like in Hinduism, Judaism too has a thousand Holy Names of the Lord (though like almost all religions claim that there is only One Ultimate God) some were considered too holy to be even uttered, one among the names is '**EL SHADDAI**' and one of its meanings is "**The One with the golden-locks**"(blonde hair) and one Name of the Lord in Tamil is '**SHEN SHADDIYON**', which literally means "***One with golden-red colored fiery locks***"!

Apart from the body, mind and subtle-bodies the real actual person is the Self or the Soul that is ever present within when the person is alive and leaves along with the subtle and spiritual bodies when the body after death taking birth again and again gaining experiences, earning merits and de-merits, exhausting them in the process, evolving and finally getting physical *and* spiritual liberation.

Plato and Socrates on successive births: Plato:" *Life in the universe would have gone out of existence if there were no succeeding births.*"

Socrates:" *If death had been only the end of all, the wicked would have had a bargain in dying; for they would have been happily quit not only of those bodies but of their own evil together with their souls. But now in as much as the soul is manifestly immortal there is no release or salvation from evil, except attainment of the highest virtues and wisdom.*"

Man is on the top-most rung in the ladder that is *his* evolutionary-cycle, he takes precisely eighty-four thousand (84,000) births (according to the Lord Himself in the 'Sri Shiva Rahasya'), starting from the five basic elements, to single celled living beings, tograss, shrubs, plants, trees, insects, reptiles, birds, fish, animals, domestic-animals and finally man over billions of years. Man evolves over 6000 births (in the human-form alone), taking birth at first among cannibals, savages, rapists, sadists, thieves, robbers and murderers, after much suffering and torment, he starts to hate wickedness and violence and yearns for peace, contentment and love towards all living beings and thus takes birth amidst like-minded people and further evolves. He finally realizes that he is still a prisoner ensnared in desires, lusts and cravings. He has to transcend hates and likes, the beautifull and ugly, good and bad, the *"pair of opposites"* for de-merits or sins shackles one in iron-chains while merits earn him golden-chains. Performing good deeds and showing love to all beings without expecting anything in return only ensures total freedom as taught by Lord Krishna to the warrior-prince Arjuna on the battle-field in the Bhagavad Gita and by the Tamil Siddhar (Perfected Being) Thiruvalluvar who in his Thirukural further says that no more sufferings are there for the one who transcends the pair of opposites, performs penance (*tapas* or *thavam*) which are actions or duties without yearning for the fruits of his labor that eradicates impurities and therefore re-writes his own destiny ("*Thavam seyvaar thum karmam seyvaar…*")!

There are eighteen evolutionary-cycles including that of man evolving simultaneously like that of the angels, demons, titans known as 'Devas','Asuras','Rakshasas' etc., going on in various planes and dimensions in what is known as '224 *bhuvanas*' or global-constellations. Each cycle is ensnared in its own space-time, for example a day-time for the angels is equal to one earth-year and a day-time *alone* of Lord Brahma the Creator is 4.32 billion earth-years!

There are 14 planes in what is known as the 7 "*upper worlds*" and 7 "*lower worlds*" containing countless universes, while our world, the solar-system and the universe being the lowest-plane in the upper-worlds.

Man takes birth in the other evolutionary cycles also and thus has the qualities of not only the plant, the snake, deer, rabbit, fox etc., but also that of the angel (who is naturally wise, docile and good) and of the demon and titan who are dull and filled with jealousy, lust and anger.

Only man has the capability to evolve further and attain liberation for only he possesses the mind in a fully developed state and can thus discriminate, transcend the lower-mind that is related to the animal or serpentine-brain (the medulla oblongata that modern research says governs basic but vital functions like the breathing-process and functioning of the heart etc.,) activate the *higher-mind* (and the higher-regions of the brain) which according to the Yogi and Siddhar is the realm of infinite possibilities and from where orders are issued when the breathing turns slow and deep and even stops, for such a perfected person stopping even functioning of the heart and keeping the body in a sort of suspended state of animation is also a possibility.

Such a person can defy death (Trilinga Swami used to meditate continuously for six months at a time under the deep-waters of the river Ganges and Sadasiva Brahmendra once while in a state of Samadhi on the banks of the river Kaveri was covered suddenly by mud when the river ran in spate and was uncovered accidently when a farmer's plough struck his buried head months later, though bleeding profusely the Yogi simply walked-off!) and consciously leave his body at the time of his reckoning and this is known as '*iccha mrityu*' in Sanskrit and the "art of deathlessness" is known as '*sahakalai*' in Tamil. Some perfected beings attain the state of *Samadhi* and leave the physical body behind which would never ever decompose and if needed in future, he himself or another elevated soul could re-enter the body and function for the welfare of one and all like Adi Sankara, Thirumoolar, Shirdi Sai Baba and many others did.

Some Yogis attain the state of *'Jiva Samadhi'* in which by 'internal breathing' (*"ullh moochi"* in Tamil) the breath is made to rise by yogic-means through the *'sushumna nadi'* which is the most vital astral-nerve (even more than the left and right nostril-breath known in Yoga as the sun and moon for they possess those qualities and yin and yang to the Chinese) that passes through the spinal column from the base of the spine right up to the crown of the head, connecting all the *'Chakras'* which are psychic-centres and energy-vortexes and piercing a secret and mystical-cavity lying between the 'inner-tounge' (*'Unnakku'* or *'annakku'* in Tamil) and the crown of the head whereby the body is kept alive for eons if necessary.

Some persons de-materialize after having attained the golden radiant-form (the body of Light known as *'Jyotir maya deha'* in Sanskrit and *'Jnana deham'* (Wisdom Body) or *'ollhi udal'* in Tamil) that is available only after *final-death* and in 'Ultimate' Heaven. Few persons have de-materialized and some even in the presence of many onlookers like Mira, Andal, Pattinathar, Lord Chaitanya and Saint Ramalingam who disappeared in 1872.

The person who consciously transcends the confines of the physical and literally crosses or breaks the 'Universe-body barrier' (*"Anda kosa yellai"* according to Thiruvarur Rathinasabapathy Pillai in his 'Thiruvasagamum Sivaraja Yogamum') which is a ultra-subtle barrier that exists 12 inches or so above the head and surrounds the body is a *'Purna Yogi'* or a full-blown Yogi, a Perfected Being who transcends both Space and Time, becomes ageless, attains all knowledge *and* Divine Wisdom and could be at any point in space or at various points as he wishes and fancies.

The timeless Vedas as well as many ancient Indian texts and the Siddhars and Yogis of india have claimed that man's true nature is the Divine (*'Tat Tvam Assi'* – "That thou art" and Thirumoolar's Thirumandiram:" *Jiva (the individual Soul) and Siva are no different"*).

Many of the Apostles of Jesus Christ (who himself was Perfect) did attain almost the perfect-state for the apostle Paul was bit by a poisonous viper and the poison did not affect him in the least as foretold by Jesus in the Holy Bible, Mark 17-18 that they will pick up snakes…and when they drink deadly poison it would not affect them. And when the Lord asked the apostles to go and preach to the world the words that he had said, they in turn asked how they could since different people spoke various unknown languages, Jesus said that the Holy Spirit would enter their tounges and they would be able to speak in those new languages, and it happened like that!

Later on saints like Anthony of Padua were able to 'Teleport' and appear in two places at the same time, make even other people levitate and make animals, birds and fish listen to his holy sermons.

Imams of ancient Iran had like Elijah de-materialized and Sufi saints like Moulanna Jalladun Rumi and Manzur attained enlightenment and the latter who had claimed *'Anal haq!'* or "Iam the Truth" was cut to pieces on the orders of the Badshah, but the cut pieces continued to claim 'anal haq', even when the flesh and bones were burnt, the ashes are said to have repeatedly claimed the same words

ACKNOWLEDGEMENTS

When Carl Sagan the astronomer as Director of NASA and SETI (search for extra-terrestrial intelligence) decided to send the 'Voyager' a space-craft carrying a golden-record inscribed with figures and letters explaining life on earth for a chance encounter with an alien-intelligence, he chose the 50 letters of the Sanskrit alphabets.

Carl Sagan in 'Contact' says that he chose those letters for they also happened to be the 'Prime Alphabets' of the Chinese (though there are more than 50 to 60,000 alphabets in the Chinese language) and Japanese language alphabets and they within them contained *all* sounds that could emanate from any sound-source.

When I read 'Contact' more than two decades ago, I instantly remembered Thirumoolar who is a Tamil Siddhar who after receiving direct initiation from Lord Siva Himself in *'Kailash'* the Primal-Heaven, took *Avatar* (which literally means 'descending' and if necessary entering a body) by entering the body of a dead sheperd lived for 3000 years on earth and in his Yogic-Vedic-Masterpiece 'Thirumandiram' stated:" *Fifty letters alone are all Vedas.... fifty letters become five letters*". Thirumoolar goes on to add that eight persons were sent by the Lord to spread and teach the Words of the Lord, he was to teach it in Tamil(the language of the south), while Patanjali was to teach it in Sanskrit (the language of the north). The present day Tamil alphabet has only 30 'Prime alphabets' or vowel-consonants but in the era prior to the Tamil 'round-letter' time (*vatta ellhuthu*) there existed only 50 alphabets in total and they ultimately are contained in the five 'Life-letters' or 'Seed-letters', the vowels 'A, E, I, O, U' or 'SI VA YA NA MA'. Thirumoolar goes on to add that (like the Holy Bible says in the fourth gospel, John 1;1, 2 that In the beginning was the word, and the word was with god and the word became the flesh, the word was God") everything arose from those words: Thirumandiram 910:" *One the supreme bliss, Thus chant the mantra you shall have bliss, bliss has its source in letters five; A-I-U-E-O and Aum the life vowels they are; they become the five letter mantra and joy that is within joy; bliss lies in the seed-letter five; Hum-Hrim-Ham-Ksham-Am, are they.*"

Swami Sivananda's 'Kundalini Yoga' gives detailed explanation on how the 50 letters exist as 50 sound-vibrations(mantras)spread among the six vital chakras in the subtle-bodies of man and when the "*Kundalini*" or the 'Cosmic-Energy'(the Creative-Energy of the Lord) that lies at slumber in latent-form at the 'muladhara chakra' at the base of the spine in its deadly fiery-form (as it does in the core of the earth as well as all the heavenly bodies) is woken by yogic-means, made to rise slowly coaxed up and on its ascent activating the other chakras and finally when it flows into the 'Sahasra chakra' at the crown of the head, the person attains '*Superconsciousness*', he becomes a '*Full-blown Yogi*' who comes to know all languages, the languages of the beasts and birds and even all alien languages.

Though Bertrand Russell claimed:" *What science cannot tell us mankind cannot know!*" Elevated and illumined people receive inspiration and messages in dreams and visions just as Niels Bohr had visioned the atom model and Francis Harry Crick the DNA chain, so man does in a higher state of consciousness get answers to scientific problems and also in other fields like music and art, Michelangelo to from where he gets his ideas:" … *perhaps from god!*" – 'Agony and Ecstasy' by Irvin Stone.

The adorable character 'Mickey Mouse' is etched in stone dated to the 13th century found in Mexico though it became famous after it was visioned and drawn by Walt Disney in the 20th century! Carl Jung the pupil of Sigmund Freud says that no one is born a '*tabula rasa*', that is with a clean-slate, we all carry memories of our experiences gathered right from the time we were single-celled protozoa and "*blocked-off memories*" have recordings of all experiences and a "*collective unconsciousness*" of entire mankind contains Vedic, Biblical and other ancient mythological stories and characters that give shape to the characters in our dreams, nightmares and inspirations.

Jonas Salk:" *At an early stage in the evolutionary process there had formed what has been referred to as 'the thread of life' – the self-copying tape-like molecule* that contains the code which transmits to each succeeded generation the information which, when decoded, forms the organism prescribed in it. This code contains the 'wisdom' of previous generations of living things…". "From the moment of conception, and also at birth, each of us is essentially a 'package of potential'."

Great scientists like Albert Einstein and Jonas Salk accept that humanity should be grateful to the services rendered by God's representatives, Einstein:" *Humanity has every reason to place the proclaimers of high moral standards and values above the discoveries of objective truth. What humanity owes to personalities like Buddha, Moses and Jesus ranks for me higher than all the achievements of the enquiring and constructive mind?*"

'Acquired Savant Syndrome','Foreign Accent Syndrome' and many other syndromes are in the news now according to which many diverse and un-imaginable latent-powers and knowledge like people talking in previously unlearnt languages, regaining arts like music, mathematics etc.,(and becoming geniuses in those particular fields!) after receiving sudden blows or knocks to the head. These sudden bursts of talents could be explained fully by accepting the fact the ancient Indian claim that man takes numerous births and the knowledge as well as fruits of those good or bad deeds committed are never ever destroyed for like many 'recalls', Lord Buddha is said to have in a flash remembered 400 of his previous lives when he attained enlightenment, the life of an eagle, snake, hare, deer …! But even that is not '*Total Recall*'.

The Full-blown Yogi attains '*Total Recall*', the '*64 Arts*' or "*64 branches of Knowledge*" known as the '*kalai Tattva*' in Tamil that includes astronomy, astrology, painting, sculpting, dancing, music, archery, fencing, wrestling, engineering, medicine, science, prose, poetry etc., he in fact becomes a *Master* of all subjects. He also attains 'Divine Wisdom' or '*Para Vidya*' while the former is 'inferior knowledge', this is 'Superior Knowledge' for it contains all Divine-secrets and the Wisdom of the Lord. The Yogi then transcends the '*Kala Tattva*' or 'Time concept' and thus becomes ageless. He finally acquires the '*Siva Tattvas*' which are the Five-Qualities of the Primal Lord – The Power to *Create, Sustain, Annihilate, Veil* and *Grace*.

The full-blown Yogi also attains eight enormous Supernatural Powers known as '*Ashtanga Siddhis*'in Sanskrit and '*Attamaha siddhi*' in Tamil which are 'anima','mahima,'lagima','garima','prapti','parakamya','vasitva'&'istva' Thirumoolar on the the eight great Siddhis or 'Perfections' or Supernatural Powers, Thirumandiram 668:" *To become tiny as the atom within the atom (anima); to become big in unshakeable proportions(mahima); To become as light as vapor in levitation(laghima); To become heavy as a mountain(garima); To enter into other bodies in transmigration(prapti); To be in all things, omni-pervasive(prakamya); To be Lord of all creation in omnipotence(istvam); To be everywhere in omnipresence(vasitvam) – these eight are siddhis great."*

He also attains many 'minor' powers like being able to cure incurable diseases, bring the dead back to life, turn base-metal into gold, look into and read other living-form's minds, look into the earth and depths of the oceans and point-out treasures, walk on water, on air, in fire etc.,. But the Yogi shuns these powers for like a deadly serpent guards a rare gem, they prove to be a hindrance to attain the final goal which is spiritual liberation. But if it is God's Will, the Yogi does exhibit his powers like: Saint Jnanasambhandar converted female palmyra trees into male-trees so as to help a poor farmer and brought back to life *'Poombhavai'* as a grown-up girl four years after she died after being bitten by a cobra, her body was burnt to ashes and kept in an urn by her father 'Sivanesan'; Adi Sankara out of compassion brought forth a rain of golden-nuggets within the hut of kind-hearted poor lady; Ayya Vaikuntar parted the waters of the Bay of Bengal (in Tiruchendur) entered the ocean (like Moses parted the waters of the red-sea) and returned after three days as the *Avatar* of Lord Narayana to preach that all were equal before the Lord and perform many miracles like curing deadly diseases and taming wild tigers etc., and predicting future happenings of the world.

Though astro-physicists like Stephen Hawking have their deep doubts on interstellar travel: *"I am afraid that however clever we may become we will never be able to travel faster than light. If we could travel than light we could go back in time. We have not seen any tourists from the future that means that travel to other stars is going to be a slow and tedious business. Using rockets rather than warp drives. A 100,000 year round trip to the center of the galaxy. In that time the human race will have changed beyond recognition, if it has not wiped itself out."* – There are numerous instances where the world over the ages has witnessed and recorded many interstellar travels and visits. Apart from ancient Egyptian and Greek gods who are considered to be mere myths, 'Amaterasu' the Sun-Godess, grand-mother of the God Niniji who came down from heaven to rule Nippon (Japan) was the great grand-father of the mortal emperor 'Jinmu-Tenno' founder of the Imperial dynasty 2500 years ago. The Sun-Godess had landed on Mount Fujiyama,(the main reason of it being considered holy) and the Orb and Sword of the Sun-God was presented to be preserved as royal relics, which are still being held in deep reverence in the Imperial Palace of the Royal Family; The Holy Bible says that Phillip and Elijah were taken away by a whirlwind, a *chariot with horses of fire took them away*; The Holy Prophet Mohammed took a 'space journey' riding the 'ul burraq' a craft which resembled a horse but had the face of a woman and tail of a peacock, which could span the horizon with just one step. The Prophet rode past the 'seven heavens' and finally reached Ultimate Heaven, the 'inner-circle of heaven', the 'Kurrat un nar'('Empyrean' according to Milton's 'Paradise Lost' and 'Premum mobile' to Dante)where he saw all the 'Malaks' or Angels at prayer, met Solomon, Moses, Jesus(who is also considered a Prophet in Islam) and finally had audience with Allah the Almighty and All Merciful; According to the native Indian history the Sun God landed on Sun-island on lake Titicaca and a festival is still celebrated to honor the occasion; The Dogon tribal people claim that their forefathers had come from the star Sirius in a huge ship and once in fifty-two years celebrate their home-coming by dancing donning straw masks that resemble helmets worn by astronauts. What is interesting is Sirius is visible as it falls on a direct-line from earth once in fifty-two years!

Nowhere else were there frequent alien visits to compare to that of India – in the 'Kandha Purana' war that took place on earth in the *Kreta Yuga* more than 3 million years ago, it is mentioned that 'Sooran' the Asura King ruled over 1008 universes(*1008 andam*), possessed deadly missiles and weapons of mass destruction and had 'vimanas' or flying-crafts that had *stealth-technology*, could hover over land and water, could disappear and appear at will, could appear at many places at the same time and had various magical contriviances and the battle that place over land, under water and in the skies and was finally killed by Lord Muruga's *'Vel'* "the missile with the lengthy-flame" (*"nedunchudar Vel"*) that was re-usable and voice-activated and who Himself rode the *'Peacock-Craft'* which is described in the Tamil Classic 'Thirupugazh' as *"the hero who roams about the worlds riding the* peacock that is a craft made of red burnished-gold" ("*Sempon mayil yenum theril yeri ulaavi varum Veerarae*") moreover after Lord Muruga's vanquishment of the asuras or titans,'Kandhar Alankaram' says that all the gods flew in their individual vimanas from Thiruparakundram (near Madurai) to 'Amaravathi' the capital city of the Devas or Angels realm 'Indra Lokam' or 'Swarga Lokam' (Heaven) at 'thought-speed' (*mano veham*); In the epic Ramayana, Ravana the King of Sri Lanka captured the Pushpaka vimana a flying craft built by Mayan the architect of the Devas or Angels for Kubera the Lord of riches of the celestial region, it was utilized in the battle and later after the victory, Lord Rama flew back to his kingdom in North India taking along with him Sita, Lakshmana, Vibishana the newly crowned king of Sri Lanka among others; The Srimad Bhagavata mentions of many flying-crafts like the '*rotating firebrand*' and of the three great spaceships vanquished with a single missile by Lord Shiva which were so huge that they resembled *three 'floating cities'* that had ponds and waterfalls within them and had stealth-technology among other wonders; Sri Suka in the Srimad Bhagavata Purana tells of the "*effulgent car that was as swift as the sun*" of Priavarata "*the tracks of which dug up our seven oceans*"...... !

The world reknown astro-physicist Stephen Hawking has in his book 'A Brief History of Time' stated that 'quarks' which make the electron, proton and neutron could be or near to the 'elementary particles' of nature, but six 'flavors' of quarks have been identified and hence though we are not absolutely certain, these could be the elementary particles or the "basic building blocks of nature". But Vedanta and Saiva Siddhanta emphatically state that '*Nada Bindu*' ('Nadha Vindhu' in Tamil) - "The Eternal Sound-Light Continuum" are the basic building blocks of nature. The Eternal Sound-Light pulse which in fact is the *Formless–State* of the Lord, according to the Siddhars and Full-blown Yogis exist as the 'Holy Feet' of the Lord at the crown of the head of man, the one who visions it and yogically attains the Source and merges with it, is like the rain-drops and river-waters that once again mingles with the ocean, is no different from the Lord!

Contrary to what the world thinks that the mighty always triumph, during the Second World War when mighty rulers like Roosevelt, Churchill and Stalin planned their maneouvres of their mighty forces on a grand scale, scientists like Einstein, Planck and Oppenheimer pondered over splitting the miniscule atom in laboratories and it was the latter which caused the abrupt fall of the Axis forces. Similarly it is the humble individual like Mahatma Gandhi, Mother Teresa, Martin Luther King, Nelson Mandela, Abraham Lincoln, Lord Buddha, Lord Mahavira, Lord Jesus, who ultimately triumph and are remembered for their greatness attained through serving mankind and by their humility. The Lord in the 'Shiva Sutras' explains that like when the atom is sought after and split infinite energy is released, when the mind of man is obliterated through pranayama infinite knowledge is revealed.

Only compassion, sympathy and emphathy shown by the individual toward all living-beings would bring forth peace, harmony and joy in the world.

The unfolding of man has to be like though we know not the mysteries present within the atom which is said to be 90% empty space, neither of the vastness, depth and various dimensions of space (Carl Sagan in 'Cosmos' and 'Broca's Brain' claims that there are a *hundred billion* stars in our galaxy *alone* and estimates that there could be a *billion black holes* in each galaxy ...) and the late Dr.Ramamurthi of Chennai who has said that there are more than 100 billion neurons in the human brain which could telephathically connect with the equal number of people on earth with distance being of no consequence and Michael Crichton in 'Andromeda Strain' who says that in an average human-gut which is equal in size to a normal thermos flask there are more bacteria than the global human population, but when man lets go of his ego, he is un-bound by the shackles of the body and transcends space and thus time and this is known as '*Viruthi*' in the Saiva religion of the Tamils that says:" like a circus-tent when unfolded becomes immensely big ("*padalam kudil anar pola*"), man in an expanded fully-blown state is The Infinite." Lord Krishna in the Bhagavad Gita too explains that the 'field' (*Kshetram*) that man occupies at the microcosmic-level is the human body but at the macrocosmic-level the 'knower' of the field (*Kshetranjnan*) can expand and cover the entire universe.

And in that state of expansiveness Saint Ramalingam experienced empathy with dried and shrivelled-crop and claimed:" *when ever I saw the withered-crop, I too withered!*", and when ever Lord Mahavira or Lord Rama set foot in the forests, grass, shrubs and plants would sprout-out tender leaves, flowers would bloom in the thousands, un-seasonal fruits would ripen and hang in heavy bunches, even dead trees would germinate and friend and foe like the serpent and the frog, falcon and dove, deer and the tiger would stand in unity to welcome them and cry out in joy!

The Lord is said to be in three Forms – Form, Form-Formless and Formless and man too as he evolves passes through those states – he is in his physical body; he then acquires the 'Cause-Effect Body' (*kaarana kaarya rupa*) like Jesus Christ, The 'Bab' (founder of the Ba'hai faith of Iran in the early 1800's), Lord Chaitanya, Lahiri Mahasaye and Saint Ramalingam possessed which like the flame could be seen but not within anyone's grasp, nor could be captured on film, nor hurt with any weapon or by the five elements in nature (when the Roman soldiers of Pontius Pilate at first approached the Lord, they were suddenly flung back and could arrest him only after his consent; similarly when 750 Armenian soldiers shot at the Bab with rifles, to their amazement he had disappeared though the ropes that helped to tie him up to the stakes were found burnt); he then finally attains the 'Wisdom Body'(*Jnana deha*)Formless-state and de-materializes.

Moreover the Soul exists as 'Satchitananda' – 'Sat' – Existence Absolute; 'Chit' – Knowledge Absolute; 'Ananda' – Bliss Absolute. Only realization of one's divinity has to dawn, Adi Sankara in his 'Viveka Chudamani' says that there is only *one* space and it is illusion that makes us believe that the space within a pot (*gada akasa*) merges with the space outside when the pot is broken, similarly ther is only the 'Cosmic mind' and there is no question of the individual mind merging with the Cosmic mind (after final-death or realization).

The Lord in the Shiva Rahasya, 'The Vijnana Bhairava Tantra', and Thirumandiram among others has given simple techniques through which His state could be attained. By mere 'breath-watching' and /or breath-awareness one can transcend space and time. The Lord says that "*the one who knows the secret between two breaths is no different from me.*" The 'Yoga Vashishta' speaks of 'Kahapusandha' an youthfull Yogi who lives in a secret cave north-east of Mount Kailash in the Himalayas who has been a witness to 7500 pralayas (that are global and universal-level catastrophes that happens once every 4.32 billion years) and he is in that state by watching the interval between two breaths.

The Japanese Zen masters attain 'sartori' or enlightenment by attaining 'mushin' - the state of *'no-mind'* (they had also mastered the science of the breath – when the chest is expanded in breathing, it is known as 'yo-ibuki'(in Japanese) or hard-style breathing used in combat; it is the opposite in meditation-breathing which is known as 'in-ibuki', yet both use the entire natural breathing apparatus unlike the modern-day norm that merely uses the top of the lungs) and Lord Rama in the 'Rama Gita'says: "*Thoughtless mind is Brahman*" – God.

Lao Tzu the ancient Chinese Tao Master would to any question put to him on the mysteries of life, quietly write on the river-sands 'Meditate'. Sufi saints would fall faint into a state of ecstasy by willfully holding their breath, while Moulanna Jallaludin Rumi of the 12th century Iran *'whirl-danced'* for 36 continuous hours and attained enlightenment (that is why dancers are known as 'Super-beings'), King Ravana of Sri Lanka attained Wisdom through music.

The Lord in the 'Shiva Maha Purana' says that one could be absolved of *all* his sins (and thus all diseases as modern research says that more than 80 percent of toxins could be flushed-out by proper breathing) by performing one *'Uttama Pranayama'* the highest form of pranayama. 'Prana' which is wrongly assumed to be air or oxygen is in fact the "Sum total of all forces", air or the breath that is inhaled being only the outer-manifestation of prana. In fact the siddhars say that Prana is or 'Vasi' is none other than the ultra subtle-form of the Lord ("*vasiyum Isanum ondru*"), when Prana within the body is controlled all (infinite) forces *outside* comes within the control of the person whereby the normal laws of science and nature like space, time, gravitation, speed-limits, mass, electro-magnetism etc., do not affect him.

One needs to at first delve into the state of no-mind or *'Zero Experience'* as Osho would say every now and then and this state should become a continuous one and not just when one's eyes are closed (as during meditation) as very beautifully explained in the 'Tripura Rahasya'. That continuous-state was experienced by Rabbi Abraham Heschel who after marching with Martin Luther King, commented:" *I felt as if my legs were praying when I marched with Martin Luther King.*"

It is repeatedly mentioned in the Srimad Bhagavata that Perfected-Beings like Kapila, Suka and Kardama went about the world with *"an expanded state of consciousness"* and in fact the Lord in the 'Shiva Gita' tells that the one who meditates with the "feeling of belief" (*bhava*) that he is the Lord himself encompassing the entire cosmos is most dear to Him.

It is only through Yoga (the Essenes a sect of Judaism in which Jesus was born had tenets of Yoga and in Arabic Yoga is known as 'Saluk' and the art of controlling the Pranic-force or 'Pranayama' was known as 'Habs-e-dam') that the individual and the world attains harmony and the perfect state of equilibrium (samadarshini according to Lord Krishna in the Bhagavad Gita), the state when man's brain as well as all his capabilities function in their entireity (whereas modern research says that we use less than ten percent of our brain's capacity). The illusive-Power of God is known as 'Maya' and only when this very strong veil is destroyed Divine-Wisdom would be revealed. Maya's might - The 'Bheranda Samhita':" *There is no greater force than maya which binds one to another, and to break that powerful bond, there is no greater force than Yoga."*

The Lord on Yoga in the Shiva Rahasya: *"There is nothing that cannot be attained through the Power of Yoga..."* *"Yoga is the Power of Unity – the Unity between Body, Mind and Soul is of the Human kind, that which is between Man and Nature is of the Worldwide Kind, but that which is between Man and the Lord is indeed Divine".*

CHAPTERS

1. Man was programmed to live for 100,000 years in a previous era according to the ancient Vedas; was 100 feet tall according to the Hadith a holy book of Islam; 60 feet long tombs of Caine and Abel the sons of Adam and Eve near 'Adam's Bridge' in southern India; gigantic snakes, birds and dragons ('yazhi'in Tamil, which could hold elephants in their tails that seemed to be puny in comparison) lived on earth.

2. The four 'mind-born' sons of the Creator flew down from the 'fifth heaven' in 'Fiery chariots' (agni ratha) to earth and landed on the 'Lemuria' continent millions of years ago and fast-forwarded the evolutionary process when both man and ape stood more than 60 feet tall and man had three eyes.

3. The Primal Lord above the 'Holy Trinity' and the 'Five Gods'; Life in different states in various living-forms and in 'realized' Man; The 'System Theorists' of the west and Thirumandiram claim that the worlds and all lives are one giant organism; The Perfected Being does actually become a 'Star' that adorn the skies ...

4. The Lord the Father lifted up Mount Sinai to save the Israelies (From 'Talmud To Torah' by R.P.Lawrie) just as Sri Krishna lifted Mount Govardhana for seven consecutive days to save the Gopis.

5. Earth And Everything Closely Monitored; Depths Of The Seven Oceans Dug-up by The Tracks of Priavarta's Flying-Craft (*Vimana*) According To The Srimad Bhagavata; Archangel Gabriel Taught

Adam to Grind Wheat; The Grape – Earth's First Fruit Introduced; Remarkable Similarities Between World's Most Ancient Religions of Hinduism And The Three 'Abrahamic Faiths'

6.   Evolution According To Charles Darwin, Sage Patanjali; The Apostle James in The Bible, 84,000 Births And 6000 Human Births According To 'Sri Shiva Rahasya', Saint Manickavasagar; Re-birth – Plato, Socrates, Zen Master Daito.

7.   "Blocked-off Memories",'Tabula Rasa', "Collective Unconscious" & 'Total Recall' – Carl Jung; Carl Sagan on 'Habitable Zones' in the Immediate Neighborhood

8.   Eighteen Evolutionary Cycles.

9.   Countless Cycles of Creation and Destruction; Power to arrest and Kill by Sight ('*nokku varma kalai*' in Tamil,'*Habs-I nazir*' in Arabic); Beings as tall as the Holy Ka'ba in Mecca Who Claim that Adam only the father of 'modern man' and further claim to be more than 40,000 years old; 30 other 'previous worlds'

10. Can Man be Re-programmed To Live For Eternity?; made Immune to All Diseases?; Speak All Languages? Even that of Beasts and Birds like King Solomon and the Sage Narada?; Teleport to distant places and be back in a jiffy like Saint Antony, Gurn Nanak and Saint Ramalingam?; Can He Master the '64 Arts' or 'The 64 Branches of Knowledge' And Attain Divine Wisdom?; Can Man Cure incurable Diseases, turn base metal into gold, *turn* eternally young and bring the dead back to Life like Jesus Christ, Chaitanya Prabhu and Saint Ramalingam?

11. The Quest For the 'Fountain of Youth'; DNA Programming and Natural programming; Jesus Christ in Matt.5, 48:" *Be ye perfect therefore as your heavenly father is perfect*",'Saiva Siddhanta of the Tamils:"*Like copper turns into gold when verdigris present in it is removed, man becomes the Divine when three 'malas' (stains) are removed*"; Sri Shiva Rahasya:" *The One who knows the secret between two breaths comes to know that he and I are One.*"

12. Transcending Space and Time possible by Watching the gap between two breaths – 'Yoga Vashista'; The Physical Body too should attain Perfection according to Thirumoolar and Sri Aurobindo in 'The Supramental Manifestation' and 'The Synthesis of Yoga'; Levitation of the Physical Body (*Uthapena*), Attaining the 'Cause-Effect Body'(*kaarana-kaarya rupa*), Attaining the 'Body of golden radiant-light' and finally de-materializing

13. Carl Sagan chose the 50 Sanskrit Alphabets which are also the 'Prime Alphabets' or Vowel-Consonants of the Chinese, Japanese and ancient Tamil Languages to be inscribed on a golden-record and sent into outer-space on the space-ship 'voyager' for an 'Alien' chance-encounter; Thirumandiram and Sivananda's 'Kundalini Yoga' on 50 letters existing as 50 sound-vibrations in the six Chakras of the Human body and containing All Languages and 'All Knowledge'.

14. Answers to scientific-problems like the DNA chain received through visions and Dreams; Fritjof Capra's Vision of the Cosmic-Dance of Lord Shiva in 'Tao Of Physics'

15. Issac Asimov on Intuition; Stephen Hawking on sub-atomic particles and 'Quarks' being the basic building blocks of nature in 'A Brief History of Time'; Vedanta and Saiva Siddhanta on 'Nada Bindu' (The Eternal Sound-Light Continuum)being the basic building block of nature

16. Stephen Hawking on Interstellar Travel and 'Time travel'; The ancient Japanese Royal Family being descendants of the Sun-God; Philliph and Elijah who were taken away by a whirlwind and chariots with horses of fire; Sun-God landing on 'Sun Island' on Lake Titicaca; Dogon Tribes ancestors descended from 'Sirius' the star; Tamil Classic 'kandha Puranam' mention of 'Sooran' the Asura King who ruled over '1008 Universes' (*1008 andam*) ...

17. The 'Dimension Barrier' needs to be broken just as Chuck Yeagar broke the Sound-barrier in 1947, Siddhars master's of the art of literally

hopping from one dimension to another (*koodu vittu koodu paayum vidhai*); Albert Einstein's General Theory of Realitivity,'Time Travel' and the '*granny paradox*' phenomenon; Siddhars by transcending the Chakras within the body and by breaking the 'Body-Universe Barrier' ('*anda kosa yellai*' – Thiruvavoor Rathinasabapathi Pillai's 'Thiruvasagamum Sivaraja Yogamum') break the dimension-barrier for "*what is in the universe is also within the body*", the Chakras containing the 'tattvas' or Principle-ingredients of the '14 worlds' or planes

18. 'Mushin' the State of 'No-Mind' in Zen Philosophy,'Kevala Kumbaka' the Perfect retention of Breath in Yogic-Meditation where Mind also stops; Lord Rama in Rama Gita:" thoughtless mind is Brahman" (God); Islamic (Iranian)Darvishes like Moulanna Jallaudin Rumi who 'whirldanced' and attained enlightenment, others like King Ravana of Sri Lanka through music,'Zero-experience' of Osho and Rabbi Abraham Heschel who after marching with Martin Luther King, commented:" *I felt as if my legs were praying when I marched with Martin Luther King.*"

19. The Soul – 'Satchitananda' – 'Sat' – Existence Absolute,'Chit' – Knowledge Absolute,'Ananda' – Bliss Absolute

20. Extraordinary Supernatural Powers Attained by the Full-blown Yogi

21. Michael Crichton in 'Andromeda Strain':" *There is present in the human gut microbes and bacteria that are equal to the global human population...*"; Dr.Ramamurti:" *There are as many neurons in the human brain as there are people on the earth*"; Lord Shiva in the 'Shiva Gita':" *The human body is the most intricate and complex one among all my creations*"; Issac Asimov in 'Change':"*The human body is made up of 50 trillion microscopic cells of dozens of types each containing 50 trillion atoms or more...*" "*Enzymes help to renew millions of blood cells every second...they are so small that millions can exist in a single drop of blood...*"; Carl Sagan in 'Cosmos' and 'Broca's Brain' claims that there are a hundred billion stars in our galaxy alone and estimates that there could be a billion black holes in each galaxy...

22. The Lord On Yoga - Srimad Bhagavata, book III, dis., XXIV, "Descent Of Lord Kapila"

23. Perfection Through Yoga; Total cleansing of impurities and diseases through Pranayama for Prana or 'Vasi' is the ultra subtle-Form of the Lord ("*vasiyum Isanum Ondru*" – Tamil Siddhars); The Lord in the 'Sri Shiva Rahasya: "There is nothing that cannot be attained through the Power of Yoga…" "*Yoga is the Power of Unity – the Unity between Body, Mind and Soul is of the Human kind, that which is between Man and Nature is of the Worldwide Kind, but that which is between Man and the Lord is indeed Divine*".

24. One needs to realize his state of infinity to Become the Infinite; Lord Krishna in the Bhagavad Gita:" *The field that we occupy at the microcosmic-level is limited to the human body but when expanded to the macrocosmic, it could cover the entire universe*"; The new-born human baby too experiences its state of infinity until ego sets in after it is eight or nine months old – modern research; 'Sri Shiva Rahasya' - The highest form of meditation and the one most dear to the Lord is to meditate with the 'feel' (*bhava*) that one is the Lord Himself extending to infinity; J.Krishnamurti:" *It is all about space*"; Srimad Bhagavata:" *The Perfected-One like Kapila, Kardama and Sri Suka went about the world with an expanded state of consciousness*"

25. Attainment of 'Eternal Youth' Through Pranayama – Thirumoolar, Bogar, Sivavakkiar, the Kanchi Sankaracharya in 'The Vedas'

26. Mythological, Vedic, Biblical and other characters, the 'archetypes' (even 'Mickey Mouse') are deeply engrained in the "collective unconsciousness" and "blocked-off memories" – Carl Jung

27. Infinite Energy, Infinite Space and Infinite Knowledge of Man – David Bohm's "Zero-point Energy"; 'Shiva Sutras' on the infinite power held within an atom and infinite powers within man.

28. Everything Is Born Of That Supreme Sound; My Five Powers Divine When obscured by My Mighty Magic they become limited and the being who holds them is known as Soul – Sri Shiva Rahasya

29. Thus the Soul is born as the sixth in the midst of the five. He is the power-holder and their master even as I am the Holder of the Five Powers Divine – Sri Shiva Rahasya

30. The Ten Powers Of God when obscured and greatly reduced by Maya, they are imperfect human powers. When free and unobstructed, they are indeed Infinite and Divine. They are the Yogic Powers of Buddhahood – Sri Shiva Rahasya

31. Amongst the Righteous Nations the Holy Land of India shall ever be the first – The Lord in Sri Shiva Rahasya

32. Man Needs the Grace of a Human or Divine Guru To Realize Unity Through The Practise of Yoga – The Lord in Sri Shiva Rahasya

33. The Greatest of Yogas – Sri Shiva Rahasya

34. The Soul is The Supreme Spirit, Hence Should Realize He is Beyond All Limitations; Transcending The Three 'Malas' (Stains) – Sri Shiva Rahasya

35. Yoga And Dharma (Righteousness) Are One And The Same; Among The Five Castes Of Man, The Yogi Is The Head Who Spreads My Word Of Truth –Sri Shiva Rahasya

36. The Soul Drinks The Milk Of Heaven Which Is Attained By Renunciation And Not Attachment; The Yogi Who Learnt The Art Of Letting-go By Watching The Wise Heron

37. God's Signs Of Two Kinds, The Enduring Ones Like The Sun And Moon And Passing Ones Like Visions And Dreams – Sri Shiva Rahasya

38. The People of India Alone Remained Faithful To My Law; The Holy Land of India, the Abode of Light (Bharat) which shines like unto a jewel on this Earth – Sri Shiva Rahasya

39. The total discarding of the mind is alone victory, achievement, bliss, yoga, wisdom and liberation. The sacrifice of the mind is, in fact, the totality of all sacred sacrifices – Ribu Gita

40. Totality of all Knowledge attained in the Blissful-state of 'no-mind' – Ribu Gita:

41. "One is absolved of all his sins and remains established in Brahman-Self" – Ribu Gita

42. The True World Guru (Teacher) is the one who teaches that one is the Absolutely Thought-Free, Blissful, Infinite Self – Ribu Gita:

43. True Liberation (Moksha) is steady abidance in the pure thought-free Alert-Awareness-Self only – Ribu Gita

44. The Three-fold impurities of Maya the dark Veil of ignorance has to be Transcended to reveal one's Divinity and thus lead from agony to ecstasy

45. The Faithful Yogi conquers old age and death and becomes Master of his own life and becomes a 'Siddha' a Perfect-One, attains Divine Wisdom, the Eight Great Supernatural Powers, attains celestial bodies of radiance and enjoys the fruits of heaven here and now –Sri Shiva Rahasya

46. Erasing the imprints (karma) on the Soul and renunciation makes one to ascend to the higher and the Highest of Planes – Sri Shiva Rahasya

47. The sight of the third-eye of Wisdom alone reveals Truth as it is; he sees not the multitude but as the one; When he realises the whole diversity of living things as existing in the One and as born of that One, he attains the Highest; When he sees the Absolute Self as a real

experience, and the entire Universe as immaterial like an illusion, he experiences the Highest Bliss (Paramananda); there is nothing in the Three Worlds save God, Soul and Mind. When the Mind has been stilled, Soul and God alone remain, when Soul is no longer distracted by Mind, he sees God face to face; Enlightened Ones in Heaven names are established among the Radiant Stars. – Sri Shiva Rahasya

48. Cycles of Creation, Sustenance and Destruction as waves united in eternal continuum; He who knows this, with concentrated mind, enters My World of Uncreated Light by the secret gateway between two moments and goes to Everlasting Life; man shall strive to become Perfect even as I Myself am The Most Perfect; Verily, man is born to strive for Perfection. For he that seeks Perfection is a Seeker of Truth; He who seeks Truth seeks his True Home. No Soul shall ever find peace till he has found his True Home. Home is that Place where a man finds Peace. Therefore the life of man is a quest for Peace; And Peace is found in Perfection, there is no Peace where there is no Perfection; I grant many lives to a Soul that he may steadily grow in wisdom and become wise. For, no creature that is born imperfect attains Perfection in one lifetime. To expect man to become Perfect after one brief life would be unjust and unwise – Sri Shiva Rahasya

49. Those that live in harmony with Creation (Nature) live in Unity with the Lord; thus, from Wish, to Thought, to Word, the World came into being at My Divine Command. Everything is born of That Supreme Sound. Even the Divine Form you are now beholding with your eyes is a Manifestation of That; I Am That Supreme Reality. I am Boundless Freedom and Might and My Powers are Five: Omnipotence, Omniscience, Infinite Fullness-and-Satisfaction, Omnipresence and Eternity. These are My Five Powers Divine. When obscured by My Mighty Magic they become limited and the being who holds them is known as Soul. Thus the Soul is born as the sixth in the midst of the five. He is the power-holder and their master even as I am the Holder of the Five Powers Divine; The Awakened Ones, the Buddhas, they alone know that Maya is the Mother and I Alone am the Father of the multitude of creatures born in this World.

50. He who understands that everything is made of consciousness knows everything.

51. The Soul having become imperfect on his descent to Earth must become Perfect again to return unto the Perfect One. For only that which is Perfect can join Perfection. The imperfect is doomed to ever abide in separation from Supreme Perfection. Yoga is the means whereby a Soul is made Perfect and pleasing to the Lord; When other faiths have passed away, Yoga will prevail. Then Perfection shall rule over the World.

52. The Alpha and Omega of Yoga explained in one line in the 49th Sutra of Sage Patanjali's Yoga Sutras.

53. Evolution is the advancement of lower froms of life to higher ones over various lives - Sage Patanjali

54. Sage Patanjali on Pranayama (art of regulating the Pranic-energy through the vital-breath)

55. Sage Patanjali on restraining the breathing-process for extended and un-limited period of time

56. Patanjali on attainment of Divine-Wisdom through pranayama

57. The three levels of meditation - pratyahara, dharana, dhyana - Sage Patanjali

58. Total recall of all past-life memories of one's own and of other people's minds – Patanjali

59. Acquiring the prowess of an elephant and understanding the languages of beasts and birds – Patanjali

60. David and Solomon had Knowledge of the beasts and birds – Holy Qu'ran; sura XXVII. 15, 16

61. When past and present are compressed into a single-point, realm of timelessness result – Patanjali

62. Swami Vivekananda on Time-Phenomena (1890's); Thomas Mann (1924)

63. Hunger and thirst can be transcended and sight of Siddhars (perfected beings) could be attained – Patanjali

64. Practice of Yoga at dawn, noon and dusk gets rid of the 3 'poisons', hence turns one young; Thirumandiram

65. Control of seminal ejaculation and dieting prolongs life; you become the Lord; Thirumandiram

66. Man can vision the past, present and future (trikala jnana), ambrosia flows hence beyond clutches of hunger and thirst; Thirumandiram

67. Man 'turns' young by 'internal-breathing', attains immortality when ambrosia flows down through secret mystic-opening; Thirumandiram 805:

68. Beautiful maiden are attracted when Kundalini (the Cosmic-Energy) rises to the cranium-top; Thirumandiram 736

69. The realized person and the omni-present state – Adi Sankara's Viveka Chudamani

70. Cessation of thoughts brings about state of no-mind, result being spontaneous-state of Divine-Bliss - Adi Sankara's Viveka Chudamani

71. Stand apart from the body, be a witness and realize that you are the Supreme - Adi Sankara's Viveka Chudamani

72. Meditate on the Self as the vast expanse of space – Adi Sankara's Viveka Chudamani

73. Omnipresence of the soul - Adi Sankara's Viveka Chudamani

74. The Perfected-being is in a constant state of ecstasy

75. Sins no more (salvation) when one realizes that he, the soul is none other than God - Adi Sankara's Viveka Chudamani

76. Realize your Perfection - Adi Sankara's Viveka Chudamani

77. I am in all animals (life-forms) - Adi Sankara's Viveka Chudamani

78. After realization of the Self, nothing more to know - Adi Sankara's Viveka Chudamani

79. Realized person in an expanded-state is Brahman (God) - Adi Sankara's Viveka Chudamani

80. Glorification of the body leads to misery; self-realization brings purity and divinity - Adi Sankara's Viveka Chudamani

81. Advaita (God, cosmos and man are one) – the truth through sushupthi (deep sleep-state) - Adi Sankara's Viveka Chudamani

82. Through self-experience realize the expansiveness of the soul and siddhis (supernatural powers), Oneness and Bliss – remain entrenched in that state

83. The soul possesses infinite-energy; the realized person of Divine-Wisdom is greatest among great

84. Creation as was in existence in previous-cycle – Srimad Bhagavatam

85. Not the least difference between the individual soul and God – Srimad Bhagavatam

86. Vedas transcend time and space and taught by the Lord to men and various beings of other evolutionary-cycles existing in other global-constellations in other dimensions - Srimad Bhagavatam

99. 'Kailash' the realm of Lord Shiva filled with celestial earth-like living forms as well as extinct ones and one-footed and eight-footed animals – Srimad Bhagavatam

100. Stephen Hawking on interstellar travel

101. Deadly missiles,'stealth-warfare', aerial-cars, stun-weapons and 'life-giving' medicines and herbs in the Ramayana War – 'Sri Shiva Gita' & Ramayana

102. Rotating firebrand aerial (stealth) craft that was amphibious and as big as a miniature-city – Srimad Bhagavatam

103. Celestial-cars crammed in the skies – Srimad Bhagavatam

104. Effulgent car as swift as the sun, the tracks of which dug up the seven oceans – Srimad Bhagavatam

105. Sooran the Asura, Titan-King ruled over 1008 universes, ultimately defeated by Lord Muruga in the Kandha Puranam war in the 1st Yuga (eon) more than 30 million years ago in Southern India and the Lost continent of Kumari Nadu; Adi Sankara's 'Subramanya Bhujanga'; 'kandhar Alankaram'

106. During the Kandha Puranam war (30 million years ago) the entire world was enveloped in darkness (nuclear winter?) caused by the Asura (Titan) King Sooran, who then stood in the form of a 'mighty tree' in the midst of the ocean that measured a million miles high; Sooran eventually destroyed by Lord Muruga's 'Nedunchudar Vel' ("missile with the lengthy flame")

107. The mighty missile the 'Vel' that blasted a massive mountain into dust in the Kandha Puranam War 30 million years ago

108. The 'Peacock-Craft' that could circumvent the 14 planes and beyond within a micro-second

109. Chariot of Fire with horses of fire takes Elijah – The Holy Bible

110. Thunder, fire, smoke, trumpet-blast and violent shaking on Mount Sinai, The Holy Bible

111. The Japanese Royal Family are the direct Descendants of the Sun-God; Karna the son of the Sun-God (the Mahabharata warrior); Indians living on shores of Lake Titicaca descendants of Sun-God

112. The ancestors of the Dogon tribes of South Mali came from Sirius the Star

113. The Brahmastra – a retractable missile that scorched the upper, middle and lower worlds – Srimad Bhagavatam

114. 'Stun weapons' in the Ramayana war (1.7 million years ago)

115. Atom bomb in the Mahabharata war (3500 B.C.); Dr.J.Robert Oppenheimer remembered a passage from the Mahabharata after seeing the first atom bomb explode at Alamogordo, U.S.A. in 1945

116. Guru Dronacharya presented Druyodhana a body-armour that could not be pierced by any weapon – Mahabharata,'Drona parva' – Arjuna & Karna presented with similar armour

117. Cloning performed by Sage Vyasa 5500 years ago

118. Suka sated in Self-Realization, a master of Yoga, is forever 16 years old – Srimad Bhagavatam

119. Only Wise men experience Supreme Bliss – Srimad Bhagavatam

120. Gains of 'Uttama Pranayama' – becomes master of lions, tigers and elephants; gets resolved of all sins; advanced Spiritual-advancement – Sanatkumara (the mind-born son of Brahma the Creator) to Vyasa in 'Shiva Maha Purana'

121. "Like *the snake sheds its wasted-skin, man is resolved of all his sins when he meditates on Me*" – Lord Shiva to Dhurvasa in 'Shiva Maha Purana'

122. Man can quit the physical body (without dying) – Srimad Bhagavatam

123. The Lord is in the Form and Formless state – Srimad Bhagavatam

124. In an ancient civilization that predated the Vedic and Chaldean, there is mention of the Glorious body – The Mother (of Pondicherry) in 'Questions and Answers, 1957'; radiant-luminous body – the Jyotirmaya deha of Vaishnavites; transformation of body into gold – Tamil Siddhar Thirumoolar

125. *Perfection is the true aim of all culture...* - Sri Aurobindo in, 'The Supramental Manifestation'; Thirumandiram – attainment of perfection through self-analysis of the body and Realization of the Self; body the microcosm, universe the macrocosm, all of interdimensional-space can be traversed

126. Transition of the Physical body from imperfection to Perfection could take a thousand years! – Sri Aurobindo, The Mother of Pondicherry

127. Ayn Rand on Human Perfection in 'Atlas Shrugged', 'The Fountainhead'; Ayn Rand:" My philosophy, in essence is the concept of man as a heroic being, with his own happiness as the moral purpose of his life..." Roark – "the truth remains that he exists in everyone – the Self sufficient ego"

128. Most ideas, thought-provocations and diseases originate in the Spiritual or finer bodies of man; We are in the midst of a sea of tremendous vibrations – The Mother, Micheangelo, Thiruvalluvar

129. "There exists an underground reservoir of aggregated memories through which minds may communicate" – Carl Jung, Arthur Koestler, Adrian Dobbs, The Mother, Dr.Ramamurti

130. *"Two of the most advanced fields of modern science, higher mathematics and particle physics are sliding into the fantastic world of phenomena such as 'anti-matter', "the four-dimensional universe",'imaginary-masses' and electrons which "move backward in time"* – Sir Cyril Burt

131. Stephen Hawking to Nigel Farndale:*" There have not been any significant changes in the human DNA in the past 10,000 years... Our computers have an advantage of speed but show no sign of intelligence; our present computers are less complex than the brain of an earthworm.... We can be quick-witted or very intelligent, but not both;* Carl Jung, Adi Sankara, Thirumandiram, Holy Bible, Hanuman

132. Cycle of death and birth – Plato, Socrates, Zen Master Daito, Lord Krishna

133. Reply to Sadhu Sundar Singh's (Christian Preacher) criticism on Yogic-meditation and the Yoga-System; Essenes of Judaism, Sufism, Islam, Pythagaros, Ch'an, Zen, Buddhism; Holy Bible, Thirumandiram

134. Swami Vivekananda ('Bhakti Yoga'): "…. One's love and knowledge of one's own religion should be deep and the knowledge and acceptance of other religions should also be broad

135. Dr.Carl Jung - Yoga superior to gymnastics and breathing-exercises; Yoga is the perfect and appropriate method of fusing body and mind; a psychological disposition which makes possible intuitions that transcend consciousness

136. Recognition of Superconsciousness which in its grandeur is the exact opposite of the subconscious mind conceived by Sigmund Freud (From 'Autobiography of a Yogi' by Paramahansa Yogananda

137. Sir jagadis Chandra Bose:*"...to my amazement, I found boundary lines vanishing, and points of contact emerging between the realms of the living and the non-living."*

163. 'Empyrean' – the highest heaven – "Kurrat un nar "– Holy Qu'ran

164. Man can disappear and re-appear at will – Patanjali' Yoga Sutra; Thirumandiram; "Cloak of invisibility"; Albert Einstein's "Unified Field Thoery"; Sadasiva Brahmendra & Swami Ramalingam's "Cause-effect body" (kaarana-kaarya rupam and teleportaion); St.Appar, Goraknath, Swami Nityananda of Vadakara,'Tai Chi' Founder Chang San Feng; Charles Berlitz, John Gribbin; Lord Rama in Kamba Ramayanam, Lord Buddha, Lord Mahavira, Lord Krishna – the 'Kshetra' – the field extends to infinity in Bhagavad Gita

165. Rotating 'Black Holes' Connect Multiple Universes and Different Times

166. "The Religious leaders of the world had forgotten their common origin … Moses, Jesus and Mohammed were equal Prophets, mirroring God's glory, messengers bearing the imprint of the great Creator". "Later on, Zoroaster, Buddha, Confucius, Krishna, Lao and Baha'u'llah, the last great manifestation of the Divine Being…" The 'Bab' disappeared after being shot by 750 Armenian soldiers in front of thousands…

167. The Self – the Soul is the 'True Man' concealed within the body, it is the Soul of the Universe, the Lord of Time, the Great Lord, the Perfect One and is a Witness to everything as he is preent everywhere; That imperishable core is part of My Eternal Self; Man is called 'man' (Manu) because he is determined by his mind, verily what he thinks he becomes, elevating himself by noble thoughts, he once again becomes Divine; the Soul is pristinely Pure otherwise it could never become Perfect even in hundreds of lifetimes – Sri Shiva Rahasya

168. Man is born with different kinds of Physical bodies and minds that correspond with inner latent tendencies developed over past lives; everything is born of the mind and the mind is nothing but the light of the soul tinted by latent tendencies of past lives; The world was created not in vain but with a purpose, Truth remedy over all sorrows; wisemen regard this Universe as made of knowledge

169. Yoga is the Power of Unity – *the Unity between Body, Mind and Soul is of the Human kind, that which is between Man and Nature is of the Worldwide Kind, but that which is between Man and the Lord is indeed Divine*

170. The Soul enveloped in 84,000 Veils – corresponding to the 84,000 births man takes – 42,000 births as inanimate forms auch as stones, rocks and other things made of the five basic elements; 15,000 as half-sentinent things like plants and trees;12,000 in sentinent things like insects and worms;9,000 as land, water and airborne creatures and 6000 in Human form

171. *The Self doesn't have to be Realized for it has already been Realized; Realize with a still mind the state between sleep and wakefulness, the gap between two perceptions; the mind should be brought to the condition of a new-born baby; One should also be free from the thought of "I see", only by transcending Will, sensation or thought, only then is Perfection possible* – Tripura Rahasya

172. The Perfect state of Samadhi (Oneness) not experienced by merely being in that state for a couple of hours by closing on'e eyes and stilling the thought-waves, One should always be in Perfect Equlibrium (samadharshini) – Tripura Rahasya

173. King Janaka to sage Ashtavakra on the infinite pervasiveness of the Soul and by realizing it by withdrawing the mind from objects – Tripura Rahasya

174. The Fire of Yoga burns the fetters of ignorance and sin; The greatest form of Yoga is that of one meditating upon oneself as identical with God's Immanent Infinite Being (practiced even by gods - angels) that leads to God-Realization and Perfection in this very life and joys of heaven experienced at the very moment, on earth – Sri Shiva Rahasya

175. Perfection not attained in One Life-Time; World is ruled by Radiant-Ones who are Rays of God's Own Light; Yoga is living in Unity with Truth, the Person knows neither grief nor pain; Yogis who have attained Perfection are the Jewels of God's Creation who sit in the

Assembly of Holy Sages; The Yogis task is to reveal God's Will to the world; The Land where Yogis are Honored shall be known as the Land of Righteousness (dharmabhumi) – Sri Shiva Rahasya

176. A Great Man is Ever Desirous to Know Things of the Soul, Whilst others follow their craving for things material; Knowledge is of Three Kinds – Hearsay, Reason and Direct Experience; The Un-awakened Soul shrouded in a Power called Material-Energy (Prakriti), upper part of the dark shroud is the Intellect (buddhi), lower part is the Mind (manas) – Sri Shiva Rahasya

177. The One who understands the Twenty-Five Life-Principles is a Free and Happy Soul, but He who understands the Greatest Secret of Maya is One with God who Knows the Thirty-Six Principles Knows Everything and All – Sri Shiva Rahasya

178. Everyone is a Spark of Heaven; The Thirty-Six Principles are to be Ascended gradually, the Knower knows the Secret of All Numbers and Everything; Liberating himself from bondage of the Mind by means of Yoga, he turns from finite to Infinite, from speck of stardust to Sea of Divine Radiance, from Man-God to God–Man; Yoga is therefore to be known as the Expansion of the human soul to Cosmic Dimensions; Man is born to strive for Perfection, that One is the Seeker of Truth, he who seeks Truth seeks his True Home, Home is where man finds Peace, Peace is found in Perfection, man's life is quest for Peace – Sri Shiva Rahasya

179. It is through the Power of Unity that man is united with the body, through the Power of Unity, Enlightened Man is united with the Awakened Soul; Through The Power of Unity, all conflicts are ended and Peace is established in the World, the Power that brings a thousand things together and preserves the life of everything; By the Power of Yoga Peace is restored to a troubled mind, by the Power of Yoga man is united with the Lord, by the Power of Yoga the brotherhood of man and Unity of Life are preserved; By the Power of Yoga God's Kingdom is Established on Earth, There is nothing that cannot be achieved by the Power of Yoga – Sri Shiva Rahasya

180. The Three States – The Waking, Dreaming And Dreamless are known to All, the Fourth state – 'Turiya' is known by the Yogi, the Fifth is known only by the All Knowing One; The One who Realizes the Fourth State is an Awakened One, a Buddha; But he who conquers Sleep is a Great Yogi and a Well-Awakened (Prabuddha). He is a Great Hero (Maha Vira) and a Vanquisher of Death – Sri Shiva Rahasya

181. The Lord leads the holy Sages through a secret cleft in the walls of the mighty mount Kailash in the Himalayas and shows them various worlds (in various planes and other dimensions) and their beings and ultimately the Ultimate Heaven – Sri Shiva Rahasya

182. The greatest Yoga according to the Lord Himself is when one meditates with the 'bhava' – feel and belief that he and the Transcendental Immanent Lord are One – Sri Shiva Rahasya

183. The Four Goals of Life and Supreme Perfection attained in the present life for he is born of Divine Perfection – Sir Shiva Rahasya

184. Those who attain perfection know the greatest Joy of all; Only the one who goes with Unity with the Lord transcends the veil of Maya, he alone is a man of Unity – an Yogi, a Perfect One – a Siddha – Sri Shiva Rahasya

185. Microbes *converse* with human cells according to microbiologists;"*they function like our mother…. We should love them… we are in equilibrium.*"

186. Various States of the Mind: "The *Saiva Siddhanta Philosophy of the Tamils is the most elaborate, influential and undoubtedly the most valuable of all religions…*" - Rev.G.U.Pope of Oxford University; Modern Science; Saiva Siddhanta Philosophy

187. Parallels in all Religions and all Philosophies

188. We are all named before birth! – Holy Bible, Saiva Siddhanta

189. All Messages are imprinted in the Genes! Can Man be re-programmed to become a Superman? – 80 to 100 feet tall man according to Vedas, Tamil Siddhars, Hadith of Islam; 100,000 years life-span of man in 'Kreta Yuga' more than 3 million years ago; 'Deathless –state' attained by Siddhars; 'Acquired Savant Syndrome', 'Acquired Foreign Accent Syndrome', 'Total Recall' is attainment of the '64 Arts' ('Kalai Tattvas') and recollection of experiences of more than 84,000 past lives, of One's Divinity; Lord Buddha, Lord Chaitanya, Ramalingam Swami, Shirdi Sai Baba

190. Fifty Letters Contain All World Languages - All world languages are contained in the 50 Sanskrit Alphabets, ancient Tamil, Japanese & Chinese Vowel-Consonants – Carl Sagan, Thirumandiram, Kanchi Sankaracharya, and Holy Bible

191. 'Aum' and its Significance – The Bible, Heraclitus and 'Logos', The Vedas, The Kado Upanishad, Thirumandiram

192. Mantras Which Are Sound-Vibrations 'Protects', Heals And Has A Positive-Influence In All Life-Forms

193. Birds Live In a World Expanded From Ours – National Geographic

194. 'Jonathan Livingston Seagull' By Richard Bach on "The Strive For Perfection"; on 'Teleportation'

195. Realizing the Entire Universe Withing Themselves And The Self As Permeating The Entire Universe – Srimad Bhagavata

196. The Humble Fruit Fly Like the shark, Crocodile, dolphin, Seal, Penguin, Spider, Ant, Bat, Beetle, Snake, Termite, Trees & Many Others In Nature Have Attained Perfection

197. The First Revelations of The Lord Were Revealed in Both Sanskrit and Tamil

198. The Three Philosophies and States that Define All of Mankind – Lord Rama, Hanuman, Ramakrishna Paramahamsa

199. After Death, Man lives in the 'Other World' for some time with His Name, Body-shape and Sex – Holy Bible, Holy Quran, Thirukural, Thirumandiram, Bhagavad Gita, Ramayana, Mahabharata, Silapathikaram, Swami Abhedhananda, Auvviar, 291st Guru Maharaj of Madurain Adheenam

Conclussion

Man Was Programmed To Live For A Hundred Thousand (100,000) Years; Man (Adam According to the Hadith) Was A Hundred (100) Feet Tall", Holy Bible, Genesis: *There were giants on earth in those days",* **"***Man was as tall as a fully grown Palmyra tree***" According to the Tamil Siddhars; Tombs Of Caine and Abel Near 'Adam's Bridge' in Southern India; Elephant-Killer/constrictor Snakes, Gigantic Birds, Dragons ('Yazhi' in Tamil) Lived on Earth**

Man according to the timeless Vedas was *programmed* to live for 100,000 (hundred thousand) years in an early era (in the present one it is 100 years) and his *average* height was 32 feet but even stood 100 feet tall! Siddhars (Siddhas in Sanskrit) who are *Perfected beings* of the Tamil land like Bogar mention specifically that man in earlier eras stood "*… as tall as a fully-grown palmyra tree*" which even now in ideal conditions grows fifty to sixty feet tall. The *Hadith* a holy book of Islam containing anecdotes of the holy Prophets too mentions that when Adam was banished from heaven and when he landed on mount Sarandip in Sri Lanka, he stood 60 cubits or a *100 feet* tall. To substantiate this claim there exists even now the tombs of Cain and Abel the sons of Adam and Eve which measure 50 to 60 feet long in a Moslem Dargah at Rameshwaram which is a coastal town of southern India that stands connected to the *'Adam's bridge'* that runs from Sri Lanka and India. Just as Genesis in the Bible says that there were giants on earth in those days and that giants were the sons of fallen angels; Islam says that the skeletons of giants were so huge that animals like the fox and jackals would utilize the eye-sockets and nasal-cavities of the skulls as nesting places! One can now see photos of huge giant human-skeletons that have been recently excavated in Arabian deserts that are available on google.

1

Though the Holy Bible says that Adam lived for 930 years, ancient Indian epics like the Ramayana say that Emperor Dasaratha the father of Lord Rama lived for 60,000 years and the 'Tripura Rahasya'says that even in an earlier era known as the '*Kreta Yuga*' about 30 million years ago many a king lived for 80,000 and even 100,000 years.

Birds and animals were also huge like the mammoth and dinosaur whose fossils and bodies that are still preserved in ice and rock-sediments we find today. It is mentioned in the Kamba Ramayana that there were huge snakes ('*anaicondran*' literally means 'elephant-killer' and sounds very similar to anaconda)that could constrict and kill an elephant and the Tamil Siddhars say that there was a huge bird that could snatch and carry away animals that were ten times the weight of elephants known as the '*andabahirandam*' and there are stone-carvings found in ancient temples depicting an extinct enormous gigantic dragon-like creature known as the '*Yazhi*' (pronounced as 'yallhi' in Tamil) holding in their tails elephants which seem puny in size in comparison to their own.

The Four 'Mind-Born' Sons (*Manasa Puthra*) Of The Creator Flew Down To Earth From The 'Fifth-Heaven' in 'Fiery Chariots' (*Agni ratha*) Hundreds Of Millions Of Years Ago And 'Fast-forwarded' The Evolutionary-Process'; The Four Holy Men Stayed On Earth For 400,000 Years, Lord Sanarkumara 18 Years Old For Eternity

Hundreds of millions of years ago the four 'mind-born' (*manasa puthra*) sons of the Creator flew down from the fifth Plane (known as *Sathya loka*, there are fourteen planes in what is known as *seven upper planes* and *seven lower planes* containing countless universes and ours is *Bhu loka* the lowest and first among the upper planes) in 'fiery Chariots' (*Agni ratha*) that flew at 'thought-speed' (*mano veha*) landed on a great mass of tree-covered mountainous-land that existed below southern India and extended all the way beyond Australia and New Zealand in the south and South America in the west, Java, Sumatra and the African continent in the east, which later came to be known as the *Lemuria continent*. The four holy beings along with their assistants stayed on earth for more than 400,000 years, fast-forwarded the evolutionary process, greatly reduced the height of man *and* ape who were *both* more than 50 to 60feet tall and possessed *three* eyes at that time, got rid of several species of life-forms that proved to be a hindrance to the growth of the evolutionary process as a whole and introduced new ones when found necessary. Among the four holy beings (known as *sanahathi munis*) who had received direct initiation from the Primal Lord Shiva Himself, *Lord Sanarkumara* is said to be *18 years old* for *eternity*.

Primal Lord is Above The Holy Trinity And The 'Penta Gods' (Five Gods); Life in Different States in Varied Life-Forms And in Realized-Man; 'System Theorists' And The Tamil Siddhar's Thirumandiram Claim That The Cosmos is One Single Entity; The Perfected Being does literally become a 'Star' adorning the sky; God knows the number of stars and calls them all by name:

Though the Lord is One, he acts in a multitude of ways, the Saiva tradition in particular says that Five are the main Acts – the Power to Create, to Sustain, to Annihilate, to Veil and to Grace (though Christianity and the ancient Egyptians believe in three – *The Holy Trinity as the Father, Son and Holy Spirit* and the latter knowing them as *Osiris, Isis and Horus*); there are an hierarchy of Devas or Angels who are empowered to control all heavenly bodies and all of nature; all the rivers, lakes, mountains, seas and oceans are goverened by elevated souls; in fact all living forms and what seem to be the inanimate are aspects of the Lord. Life is said to be in the deep sleep-state in stones, in the sleep-state in plants and trees, in the dream-state in animals, in the woken-state in the conscious-man, and in the eternally happy-state in the Superconscious or Realized man. Though the souls seem to be infinite, they like little waves that arise on the surface of the mighty ocean, are mere sparks of the infinite-fire that is the Lord and like rain-drops and mighty rivers merge into the ocean, ultimately merge with the Lord.

The 'System Theorists' in western countries believe that like many cells constitute an organ and many organs constitute a body, the countless living-forms could constitute the earth and a Japanese scientist claims that the earth is a gigantic living organism that breathes once a day – but it is the ancient Indian cultures that emphatically state that like the human-soul (of which we are not aware of either), the earth, the sun, stars and in fact all the heavenly bodies are goverened by an individual soul which are all part of the Cosmic Soul – Thirumoolar the Tamil Siddhar in his Thirumandiram:" *One alone created the worlds seven; One alone sustains the worlds seven; One alone annihilates the worlds seven;* **One alone is all the worlds and all lives too.**"

Sage Parasara the father of sage Vyasa (the codifier of the Vedas as well as most Puranas) pointed out a star in the 'Seven-Star Constellation'(Sabdha Rishi Mandala) to 'Dvaiba' asVyasa was known as a lad, and said, "*He is my grand-father 'Maha Rishi Vashista'.*" When Vyasa asked his father whether he too would become a star, sage Prasara replied," *Yes, according to the Vedas those who live a virtuous, righteous life and protect the Veda-Dharma, would take birth as a star.*"

Two Harvard University astronomers have discovered a "great wall" of galaxies that they estimate to be 500 million light-years long, 200 million light-years wide, and 15 million light-years thick (one light-year is 5.88 trillion miles). Yet God knows each of them by their names according to the Holy Bible, Psalm 143:3-4.

The Lord The Father Lifted Up Mount Sinai And As Krishna Lifted Up the Mount Govardhana

'From Talmud To Torah' – R.P.Lawrie
Torah the Cement

The Bible Rabbis have driven home this moral by declaring that when the Israelites stood trembling at the foot of Mount Sinai, God lifted the mountain over them and said, "If you accept My Torah well and good; but if not, here shall be your grave."

What saved the Israelites after their release from Egypt, from splitting up into tiny fragments and being swallowed up by the surrounding peoples, was this possession which they held in common- The Torah was, as it were, the cement which made them adhere and gave them strength to hold fast.

When Lord Indra the Lord of the Devas or Angels brought down a deadly rain of water, stones and rocks upon the cow-herders and Gopis of Brindavan, angered and jealous by them praying to Lord Krishna instead of him, Lord Krishna came to their rescue. Krishna lifted up Mount Govardhana and balanced it at the tip of his little finger and held it for three consecutive days thus protecting them from the deadly onslaught. Only after Indra realized his folly and surrendered at the Holy Feet of the Lord, did the Primal Lord put down the mountain – Srimad Bhagavata.

Earth And Everything Cosely Monitored; Depths Of The Seven Oceans Dug-up by The Tracks of A Flying-Craft (*Vimana*) According To The Srimad Bhagavata; Archangel Gabriel Taught Adam to Grind Wheat; The Grape – Earth's First Fruit Introduced; Remarkable Similarities Between World's Most Ancient Religions of Hinduism And The Three 'Abrahamic Faiths'

That we are closely monitored, guided and led can be understood for it is even mentioned in the Srimad Bhagavata that ages ago the fellies or tracks of the *vimana* or flying-craft ("*.... the effulgent car that was as swift as the sun*") of Priavarata dug up the seven oceans and Islam tells us that Archangel Gabriel taught Adam apart from morals, how to make bread by grinding wheat between two stones and introduced earth's first fruit, the grape. Moreover this claim could be established by going into the two most ancient religions of the world Judaism (that includes the three 'Abrahamic Faiths' – Judaism, Christianity and Islam) and Hinduism have various Prophets and Visionaries and which have remarkable similarities: Like in Hinduism, Judaism too has a thousand Holy Names of the Lord some were considered too holy to be even uttered, one among the names is '**EL SHADDAI**' and one of its meanings is "**The One with the golden-locks**"(blonde hair) and one Name of the Lord in Tamil is '**SHEN SHADDIYON**', which literally means "***One with golden-red colored fiery locks***"!; The '**Aum**' or 'Ohm' of Hinduism,'**Amen**' of Christianity,'**Amin**' of Islam and '**Hum**' of Tibetan Buddhism seem remarkably similar; The Lord is addressed as '**Abba**'(Father) in the Hebrew texts while in Tamil He is addressed as '**Appa**'(Father); Apart from the '**Torah**' another Holy very secretive mystical Holy book of Judaism is the '**KABBALA**' which means "*the shining frontal-skull*" and in Yoga there is a breathing-technique known as '**Kabbala bheti**' through the practice of which one's forehead or cranium or kabbala shines with the light or radiance of Wisdom!; The 'Heavenly-Vehicle' or flying-craft,'*El Burraq*' mentioned in the Holy Qu'ran and '*Kamadhenu*' (the Heavenly cow) mentioned often in ancient Indian texts are remarkably similar – while the former has the face of a woman, body of a horse and tail of a peacock, the latter is almost the same excepting it has the body of a cow; The Crafts used by the Lord mentioned in both the Holy Bible and Indian texts have the foot and hooves of a 'Calf' or a 'Bull' – telescopic landing gear?; The **Prophet Ezekiel** in the **Holy Bible** visions God who comes through a whirlwind with the sound of roaring flood-waters and blowing of ram-horns and trumpets with flashing lights and he sees God having '**four-faces**', in all Hindu texts the Creator is known as '**Nanmukan**' – the '**four-faced One**'!

Evolution According To Charles Darwin, Sage Patanjali; James in The Bible,84,000 Births And 6000 Human Births According To 'Sri Shiva Rahasya', Saint Manickavasagar; Re-birth – Plato, Socrates, Zen Master Daito

Evolution as defined by naturalist like Charles Darwin deals only with the physical aspect and regarding the mind itself they have very little to say, in Darwin's own words in 'Origin of Species': "*Many instincts are so wonderful that their development will appear to the reader a difficulty sufficient to overthrow my whole theory. I may here premise that I have nothing to do with the origin of the mental powers, any more than I have with that of of life itself.*" Many instincts like ducklings taking to water immediately after hatching, fish like salmon migrating over thousands of miles in ocean-waters and returning back to their exact place of birth to once again spawn and die and birds and butterflies which also migrate by flying over land and sea travelling distances more than even our modern commercial jets like the 'artic tern' does, convinces us that the path they tread had been performed by their fore-fathers countless times over numerous births for it to be ingrained into their memory or their genes as scientists would say.

Evolution (*Parinama*) according to Sage Patanjali is the gradual advancement of lower forms of life to higher ones over *various births*.

Though we seem to think that we live for a long time, the truth is as is mentioned in the Holy Bible too in James 4:14 that Life is only a vapor that appears for a moment and then vanishes in the Cosmic calendar a life-time exists for but a moment. We needn't worry about that too much for unlike we think that we live for one life-time, the Lord in 'Sri Shiva Rahasya' says that man takes *84,000 births* – we take thousands of births first as the five basic elements in nature – earth, water, fire, air and space; thousands again as grass, shrubs, plants and trees; thousands again in the animal and bird kingdom; *6000 lives* in the human-form itself! Manickavasagar a Tamil Saint of the 5th century A.D. in his Thiruvasagam had also elaborated:" *from a blade of grass to shrubs, plants, creepers, trees, birds, animals, snakes, man, ghost, god (Angel) through all life-forms I have evolved, grown worn and tired in the endless cycle my Lord!*"

Plato:" *Life in the universe would have gone out of existence if there were no succeeding births.*"

Socrates:" *If death had been only the end of all, the wicked would have had a bargain in dying; for they would have been happily quit not only of those bodies but of their own evil together with their souls. But now in as much as the soul is manifestly immortal there is no release or salvation from evil, except attainment of the highest virtues and wisdom.*"

When the Zen Master Daito saw the Emperor Godaigo who was a student of Zen, the master said:" *We were parted many thousands of kalpas ago, yet we have not been separated even for a moment. We are facing each other all day long, yet we have never met.*"

"Blocked-off Memories",'Tabula Rasa', "Collective Unconscious" & 'Total Recall' – Carl Jung; Carl Sagan on 'Habitable Zones' in the Immediate Neighborhood

Does modern science accept the fact that we take numerous births and is there intelligence out there in space? Well, they seem to, but speak in a different language, Carl Jung the pupil of Sigmund Freud the father of modern day psychology and psychiatry says that we possess "*blocked-off memories*" that contain memories of experiences that we had as of animals, birds and even protozoa, which were all imprinted in our genes and passed on through our DNA.

Carl Jung further claims that no one is born a '*tabula rasa*', that is with a blank state of mind. As the body carries features specifically human yet individually varied, so does the psychic organism. The psyche preserves an unconscious stratum of elements going back to the invertebrates and ultimately the protozoa. Jung speaks of a hypothetical peeling of the *collective unconscious*, layer by layer, down to the psychology of the amoeba. And Carl Sagan the renowned astronomer and former Director of NASA as well as SETI (search for extra terrestrial intelligence) in 'Contact' and 'Cosmos' says that there are many planets in the *habitable zone* which could contain life and that atleast 18000 planets could have life in our *immediate neighborhood*.

18 Evolutionary-Cycles

Evolution takes place over thousands of births over billions of years and this Transition takes place in *224* '*bhuvanas*' or global-constellations spread over 14 planes. There are totally 18 'evolutionary cycles' including the human that are progressing simultaneously like that of the 'Devas' (Angels),'Asuras' (Titans),'Rakshasas' (Demons),'Ghandarvas' & 'Kinnarvas' (Celestial bards, singers & dancers),'Nagas' (possessing Serpentine bodies with human-like faces of the nether worlds) etc. The Holy Qu'ran states that huge bird-like creatures with human-heads and wild ferocious animals with human-heads that bite and eat the living flesh of other creatures of the nether worlds. Each are ensnared in their own '*space-time*' for a day for the Angels is equal to one earth-year and a day for the Creator whose realm is the fifth plane is 4.32 billion earth-years and night again another 4.32 billion years!

Multitudes of Cycles of Creation And Destruction; Power to Kill by Sight (*'nokku varmam'* in Tamil,*'Habs-I nazir'* in Arabic); Beings as tall as the Holy Ka'ba in Mecca Who Claim to be morethan 40,000 years old; 30 other 'previous worlds'

Apart from many lost civilizations like Atlantis and 'Kumari Kandam' (lost continent that existed below southern India) many buried civilizations are still being unearthed among others all over the globe, like in China and North America also. That there were many cycles of creation and destruction is not mentioned only in ancient texts, for a Sufi saint the celebrated Shaikh, Muhyi-ud-Din al-'Arabi who possessed the power to arrest a person by mere power of sight known as '*habs I nazir*'(in Arabic and '*nokku varmam*' in Tamil whereby one could disable and even kill a person from a distance) once saw three extremely tall persons circumnavigating the Holy Ka'ba in Mecca who were as tall as the Holy Ka'ba which stands nearly 38 feet tall, the saint would not let them go until they mentioned who they were and they claimed that they too were of human origin and that they were more than 40,000 years old and when upon being questioned again on how that could be since it was only 6000 years since the advent of Adam, they again claimed that *Adam was only the father of modern man* and that Allah had created *30 other worlds* preceding the present one and that they were of a previous era!

Can Man be Re-programmed To Live For Eternity?; Made Immune to All Diseases?; Speak All Languages? Even that of Beasts and Birds like King Solomon and the Sage Narada?; Teleport to distant places and be back in a jiffy like Saint Antony, Gurn Nanak and Saint Ramalingam?; Can He Master the '64 Arts' or 'The 64 Branches of Knowledge' And Attain Divine Wisdom?; Can Man Cure incurable Diseases, turn base metal into gold, turn eternally young and bring the dead back to Life like Jesus Christ, Chaitanya Prabhu and Saint Ramalingam?

Can man be re-programmed to live as many years as he had done in the first eon and grow to the height and stature of his liking? Can he be disease-free and be immune to the deadly effects of natural, extra-terrestrial as well as man-made bacteria, viruses radiation and poisons? Can he speak all languages, even that of the beasts and birds like King Solomon and the Sage Narada had done? Can he teleport himself to distant places and be back in a jiffy like Saint Antony, Guru Jnanak, Saint Ramalingam and Sadasiva Brahmendra had done? Can he be a master of all the "*64 branches of Knowledge*" (known as the '*Kalai Tattvas*' or '*Art Principles*') that includes painting, sculpting, dancing, music, literature, prose, engineering, astronomy, medicine, astrology, archery, wrestling, sword-fencing, warfare, in fact everything which itself is known as *inferior-knowledge* ('*Apara Vidya*') and attain *Divine Wisdom* (known as '*Para Vidya*')? Can he turn base metal into gold, cure in-curable diseases, bring the dead back to life like Jesus Christ, Saint Jnanasambahandar, Saint Thirunavukarasu and Sri Ragavendra did? Can he turn his own body into a golden radiant-form that no weapon nor the elements of nature affect it, *turn* eternally young as Chaitanya Maha Prabhu, Saint Ramalingam, Meera, Andal and many others had done and finally de-materialized or disappeared right in the presence of many onlookers?

The Quest For the 'Fountain of Youth'; DNA Programming and Natural programming; Jesus Christ in Matt.5,48 on being as perfect therefore as the heavenly father is perfect,'Saiva Siddhanta of the Tamils:"*Like copper turns into gold when verdigris present in it is removed, man becomes the Divine when three 'malas' (stains) are removed*"; Sri Shiva Rahasya:" *The One who knows the secret between two breaths comes to know that he and I are One.*"

Man has wondered whether it is possible to extend his life-time and his quest for the elusive elixir, the *fountain of youth* has been relentless the pace for which has grown manifold in recent times.

Modern research says that by genetic-engineering, specific genes like the ones that cause ageing have been identified and isolated so that those diseases could be cured or prevented altogether! Our DNA could be re-programmed like the DNA of the mongoose has been *naturally* programmed to be immune to snake-venom and the DNA of prostitutes in a particular country in Africa who were found to be immune to the HIV virus as found recently by a global study on AIDS done by W.H.O.

But could man become the Super-Man, the Divine-Being as the Lord Jesus Christ himself says in the Holy Bible; Matt.5.48:" *Be ye perfect therefore as your heavenly Father is perfect.*"? Well Vedanta and the Saiva Siddhanta of the Tamils very clearly and emphatically state that the true 'Self' – the Soul which is Pure Consciousness is none other than the eternal infinite cosmic Being. Like copper turns into gold when'verdigris' – the green-rust present in it is removed, when three '*malas*' or stains - ego, residues of past-lives and illusion ('*anava*','*kanma*','*maya*') are removed man is the Cosmic Being!

That one can transcend space and time is confirmed by Lord Shiva Himself in the Sri Shiva Rahasya,'The Second Light' 72': "*the one who knows the secret between two breaths comes to know that He and I are One*" He moreover says that "*movement means Time*", and in the universe the movement of the stars, sun and moon determines Time, and in the human body the chief form of movement is the one caused by Prana (the dynamic breath). In fact He goes on to add that there are only three things in the world,'God','Soul' and 'Mind', and "*when the mind is stilled by stopping the Prana, God and Soul come face to face, the Father and Son become One*".

Transcending Space and Time possible by Watching the gap between two breaths – 'Yoga Vashista'; The Physical Body too should attain Perfection according to Thirumoolar and Sri Aurobindo in 'The Supramental Manifestation' and 'The Synthesis of Yoga'; Levitation of the Physical Body (*Uthapena*), Attaining the 'Cause-Effect Body'(*kaarana-kaarya rupa*), Attaining the 'Body of golden radiant-light' and finally de-materializing

There is a very interesting incident mentioned in the 'Yoga Vashishta' where when Vashishta is questioned by the twelve year old prince Lord Rama who was being taught the tenets of Yoga on how was it possible for man to transcend Space and Time and whether he had met such a person, the Master replied in the affirmative and said that he met 'Kahapusandha' an accomplished Siddha in a secret cave north-east of mount Kailash in the Himalayas. Kahapusandha appeared in his golden-radiant form (that is available to us only in heaven), had attained the state of an eighteen year old for eternity and was a witness to 7500 'pralayas' or global and universal-level catastrophes that takes place at the end of every '*kalpa*' – 432 crore or 4.32 billion years being the day-time of Lord Brahma the Creator. When Vashishta questioned him on how he had attained that exalted-state, Kahapushanda replied that he *watched* the gap or interval between breaths which was the Infinite-State of the Lord which contained all the worlds with their respective time-zones!

The Physical body too has to turn perfect though many claim that the physical body is unclean and should not be given undue importance, Yoga stresses on the fact that the physical is the base and so has to first be strong and clean. Thirumoolar says that only after realizing that the body was the *Temple* that housed the Lord, he took utmost care to nurture and preserve the body and Sri Aurobino emphatically says in 'The Supramental Manifestation' and 'The Synthesis of Yoga' that for Perfection to be Complete, the physical too has to be Perfect. Among the first signs of attainment of Perfection is that the body becomes disease-free, attains a glow, becomes light and begins to levitate for like the string acquires the fragrance of the flowers strung on it, the physical begins to acquire the qualities of the subtle or Spiritual bodies which in Sanskrit is known as '*Uthapena*'. Like the Lord who is in the three states of 'Form','Form-Formless'and 'Formless' man too goes through the metamorphosis – he attains the 'Cause-Effect Body' (*Kaarana-Kaarya Rupa*) whereby his body like the flame can be seen but cannot be grasped nor affected by any weapon nor any of the elements in nature; he then acquires the 'Sound/Vibrant Body' (*Pranava Deha*) or the 'Radiant Light-Body' (*Jyotirmaya Deha*) or the 'Wisdom Body' (*Jnana Deha*) and finally de-materializes or disappears like the "Bab' the founder of the 'Ba'hai' faith had done in Iran in 1850 and many Perfected Beings of India like Lord Chaitanya, Pattinathar, Adi Shankara, Meera, Andal and Saint Ramalingam whose image could not be captured on film and finally like many others disappeared before many onlookers in 1872!

Carl Sagan chose the 50 Sanskrit Alphabets which are also the 'Prime Alphabets' or Vowel-Consonants of the Chinese, Japanese and ancient Tamil Languages to be inscribed on a golden-record and sent into outerspace for an 'Alien' chance-encounter; Thirumandiram and Sivananda's 'Kundalini Yoga' on 50 letters existing as 50 sound-vibrations in the six Chakras of the Human-body and containing All Languages and 'All Knowledge

Carl Sagan the astronomer and former director of NASA mentions that when S.E.T.I. (search for extra-terrestrial intelligence) decided to send a satellite the *Voyager* into outer space for a chance contact to be established with alien intelligence apart from utilizing radio-telescopes to scan multiple frequencies in space, it chose the 50 alphabets of the Sanskrit language (which also are the Tamil vowel-consonants of an earlier era) to be inscribed on a golden-record (apart from other details of our world) which are also the 'Prime Alphabets' of the Chinese (for though the Chinese language has more than 50 to 60,000 alphabets,50 are the vowel-consonants) as well as Japanese languages, for they contain the entire gamut of sounds possible. After reading Sagan's works, I instantly remembered the Tamil Siddhar Thirumoolar's Thirumandiram (thousands of years old) in which he mentions:" *Fifty letters alone are all Vedas ...*" and Sivananda's 'Kundalini Yoga' where he mentions that the six main Chakras which are energy-vortexes and psychic-spots that exist in the subtle bodies of man each contain a specific number of sound-vibrations that are activated when the 'Kundalini' or 'Cosmic-energy' lying dormant at the base-chakra below the spinal-column is aroused by yogic-means, made to flow into them, they are in total fifty in number, and when the energy attains the seventh chakra above the crown of the head, the concerned person attains superconsciousness, he becomes a *full-blown Yogi* and in an instant comes to know all languages and their texts, even that of the beasts and birds and of the nether and celestial-regions!

Answers to scientific-problems like the DNA chain received through visions and Dreams; Fritjof Capra's Vision of the Cosmic-Dance of Lord Shiva in 'Tao Of Physics'

Bertrand Russell:" *What science cannot tell us mankind cannot know?*" But even great scientists like Niels Bohr had visioned the atom model and Francis Harry Crick the DNA chain, so can man in a higher state of consciousness get answers to scientific problems? Michelangelo to from where he gets his ideas:" ... *perhaps from god!*" – 'Agony and Ecstasy' by Irvin Stone.

The adorable character 'Mickey Mouse' is etched in stone dated to the 13th century found in Mexico though it became famous after it was visioned and drawn by Walt Disney in the 20th century! Albert Einstein and Jonas Salk accept that humanity should be grateful to the services rendered by God's representatives. Einstein:" *Humanity has every reason to place the proclaimers of high moral standards and values above the discoveries of objective truth. What humanity owes to personalities like Buddha, Moses and Jesus ranks for me higher than all the achievements of the enquiring and constructive mind?*"

Indian Sages of the past had known of and visioned the '*Cosmic-Dance*' of Lord Shiva,'Fritjof Capra' in his 'Tao Of Physics' says that he had beautiful experience in which as he was was sitting by the ocean one late summer afternoon, watching the waves rolling and feeling the rhythm of his breathing, he suddenly became aware of his whole environment as being engaged in a gigantic cosmic dance. Being a physicist, he knew that the sand, rocks, water and air around him were made of vibrating molecules and atoms, and these consisted of particles which interacted with one another by creating and destroying other particlesHe knew also that the earth's atmosphere was continually bombarded by showers of 'cosmic rays', particles of high energy undergoing multiple collisions as they penetrated the air. All this was familiar to him from his research in high-energy physics, but until that moment he had only experienced it through graphs, diagrams and mathematical theories. As he sat on the beach his former experiences came to life and he 'saw' cascades of energy coming down from outer space, in which particles were created and destroyed in rhythmic pulses. He 'saw' the atoms of the elements and those of his body participating in that cosmic dance of energy. He felt its rhythm and 'heard' its sound, and at that moment he knew that was the dance of Shiva, the Lord of Dancers worshipped by the Hindus.

Issac Asimov on Intuition; Stephen Hawking on sub-atomic particles and 'Quarks' being the basic building blocks of nature; Vedanta and Saiva Siddhanta on 'Nada Bindu' (The Eternal Sound-Light Continuum) being the basic building block of nature

We are yet to determine the vastness and the various dimensions that enfolds space at the macro-level and at the micro-level which scientists call quantum mechanics, it is calculated that more than 90 percent of the inside of an atom is empty space. Up to 1930 it was presumed that the atom was the smallest particle in nature, Issac Asimov:" ... *If intuition is as important to the world as reason, and if the eastern sages are as knowledgeable about this universe as physicists are, then why not take matters into reverse? Why not use the wisdom of the east as a key to some of the unanswered questions in physics? For instance what is the basic component making up subatomic particles that physicist call a quark?"* Stephen Hawking the astro-physicist claims in 'A Brief History of Time':" *Up to about twenty years ago, it was thought that protons and neutrons were elementary particles. But in experiments in which protons were collided with other protons or electrons at high speeds indicated that they were in fact made up of smaller particles. These particles were named quarks".* And again in page 70 he adds:" *And so we know that particles that were thought to be elementary twenty years ago are in fact, made up of smaller particles. May these as we go to still higher energies in turn to be made from still smaller particle? This is certainly possible but we do have now theoretical reasons for believing that we have, or are very near to knowledge of the ultimate building blocks of nature."* Hawking further claims that there are *six varieties of quarks* so one can imagine the amount of energy that would be available when further smaller particles and the technology to split or fuse them would be available to us! In fact the Vedanta and Saiva Siddhanta texts of the Tamils say that the eternal sound-light pulse or vibrations the 'Sound-Light Continuum' (*Nada Bindu* in Sanskrit; *Nadha Vindhu* in Tamil) are *the ultimate building blocks of nature* and that *the two are the formless-states of the Lord* apart from the Potential (male aspect) and the Dynamic (female aspect; energy), Thirumandiram 106: "*Siva the first, then the Three, and the following, with whom flourished Bindu and Nada, Nine are they all, yet one and the same – All these but names of Sankara (Siva) First.".* It is further said that at the time of the *maha pralaya* or the great deluge when all the planets, satellites, stars and heavenly bodies of the first three planes including the 1^(st) plane which has our solar system would be destroyed completely and all material would revert back to their original form which is the eternal sound-light continuum, one cannot even imagine the deadly 'big-bang' that would be caused by the enormous release of energy!

Stephen Hawking on Interstellar Travel and 'Time travel'; The ancient Japanese Royal Family being descendants of the Sun-God; Philliph and Elijah "*taken away by a whirlwind and chariots with horses of fire*"; **Sun-God landing on 'Sun Island' on Lake Titicaca; Dogon Tribes ancestors descended from 'Sirius' the star; Tamil Classic 'kandha Puranam' mention of 'Sooran' the Asura King who ruled over '1008 Universes' (*1008 andam*), Lord Muruga's 'Peacock Craft' made of burnished red-gold (**"*sempon mayi yenum ther*"**) that flew at 'thought-speed' (*mano veham*),'Vel' the deadly missile with the lengthy-flame (**"*nedunchudar Vel*"**) that blasted to smitherns a mighty mountain, was voice-activated and reusable; Ramayana's mention of the 'Pushpaka vimana' the captured flying-craft of Lord Kubera; Srimad Bhagavata's mention of the "rotating firebrand" and three huge spaceships that were "three floating cities" destroyed by Lord Shiva that had stealth-technology and Priyavarta's craft that was** "*as swift as the effulgent sun*"**, Lord Vishnu's 'Boar Craft' that 'tunnelled' down beyond the 'seven lower-worlds'**

Though astro-physicists like Stephen Hawking have their deep doubts on interstellar travel: "*I am afraid that however clever we may become we will never be able to travel faster than light. If we could travel than light we could go back in time. We have not seen any tourists from the future that means that travel to other stars is going to be a slow and tedious business. Using rockets rather than warp drives. A 100,000 year round trip to the center of the galaxy. In that time the human race will have changed beyond recognition, if it has not wiped itself out.*" – There are numerous instances where the world over the ages has witnessed and recorded many interstellar travels and visits. Apart from ancient Egyptian and Greek gods who are considered to be mere myths, 'Amaterasu' the Sun-Godess, grand-mother of the God Niniji who came down from heaven to rule Nippon (Japan) was the great grand-father of the mortal emperor 'Jinmu-Tenno' founder of the imperial dynasty 2500 years ago. The Sun-Godess had landed on Mount Fujiyama,(the reasons of it being considered holy) and the Orb and Sword of the Sun-God was presented to be preserved as royal relics, which are still being held in deep reverence in the Imperial Palace of the Royal Family; The Holy Bible says that Phillip and Elijah were taken away by a whirlwind, a *chariot with horses of fire took them away*; According to the native Indian history the Sun God landed on Sun-island on lake Titicaca and a festival is still celebrated to honor the occasion; The Dogon tribal people claim that their forefathers had come from the star Sirius in a huge ship and once in fifty-two years celebrate their home-coming by dancing donning straw masks that resemble helmets worn by astronauts. What is interesting is Sirius is visible as it falls on a direct-line from earth once in fifty-two years!

Nowhere else were there frequent alien visits to compare to that of India – in the 'Kandha Purana' war that took place on earth in the *Kreta Yuga* more than 3 million years ago, it is mentioned that 'Sooran' the Asura King ruled over 1008 universes(*1008 andam*), possessed deadly missiles and weapons of mass destruction and had 'vimanas' or flying-crafts that had *stealth-technology*, could hover over land and water, could disappear and appear at will, could appear at many places at the same time and had various magical contriviances and the battle that place over land, under water and in the skies and was finally killed by Lord Muruga's '*Vel*' "the missile with the lengthy-flame" ("*nedunchudar Vel*") that was re-usable and voice-activated and who Himself rode the '*Peacock-Craft*' which is described in the Tamil Classic 'Thirupugazh' as "*the hero who roams about the worlds riding the peacock that is a craft made of red burnished-gold*" ("*Sempon mayil yenum theril yeri ulaavi varum Veerarae*"); In the epic Ramayana, Ravana the King of Sri Lanka captured the Pushpaka vimana a flying craft built by Mayan the architect of the Devas or Angels for Kubera the Lord of riches of the celestial region, it was utilized in the battle and later after the victory, Lord Rama flew back to his kingdom in North India taking along with him Sita, Lakshmana, Vibishana the newly crowned king of Sri Lanka among others; The Srimad Bhagavata mentions of many flying-crafts like the '*rotating firebrand*' and of the three great spaceships vanquished with a single missile by Lord Shiva which were so huge that they resembled *three 'floating cities'* that had ponds and waterfalls within them and had stealth-technology among other wonders; Sri Suka in the Srimad Bhagavata Purana tells of the *"effulgent car that was as swift as the sun"* of Priavarata *"the tracks of which dug up our seven oceans"*; In the 'Shiva Gita' Lord Rama on the advice of the Sage Agasthya performs a deadly penance along the banks of the Sarayu river whereby he partakes forest-fruits and shoots for one month, in the second month he consumes only leaves, in the third only water and in the fourth just air, he smears himself with Holy Ash and even lies only on a bed of the Holy Ash, at the end with the sound of thunder and lightning Lord Shiva appears in a *"column of Light"* and lands on the river banks riding His 'Bull-craft' (*Rishaba Vahana*), everyone including Lord Vishnu in His *'Garuda'*(Eagle), Lord Brahma in his *'Anna vahana'*(Swan), Lord vinayaka, Lord Muruga, the Lord of the eight cardinal directions, the entire hierarchy of Gods and Angels land and present Lord Rama with their powerful weapons to vanquish Ravana; 'Kandhar Alankaram' and the Skanda Purana mention that after the Devas led by Lord Muruga's victory over the Asuras, the Devas or Angels as a token of appreciation and gratitude as promised gave away Devayani the daughter of 'Indra' the Lord of the Devas and Lord Muruga, the marriage-ceremony was performed at 'Thiruparankundram' near Madurai in Tamilnadu and all the Gods Angels and heavenly-hosts had flown down to earth in their own individual vimanas and after the function Lord Muruga asked each and every one of them to board their own flying-crafts to leave for 'Amaravathy' the capital of 'Swargaloka' or Heaven and they all flew at '*thought-speed*' (*mano veham*) to reach their destination in *no-time*! Speaking of *wormholes* and *tunnels* that connect *parallel universes* that scientists now theorise, the 'Vishnu Purana' and 'Linga Purana' mentions that Lord Vishnu in the Form of a mighty boar that stood as tall as the sky, had tails of fire, *tunnelled* through the earth and the lower seven planes and went even beyond 'Baathala' the lowest of the 'worlds'.

The 'Dimension Barrier' needs to be broken just as Chuck Yeagar broke the Sound-barrier in 1947, Siddhars master's of the art of literally hopping from one dimension to another (*koodu vittu koodu paayum vidhai*); Albert Einstein's General Theory of Realitivity,'Time Travel' and the '*granny paradox*' phenomenon; Siddhars by transcending the Chakras within the body and by breaking the 'Body-Universe Barrier' ('*anda kosa yellai*' – Thiruvavoor Rathinasabapathi Pillai's 'Thiruvasagamum Sivaraja Yogamum') break the dimension-barrier for "*what is in the universe is also within the body*", the Chakras containing the 'tattvas' or Principle-ingredients of the '14 worlds' or planes

Modern Man has to break the dimension-barrier (in Tamil known this art is known as "*koodu vittu koodu paayum vidhai*" – literally meaning "jumping from one cage to another" – which the Siddhars or Perfected Beings had mastered) just as Chuck Yeagar the World War II ace-pilot broke the sound-barrier in 1947 to make interstellar journeys meaningful for even if we were able to travel at the speed of light which is 186,000 miles per second (while our present day rockets travel at 12 miles per second) it'd take us 4.3 years to reach the nearest star 'Alpha Centauri' and hundreds and thousands of years to reach other *nearby* stars,100,000 years to cross our own galaxy and 12 billion years to reach the furthest distance we can see with our most powerful telescopes and travelling beyond the speed of light would according to Albert Einstein's general theory of relativity make us travel either backward or forward in time – which would bring in the infamous *granny paradox* phenomenon whereby one could go back to the times of his granny and if he kills her, his own birth would be in question! Yogis and Siddhars who are the Perfected beings mention that *what is in the universe exists in the human body*, hence with total awareness and by yogic means when activates all the chakras in his body which all contain the *tattvas* or principles of the 14 planes and crosses the '*universe-body barrier*' ("*anda kosa yellai*" in Tamil as stated by Thiruvarur Rathinasabapathi Pillai in his 'Thiruvasagamum Siva Raja Yogamum') one is omniscient and omnipresent who is beyond the clutches of space and time and could be present anywhere in space at the time of his reckoning – Sadasiva Brahmendra, Saint Ramalingam, Saint Antony, Socrates and Trilanga Swami would teleport to distant places and be back in a jiffy while the aforesaid first two would even teleport others along with them!

'Mushin' the State of 'No-Mind' in Zen Philosophy,'Kevala Kumbaka' the Perfect retention of Breath in Yogic-Meditation where Mind also stops; Lord Rama in Rama Gita:" thoughtless mind is Brahman" (God); Islamic (Iranian)Darvishes like Moulanna Jallaudin Rumi who 'whirldanced' and attained enlightenment, others like King Ravana of Sri Lanka through music,'Zero-experience' of Osho and Rabbi Abraham Heschel who after marching with Martin Luther King, commented:" *I felt as if my legs were praying when I marched with Martin Luther King.*"

'Mushin' in Japanese is the state of '*no-mind*' which was greatly valued and sought for by the Zen masters; the Sufis of Islam knew Yoga as '*Saluk*' and Pranayama (which is the yogic technique of controlling and regulating Prana which is the dynamic sum of all forces the outer manifestation of which is the air we inhale)as '*habs-e-dam*' and by force of will would stop their breathing-process and thus fall-faint into a state of ecstasy; '*Kevala kumbhaka*' is a state known by Yoga when breathing and the mind stops in a state of meditation; Thirumoolar says that:" *where there is mind there is prana, where mind is non-existent prana is not there …*"; Patanjali in the first of his 195 'Yoga Sutras' explains Yoga as "mind in an unchanged tranquil-state is yoga" (*Yoga citta vritti nirodaha*"); Lord Rama in the 'Rama Gita':" *Thoughtless mind is Brahman*" (God); The Ribu Gita:27." *There is no such thing as the troublesome mind, no world of names and forms, not the least bit of ego. All these are nothing but the perfect Brahman-Self, which I am. In this conviction one should abide firmly, until one achieves the state of sleepless-sleep which is alert-peace-eternal.*"(Ch.16, v.7) and Lord Shiva in the 'Vijnana Bhairava Tantra' has given 112 potent techniques through which one could realize his infinite-nature which are not philosophical in nature but direct-experience techniques, the first nine of them being related with the breath for that is one thing closest to us, what keeps us alive and can never be forgotten but it is the one we are least aware of!

There are numerous ways by which realization or enlightenment is attained for the Sufi Saint Moulanna Jallaludin Rumi '*Whirl-danced*' (known as Islamic Darvishes of Iran) continuously for 36 hours, fell down unconscious and attained enlightenment; the great Sri Lankan King Ravana attained it through music; Lord Buddha through breath-watching/awareness; Tibetan monks, the Chan of China and Zen Masters of Japan by attaining the state of *no-mind*; and countless Yogis of India through countless ways whereby they attained the state of Samadhi whereby the seeker and the object become One, the state explained by J.Krishnamurti as:" *the observer becoming the observed*", and the Vedas as "*Tat tvam assi*" or "*That thou art.*" One needs to at first delve into the state of no-mind or 'Zero Experience' as Osho would say every now and then and this state should become a continuous one as very beautifully explained in the 'Tripura Rahasya'. That continuous-state was experienced by Rabbi Abraham Heschel who after marching with Martin Luther King, commented:" *I felt as if my legs were praying when I marched with Martin Luther King.*"

The Soul – 'Satchitananda' – 'Sat' – Existence Absolute,'Chit' – Knowledge Absolute,'Ananda' – Bliss Absolute

The Self or the Soul's complexity is revealed by it being known as 'Satchitananda' – 'Sat' means *Existence Absolute*; 'Chit' – *Knowledge Absolute*; 'Ananda' – *Bliss Absolute*. The Self-Realized person is thus infinite, possesses Infinite or Divine Knowledge and is the personification of Bliss (the Holy Bible:" *the peace of god that surpasses all human understanding*"). Compassion and Grace flows out spontaneously so that all living-forms were positively affected in their vicinity – Saint Ramalingam out of empathy and due to his expanded state of consciousness would actually *feel* and *experience* the pain of a plant or creeper and claim:" *I too withered whenever I saw a withered crop!*"; an enraged charging wild elephant instantly calmed down before Lord Buddha while his followers scattered ot of fear, this was possible for his consciousness is said to have expanded to a circumference of fifty miles!; whenever Lord Rama, Lord Chaitanya or Lord Mahavira (the founder of Jainism) entered a forest, new shoots of grass would sprout, flowers would bloom in the thousands, un-seasonal fruits would ripen, dead-trees would take to life, birds and animals would cry ot of joy, while deer and tiger, snake and frog, friends and foes would stand united in welcoming them!

Extraordinary Supernatural Powers Attained by the Full-blown Yogi

According to Yogic Science man whose Self or the Soul is nothing but Pure Consciousness is no different from God (The Tamil Siddhar 'Thirumoolar' in his 'Thirumandiram':" *Jiva is no different from Siva...*") and could recollect the '64 arts' or branches of knowledge ('Kalai tattvas') which includes astronomy, astrology, mathematics, language, prose, poetry, grammar, dance, music, painting, sculpting, archery, wrestling, fencing, engineering, medicine, in fact everything and all this is said to be of *inferior knowledge* (known as 'apara vidhya'), he can even attain superior knowledge or *Divine Wisdom* ('Para Vidhya') whereby he can cure incurable diseases, turn base metal into gold, turn eternally young ('Kala tattva' or Time-principle) and in fact acquire the five acts of the Almighty: the power to Create, to Sustain, to Annihilate, to Veil and to Grace. The Yogi also attains the 'Eight Great Supernatural Powers'('Ashtanga Siddhis'): *anima, mahima, lagima, garima, prapti, parakamya, vasitva, istva* – whereby he can trun his body tinier than an atom, blow it into infinite proportions, turn it lighter than air, make it incredibly heavy, attain all that he desires, teleport into other bodies and various distant places in space, bring all living beings and all of nature under his command.

Though the full-blown Yogi attains enormous Supernatural-Powers he shuns them for like the thorns guard a beautiful rose or the snake a gem, they prove to be hindrance to final spiritual-liberation. One needs the humbleness of a Socrates who said:" *I know that I know nothing*" and the non-desiring mentality of the sage Narada who when asked by God who appeared before him to claim any boon declined to do so and when was requested to again, replied:" *please give me the mentality for not wishing for another boon!*"

And finally to attain the Divine, the Tamil sage Thiruvalluvar in his Thirukural has said:"*thavam seyvaar thun karmam seyvaar...*"- that only those who perform Penance (meditation and effort of any sort that burns or eradicates one of impurities) create their destiny, all others due to lustfull cravings and desires are entangled in misrey and pain. He further says that no more is there grief for the person who transcends the pair of opposites (like good and bad; beautiful and ugly; joy and sorrow) by surrendering himself at the Holy Feet of the Lord (who is beyond the pair of opposites). Saiva Siddhanta clearly says that The Holy Feet of the Lord is present in ultra-subtle Form as The Eternal Sound-Light Continuum' (Nada Bindu or Nadha Vindhu) at the crown of one's head. Modern science has only recently discovered that many involuntary-functions like the pumping of the heart and the breathing-process get their electrical-pulse orders from the animal or *serpentine-brain* - medulla oblongata, but the Yogi and the Siddhars have known for eons that when the breathing-process becomes slower and deeper, signals are received from the higher regions of the brain and ultimately all orders originate from *above* the crown of the head. By going to the *Source* all activities including that of the heart, lungs, brain, the lower and higher mind and *all* of Nature could be thus controlled. Adi Sankara in his 'Viveka Chudamani' says that like the space within a pot (*gada akasa*) and without are one, the individual and the Cosmic Mind are one, only realization has to dawn.

Michael Crichton in 'Andromeda Strain':" *There is present in the human gut microbes and bacteria that are equal to the global human population...";* **Dr.Ramamurti:"** *There are as many neurons in the human brain as there are people on the earth*"; **Lord Shiva in the 'Shiva Gita':"** *The human body is the most intricate and complex one among all my creations*"; **Issac Asimov in 'Change':"***The human body is made up of 50 trillion microscopic cells of dozens of types each containing 50 trillion atoms or more..." "Enzymes help to renew millions of blood cells every second... they are so small that millions can exist in a single drop of blood...";* **Carl Sagan in 'Cosmos' and 'Broca's Brain' claims that there are a hundred billion stars in our galaxy alone and estimates that there could be a billion black holes in each galaxy...; The presence of the 'Cosmic Energy' (Kundalini or Serpentine-Fire) in its fiery-form at the core of the earth, all heavenly-bodies and at the base of the human spinal-column act as natural magnets to 'propel' the human body to levitate and teleport by utilizing the "same poles repel" formula as did Albert Einstein's "unified Field Theory" help teleport the U.S. Naval ship 'Eldrige' from Philadelphia to Boston in 1947; Just as modern science claims that the**

atom possesses infinite energy, the 'Shiva Sutras' says that similarly when the human mind is obliterated by means of Pranayama, infinite Knowledge is revealed

We know very little of what is going on in the micro as well the macro-level – Michael Crichton in 'The Andromeda Strain' says that there is present in the human gut which is equal in size to an ordinary thermos flask microbes and bacteria in numbers on par with the global human population; the late neuro-surgeon Dr.Ramamurti of Chennai had quoted that there are as more neurons in the human brain as there are people on this planet which would be about a hundred billion in number and that telephathic contact between two persons is possible with distance not being of consequence; Lord Shiva in the 'Shiva Gita' tells that the human body is the most intricate and complicated one among all His Creations - "*the adult human being is made up of 50,000,000,000,000 or fifty trillion microscopic cells of dozens of types, each containing 50 trillion atoms or more*" – Isaac Asimov in 'Change'; Enzymes help to renew some 3 million blood cells in the human body every second, they are so small that millions can exist in a single drop of blood; a molecule of the enzyme ptyalin in human saliva can split 50,000 molecules of starch into simpler sugar molecules that the body can absorb while itself remaining unchanged; there are *over a hundred billion stars in our galaxy alone* and Carl Sagan estimates that there could be a *billion black-holes in each galaxy* with the *average distance* between them being 40 light-years which is just a hop and a jump on the cosmic scale; "*quasar seem to be violent galactic explosions that destroy millions of worlds, many of them perhaps inhabited*" – Carl Sagan in 'Broca's Brain'; Bats in the millions which find shelter under the golden-gate bridge in San Francisco consume 150 tons of insects in a single night in the skies over fruit orchards in the neighboring states also thus helping out the farmer; the homing pigeon has in its head tiny deposits of an iron oxide known as magnetite or lodestone which it utilizes to keep track with the earth's magnetic-field to navigate and the very same metal was used to make man's first compass; our earth is constantly bombarded by not less than two thousand meteorites per day some of them equal to the size of an average sized car but most of them are either deflected or are burnt to ashes by the various stratospheric layers; solar flares and ultra-violet rays too are a constant threat but the ozone-layer filters them out; Dr.Ramachandran has written vastly on 'phantom limbs', but about fifty years earlier the 291ˢᵗ Guru Maharaj of Madurai Adheenam had written that phantom limbs and their effects are experienced only by amputees and not by persons *born* with deformities for the 'extended' limbs do not exist in their dream or subtle bodies; Pheromones are enzymes present in many living-forms and that is what either attracts or proves repulsive between the sexes including that of mankind and researchers say that this 'chemical talk' is always going on; the earth's core contains a eight hundred mile thick ball of molten iron that due to the earth's spin acts as a magnet(as do all heavenly bodies and this fiery-form is the remnants of the *'Kundalini'* or *'Cosmic Energy' utilized by the Creator*) thus providing the north and south poles that in turn proves beneficial to us in various ways and similarly man's spinal-column base also contains the Cosmic Energy that provides a *'magnetic-field'* which is the *'Aura'* that could be utilized to levitate, teleport and perform other such *Supernatural* acts like 'mag-lev' trains levitate by using the *"same poles repel"* formula and Albert Einstein in 1947 made a U.S. Naval ship the 'Eldrige' disappear and teleport by using a magnetic-field by applying the *"unified field theory"* in the infamous 'Philadelphia Experiment'; we for the past few decades know that the energy present within the atom is enormous and the 'Shiva Sutras' says that:" *just as the infinite energy present within the atom is released when it is split, infinite knowledge is revealed when the mind of man is obliterated by performing pranayama"* – we know not the mysteries present within the atom which is said to be 90% empty neither of the vastness, depth and various dimensions of space, but when man lets go of his ego, he is un-bound by the shackles of the body and transcends space and thus time and like as the Saiva religion of the Tamils says:" like a circus-tent when unfolded becomes immensely big (*"padalam kudil anar pola virutthi adaivadhu "*), man in an expanded fully blown-state is The Infinite."

The Lord On Yoga - Srimad Bhagavata, book III, dis., XXIV, "Descent Of Lord Kapila"

12. The Lord said: "*In my opinion the only means to final beatitude is yoga in the form of contemplation on the Supreme Spirit, which is characterized by absolute cessation of both joy and sorrow.13. I shall now explain to you that*

very Yoga, which is perfect in every limb, and which I taught of yore to sages (like Narada), who were to hear of it, O virtuous lady.14. <u>Mind</u> *alone is* <u>held responsible</u> *for the* <u>bondage</u> *and* <u>emancipation</u> *of* <u>the soul</u>*. Attached to the objects of the senses, it leads to bondage; when, however, it develops affinity to the Supreme Person, it brings liberation to the soul.15. When the mind is purged of its mine-ness – and becomes pure, it grows indifferent to pleasure and pain and gets equipoised.16. When a mind equipped with true knowledge and dispassion as well as with Devotion, the Jiva (individual soul) then perceives the Self as One (without a second), undifferentiated, self-effulgent, subtle, indivisible, unattached and beyond Prakrti (matter), and Prakrti as reduced in strength.17-18. For striving souls there is no blissful road to god-Realization like Devotion directed towards the Lord, who is the Soul of the Universe.19. The wise consider attachment as an unyielding fetter for the soul. The same, however, serves as an open door to liberation, when it is directed towards saints."*

Perfection Through Yoga; Total cleansing of impurities and diseases through Pranayama for Prana or 'Vasi' is the ultra subtle-Form of the Lord ("vasiyum Isanum Ondru" – Tamil Siddhars); The Lord in the 'Sri Shiva Rahasya: "There is nothing that cannot be attained through the Power of Yoga..." "Yoga is the Power of Unity – the Unity between Body, Mind and Soul is of the Human kind, that which is between Man and Nature is of the Worldwide Kind, but that which is between Man and the Lord is indeed Divine".

Perfection attained through Yoga is the safest and surest method for the practice of 'Ashtanga Yoga' or eight-limbed Yoga ensures perfection of body, mind and spirit. Modern science now says that more than 80 percent of all diseases could be eradicated which includes weight-stability is attained through conscious-breathing, but the truth is all diseases would be eradicated and one would be absolved of all his sins by performing even one 'Uttama Pranayama'(highest form of pranayama) according to Lord Shiva Himself in the 'Shiva Maha Purana' and the Tamil Siddhars or Perfected Beings claim that the Dynamic-Breath or Prana or 'Vasi' in Tamil, is none other than the Subtle-Form of the Lord ("Vasiyum Isanum Ondru").

The fetters that bind the soul to the misery of the endless cycle of birth and death are three stains (known as or *'malas'* – *'anava','kanma'* and *'maya'*) only those who had transcended their ego, fruits of actions committed over innumerable past lives and the veil of illusion attain the exalted-state of liberation. What veils our true nature is Maya and this extremely powerful illusive Power of the Lord veils us in darkness (Adi Sankara calls this *'avidya'* - ignorance) and since true knowledge is not available allows us to see only things material that will decay and be no more in due course of time – to get over maya we use the weapon Yoga. The Bheranda Samhita:" *There is no greater force than maya which binds one to another, and to break that powerful bond, there is no greater force than Yoga."*

The Lord on Yoga in the Sri Shiva Rahasya: "Verily, *the World is constructed with Love and is Ever-Illumined with the Lamp of My Infinite Compassion.* **There is nothing that cannot be attained by the Power of Yoga.** *Yoga is the Path, the Goal and the Guiding Light. Yoga is the beginning and the end of all things."* **"Yoga is the Power of Unity** *– the Unity between Body, Mind and Soul is of the Human kind, that which is between Man and Nature is of the Worldwide Kind,* **but that which is between Man and the Lord is indeed Divine".**

One needs to realize his state of infinity to Become the Infinite; Lord Krishna in the Bhagavad Gita:" *The field that we occupy at the microcosmic-level is limited to the human body but when expanded to the macrocosmic, it could cover the entire universe"*; **The new-born human baby too experiences its state of infinity until ego sets in after it is eight or nine months old – modern research; 'Sri Shiva Rahasya' - The highest form of meditation and the one most dear to the Lord is to meditate with the 'feel' (***bhava***) that one is the Lord Himself extending to infinity; J.Krishnamurti:"** *It is all about space"*; **Srimad Bhagavata:"** *The Perfected-One like Kapila, Kardama and Sri Suka went about the world with an expanded state of consciousness"*

To get liberated from the vicious clutches of the endless cycle of birth and death, one has to realize his true infinite-nature: *"World* (s) *in thier entirety* ("Ulagellam unarndhu…") *though permeated, expanded into, experienced and realized would still be insufficient to Hail and realise the infinite state of the Lord"*, says the Tamil Saivaite saint Sekkizhar in his Periapuranam.

Experiencing the state of infinity is but natural for us for our true Self – the Soul which is but Pure Consciousness extends for infinity and is not bound within the body as we falsely think. Lord Krishna in the Bhagavad Gita says that we occupy a *field* and in the microcosmic-level it is limited to the body but when expanded it could cover the entire universe. Modern research too says that the new born human-baby lives and functions in a state of infinity for it *feels* that the entire world is hungry when it is hungry and is satiated when it has fed and that the state of space-limitation sets in only when it is eight or nine months old for only then does it become alarmed when an intruder comes within *its* space (of limitation).

J.Krishnamurti:" *it is all about space…*", this is true to the fullest possible sense for the purpose of our life is to realize that we are space in its totality that includes all the worlds and all lives as this song of Thirumoolar's Thirumandiram says:" *One alone created the worlds seven; One alone sustained the worlds seven; One alone annihilated the worlds seven;* **One alone is all the worlds along with all lives too.**" In the 'Shiva Gita' and the 'Sri Shiva Rahasya' the Lord says that the highest form of meditation and one dearest to Him is to meditate with the firm belief and *feel (bhava)* that one is the Lord Himself who extends to infinity. The Srimad Bhagavata mentions that when sage Vyasa called out to his son the sage Suka who had disappeared into the forests, the trees, rocks, river-waters everything responded to his calls for his son had totally merged into all life-forms and what seemed to be the inanimate! It is repeatedly mentioned in the sacred book that all the realized persons went about their lives with *"an expanded state of consciousness."*

Attainment of 'Eternal Youth' Through Pranayama – Thirumoolar, Bogar, Sivavakkiar, The Kanchi Sankaracharya in 'The Vedas'

Many Siddhars like Thirumoolar, Bogar and Sivavakkiar have written vastly on the science of the breath-process and said that '*Vasi'* or '*Prana'* which is the dynamic sum of all forces, the outer manifestation of which is the air that we inhale is none other than the Lord in ultra subtle-form ("*Vasiyum Isanum Ondru…*") Sri Chandresekharendra Saraswati, the Sankaracharya of Kanchi in 'Vedas':"*Breathing is not only necessary for keeping the body alive but the mind and mental health also depends on it to a great extent. This is because the mind which is the cause for all thought processes and breathing which is the cause of life-force are one and the same. It is possible for controlled breathing through Yoga to establish rapport with the Cosmic breath and perform beneficial acts for general as well as individual well being.…*" …"*Even if the blood vessels are severed, blood would not flow out. Yogis are able to stop the heart-beat and pulse-beat and remail buried underground in a state of quiescence. The venom of a snake or scorpion bite leaves them unaffected. All this is possible because they are able to discipline the vibrations caused by normal breathing.*"

Man has always been fascinated with eternal youth and his search for the elusive elixir or "*fountain of youth*" has been relentless and has wondered whether it is available only in the heavenly spheres for it is known as '*amrita*' or the "*food of the gods*". Yoga explains that for the full-blown Yogi the ambrosia secretes spontaneously from the '*chandra mandala*' or moon's sphere at the crown of the head which turns the person eternally young. The elixir is said to be much sweeter than that of nectar and honey and provides a constant sweet-taste in the throat of the Yogi and is therefore no more affected by hunger or thirst. Man *turns* young by '*internal-breathing*', attains immortality when ambrosia flows down through secret mystic-opening; **Thirumandiram 805:**

> "*If you can send the breath twain*
> *Into the internal tounge's upper-cavity*
> *You shall not be bound by time;*
> *And the gates of nectar will open be;*
> *Graying and wrinkling (of skin) will disappear*
> *For all to see; youthfull will the person be*
> *This is the word of the Lord Nandi (Siva).*"

AnotherPerfected Being Sivavakkiar: "*When the prana that subsides in the primal-nadi that gives shape to the body, is grasped by will-power and coaxed to rise to the cranium-top, the person even if he were old would turn into a young lad, his body would turn pink with suffused energy, this I swear upon the Holy Gracious*

Feet of the Holy Father and Mother." There are 72000 nadis or astral-nerves that run through our body among which ten are said to be vital and among these 3 – the left-nostril channel that possesses the qualities of the moon, the right-nostril channel that has the qualities of the sun and 'Sushumna' which is a channel that rises from a vital 'Chakra' - a psychic-point at the bottom of the spinal column upto the cranium-top has the qualities of 'Agni' or Fire. When the prana rises, the 'Kundalini' or 'Cosmic' energy that lies dormant at the psychic spot known as the 'muladhara chakra' (as it does in the core of our earth as well as in all heavenly bodies) also slowly rises and winds its way up and on its path of ascent activates six other vital chakras all located over strategic hormonal and nerve-plexuses like the solar plexus, heart-centre, third-eye centre in-between the eyebrows and when it finally flows into the seventh chakra known as the 'Sahasrara' at the crown of the head, the person attains *Super-consciousness* and becomes a *'Purna Yogi'* or a "*Full blown Yogi*".

A full blown Yogi *turns eternally young*; in an instant comes to know all worldly, heavenly and even languages of the beasts and birds and their texts; all of nature comes under his command; he can migrate to other bodies; he could in a jiffy teleport himself to anywhere among the *14 planes* – all this is possible for the chakras which are also '*Wisdom-centres*' contain the '*tattvas*' or principle-ingredients of the five basic elements in nature, the tattvas of the 14 planes, the 50 vowel-consonants (of the Sanskrit, ancient Tamil – for the present day alphabet has only 30 vowel-consonants, Japanese and Chinese alphabets – though the Chinese language has nearly 60,000 alphabets, it also has 50 vowel-consonants or 'prime alphabets') that covers the entire gamut of sounds possible and thus all alphabets of all languages, the 'Art' tattva as well as the 'Kala' or 'Time' concept.

Mythological, Vedic, Biblical and other characters, the 'archetypes' (even 'Mickey Mouse') are deeply engrained in the "collective unconsciousness" and "blocked-off memories" – Carl Jung

Is this talk of other worlds and alien life-forms mentioned only in ancient Indian, Greek and Egyptian texts/mythology and in the minds of elevated personalities like Milton and Shakespeare or is their other religious references and what do modern researchers, astronomers and astro-phycisits say? The sheer number of characters and mention of elves, goblins, angels etc., infused in 'The Tempest' and 'A Mid Summer's Night Dream' by the Bard places him even on a higher pedestal than that of Milton's 'Paradise Lost', but undoubtedly they delved deep within themselves to recollect those 'archetypes'. Carl Jung mentions that mythological stories and characters from ancient Biblical, Vedic and other mythological stories are ingrained as archetypes deep within our sub-consciousness and in fact these give shape to our dreams and visions. This is very true for long before Walt Disney 'created' *Mickey Mouse*, the adorable Mickey's figure has been recently found carved into stone in the South American jungles as early as in the 13th century!

The Holy Bible mentions that the apostle Paul has a vision of the *fifth heaven*; Milton mentions *Empyrean* the seventh heaven; In the Holy Qu'ran, Prophet Muhammad takes a space-journey on *El Burraq* a flying steed, he traverses the seven heavens, sees all the angels at prayer, meets Moses, Solomon, Jesus Christ and finally gets audience with Allah the Almighty; The 'Thiruvilayadal Puranam' of the Tamils mentions that the king Varaguna Pandyan had a vision of the Ultimate Heaven 'Kailash' and Sundarar and Jnanasambhandar along with multitude of others entered a "*great Pillar or column of Light*" and were *transported* Kailash the Ultimate Heaven.

Time to be derived at *needs* space for though the speed of light seems incredibly fast to us (for it travels at 186,000 miles or 300,000 kms. per second), it still takes 8 minutes to reach us from the sun, several thousands, millions and even billions of years to travel from distant stars and astro-phycisits have calculated that it takes 12 billion years to just traverse the length of our own milky way! But if we *become* space, time would become irrelevant or meaningless – the Siddhars or perfected beings had realized that if we were able to still the mind, thoughts too would cease (this greatly sought after state of '*no-mind*' known as '*mushin*' to the Japanese Zen practitioners) and thus the state of infinity – the state of the Lord is achieved. The Siddhars have pointed out a boundary known as the 'Universe-Body Limit' ('*anda kosa yellai*' in Tamil) that exists 12 inches above our head that surrounds and encompasses our body in a sort of egg-shaped bag, when through yogic-means we literally break the barrier, we become the *Cosmic-egg* and are no more bound by space nor time.

Infinite Energy, Infinite Space and Infinite Knowledge of Man – David Bohm's "Zero-point Energy"; Shiva Sutras

Like space energy too is infinite for it is the dynamic-aspect or form of the Lord as it is from from the Potential (Siva) does the Dynamic (Shakti or energy) emanate. The physicist, David Bohm, computed the *"zero-point energy"* due to quantum-mechanical fluctuations in a *single cubic centimeter of space* and arrived at the energy of 10/38 ergs. Bohm translates his ergs into the energy equivalent of about *ten billion tons of uranium!* The 'Shiva Sutras' (long before modern man had split the atom) says that like the infinite energy present within an atom is released when it is split, when the immense-mind held within the body that has infinite capabilities is destroyed by means of pranayama (Yogic-breathing technique) the consciousness in awakened and manifests in its entire immensity.

Everything Is Born Of That Supreme Sound; My Five Powers Divine When obscured by My Mighty Magic they become limited and the being who holds them is known as Soul. Thus the Soul is born as the sixth in the midst of the five. He is the power-holder and their master even as I am the Holder of the Five Powers Divine – Sri Shiva Rahasya

For this reason, the Wise Ones have called Him Shiva which means, That in Whom everything rests (Shi) and by Whose Power everything moves (Va). I Am that Shiva, the Original Ever-Living One; the Unseen and Uncreated Who Ever Is before everything that is seen and created is born or dies.

From the Stillness of My Heart a Wish was first heard and then brought to Light. The Wish was made firm in the form of Thought. The Thought was made audible as a Word. And the Word was made visible as the World.

Thus, from Wish, to Thought, to Word, the World came into being at My Divine Command. Everything is born of That Supreme Sound. Even the Divine Form you are now beholding with your eyes is a Manifestation of That.

I Am That Supreme Reality. I am Boundless Freedom and Might and My Powers are Five: Omnipotence, Omniscience, Infinite

Fullness-and-Satisfaction, Omnipresence and Eternity. These are My Five Powers Divine. When obscured by My Mighty Magic they become limited and the being who holds them is known as Soul. Thus the Soul is born as the sixth in the midst of the five. He is the power-holder and their master even as I am the Holder of the Five Powers Divine.

O Sages! First I created a Glorious World of Light, radiant as tens of millions of Suns. Therein abide the Radiant Ones and all beings that are fair and bright. Then, I enveloped Myself in Mighty Magic and created the World of man.

Of My Own Free Will I Envelop Myself in My Wondrous Power, even as the Sun conceals himself behind the Clouds created by his own heat. Verily, like unto the Sun that stands concealed behind the Clouds, even thus I conceal Myself from the World.

As in the day the light in the Sky, the Sun, is ever one but at nightfall the dark Firmament is bedecked with myriads of Stars, even so, behind the Veil of Magic I am One: ever shining in the boundless Sky of Universal Consciousness. But enshrouded in the Veil of Maya, I am myriads of Souls shining each like unto a Star in the dark night sky that envelops the Earth.

Verily, Night and Day, the Stars and the Sun, all are My eternal signs. I gave them to man that he might know the Truth at all times. The World being a manifestation of My Truth, it teaches and reveals the Truth to all who have an open heart. Unto those who follow the Path of Yoga, the World is a treasure house of precious gems, each scintillating sparks of Truth.

But to the others it is like a sealed chest that no one can open and whose secrets no one understands. The Sealed Chest is Maya. The Key is My Word of Truth. The Treasure in the Chest is the Supreme Light. Earth is the World of man, where everything is limited, divided and dark. It is not a real World being only like a dream, a World of shadows cast by a Higher Light.

I, the Great Light, am the World-Father. Maya, My Mighty Magic is the World-Mother. From our Union innumerable living Souls, all identical with their Creator, are born. Yet, deluded by My Power of Illusion, they do not recognise Me as their Maker. The Awakened Ones, the Buddhas, they alone know that Maya is the Mother and I Alone am the Father of the multitude of creatures born in this World.

He who abides under Maya's Spell is a bound Soul. He who rises above Maya is its master. Therefore, Maya is the fetter to be conquered through Sadhana or Spiritual Discipline. He, who knows the Great Secret of Maya, knows how the World comes into being. He knows how, though the Souls appear to be many, they are in reality One.

He, who knows the Secret of Maya, knows that I create the World and man creates his own perception of the World. For this reason, although the World is one, every Soul has his own perception thereof. Through My Magic Might what is One appears as many and what is many appears as One. There is nothing that cannot be accomplished by Maya, the Power of the Supreme Sovereign. But he who by the power of his thought creates a World that is equal to mine in clarity, radiance and greatness; he is Equal to My Supreme Self. Verily, he who is a Master of the World-dream, is a Master of the World. Therefore, listen you to this Great Secret of Mine.

The Soul is born of Me. His powers are born of Maya, My Great Power. From that also springs the Material Energy, the Soul's Twin. And of that, the Soul's World is born. The Five Powers Divine; Soul, Material Energy, Intellect, Ego and Lower Mind; Five Senses; Five Powers of Action; Five Perceptions; and Five Material Qualities: these are the Six Groups-of-Five. In each of these I am the Sixth, the Hidden One ever abiding in their midst. I am the Unseen Witness Who knows them each and all. Thus the Five with Myself in their midst, are Six times Six.

The Thirty-Sixth is That Which contains all, pervading and animating them from within. It consists of all Powers Divine. It Is That-Which-Alone-Is, the Unsurpassable, the Only Existing Truth known to Yogis but unknown to all others. Yogis are the People of Unity who ever strive for Union with Truth. Whatsoever does exist in Heaven, on Earth and betwixt, is a product of the 69 SHIVA RAHASYA

Thirty-Six. Verily and without doubt, there is naught else besides. He who teaches otherwise is a deceiver and most unwise. For he is only deluding himself.

The Ten Powers Of God When obscured and greatly reduced by Maya, they are imperfect human powers. When free and unobstructed, they are indeed Infinite and Divine. They are the Yogic Powers of Buddhahood – Sri Shiva Rahasya

The unawakened who deny My Revelation are as if dead. For in their delusion they know neither their true Self nor anything else that is of worth, but only the imaginations of their own mind. For them, Death is like a serpent that envelops man in his deadly coils and devours him while still alive.

But the Enlightened Yogi is never touched by Death. As he who is awake to the World is not overcome by sleep, so he who is awake to Truth is not harmed by Death. Verily, Sleep and Death cannot touch one who is Awake, even as darkness never touches the Sun.

O Sages! the body knows only itself. The mind knows the body. And the Soul knows body, mind and himself. It is for this reason that the Soul (Atma) has been called Self (Atma). For he is the Self of all three and the true Self of man.

The Soul is the Twenty-Fifth Principle, the Inner Witness who beholds the Mind, Body and outer World within his own Field of Knowledge. For this reason, he has been called, the Knower of the Field.

Beyond that, Ten more Life-Principles remain to be known. In truth, they are naught but the Glorious Powers of God: Omnipotence, Omniscience, Infinite Fullness-and-Satisfaction, Omnipresence and Eternity which are the Offshoots of His Boundless Freedom.

When obscured and greatly reduced by Maya, they are imperfect human powers. When free and unobstructed, they are indeed Infinite and Divine. They are the Yogic Powers of Buddhahood.

Amongst the Righteous Nations the Holy Land of India shall ever be the first – The Lord in Sri Shiva Rahasya

At the end of this life, if only man had no desires, he could easily ascend to the Higher Worlds above. But as he fulfils only a fraction of the total sum of desires, a great many remain to be fulfilled. Thus he is forced to descend back upon Earth by the force of his desires. This repeats itself again and again. Only when he rises above worldly desires, can man ascend to the Higher Worlds and not otherwise. This is the Eternal Law.

O noble ones! Man acts to fulfil his desires, both bad and good. As the desires, so his works too, may be right or wrong. And as his works, so his rewards are pleasant or painful. Righteous works that are done in unity with My Law and for the sake of good desires result in good rewards. But evil works; done in disobedience to My Law and for the sake of sinful desires, result in painful rewards. This is the Law of Cause and Effect, called Karma by the Wise. Every creature, whether on Earth or in the Otherworld is justly rewarded according to its works. I am Ever Compassionate and Wise.

I gave man the Day, that he might wake and Night that he might rest. I gave him fruit-giving trees and rich fields of golden grain. I gave him milk-yielding cows and cool waters full of fish. I gave him forests and caves for shelter, the Moon that he might measure time, the Great Stars for direction and the light-bestowing Sun. And I gave him the Law whereby he might live in abundance and peace. Know that all these are My Signs (Lakshana).

As a King speaks to some of his subjects face to face but to others through his ministers, envoys or messengers and to still others through signs, so I, the Lord, at appointed times reveal My Law unto the World either in Person or through My faithful devotees. They roam the Earth and bring My Word of Truth to those that wish to hear; who having heard, have the power to understand; and who having understood are moved to follow that which is True. And I also reveal My Law through certain signs that are known to the Wise.

The Wise see how the Moon follows the Sun and the Sun is stationed in the Great Sky. They see how the young calf follows the mother cow and how the herd follows the leading bull. They see how one season follows another, Night follows upon Day and Death follows Life. They see how parched fields become green again and how dense jungle turns to dust. In all this there is a sign of guidance and of warning. To some I reveal My Law overtly and to some covertly. And to still others by clear signs that are seen by all but understood only by a few. Let the Wise take heed. For he who follows My signs shall be rightly guided. As for the others, assuredly, indeed, they shall go astray.

Thus My Law is made known unto every nation in the World. Amongst these there are some that deny My Revelation and stubbornly adhere to their own law. Others accept My Law but then forget It and follow any false prophet that may come their way. Others again will seek to change the Truth. As if Truth could be changed like unto a painting on the wall! Verily, only a few hold fast unto My Truth. They shall ever be an Eternal Lamp unto the World and an Abode of Righteousness on Earth. Amongst the Righteous Nations the Holy Land of India shall ever be the first. For, amongst her noble sons and daughters dwell the most faithful followers of Truth. They ever abide by My Law even if the World were to fall to pieces or be drowned by a great flood.

Verily, My Law is heard by every Soul according to his own Karma. The righteous ones that on account of their good Karma are born amongst the Righteous Nations receive My Law in full. But those that on account of their evil Karma are born amongst the unfaithful, must content themselves with whatever fragments of My Law they may come by. For, having done a work for the sake of obtaining an end, man must reap a reward according to the nature of his intentions. Thus every man is born in the land that he deserves on his merits or sins. This is the Eternal Law. I am Ever Compassionate and Just and so is My Law.

Man Needs The Grace of A Human or Divine Guru To Realize Unity Through The Practise of Yoga – The Lord in Sri Shiva Rahasya

Second, being born of Shiva, man is essentially identical with That. As a spark of fire is identical with Fire, a ray of sunlight with the Sun and a raindrop with the Sea, so man is identical with the Supreme All-Consciousness (Parasamvid), the Mind of the Great One God (Mahadeva).

Third, the Goal of human life is to realise this Unity and Identity, called Yoga by the Wise. For Unity is the essence of Life: Life without Unity would be just Chaos and the Universe would fall apart. Nor can any man live in disunity with God.

And Fourth, Unity is to be realised through the Practice of Yoga and by the Grace of one's Spiritual Master, human or Divine. For nothing is achieved without practice nor is any goal in life attainable without a guide. Thus I have spoken the Fourfold Truth of Yoga by means whereof man goes to My Supreme Abode.

The Greatest of Yogas – Sri Shiva Rahasya

I shall now make known to you a Yoga Teaching that is easily understood by all. Therein every Seeker shall find a Path to his heart's desire and as taught by his Spiritual Guide. By means of this Teaching, My devotees see their Self, the Highest Lord, shining like the blazing Sun.

fire of Yoga quickly burns the fetters of ignorance and sins. Perfect Knowledge that leads to Liberation springs from this Yoga even as dawn springs from the Sun.

Verily, Knowledge arises from Yoga and Yoga functions by means of Knowledge. I, the Greatest God, am Delighted when one is devoted to both Yoga and Knowledge. Those who practise the Great Yoga of the Greatest God, either once, twice, three times a day or even constantly, are themselves to be known as Great Beings Divine.

First, let it be understood that Yoga is of three kinds. The first is called Bhava Yoga (the Yoga of Being), the second, Abhava Yoga (the Yoga of Non-Being) and the third, Maha Yoga (the Greatest Yoga), it being the greatest among all.

The Yoga whereby one's own inner Self is meditated upon as a living Soul in the midst of mind, body and worldly possessions is spoken of as Bhava Yoga (the Yoga of Being). It leads to the realisation of one's own individual Self, unencumbered by mental delusions. Being the Yoga of Phenomenal Existence, it should be practised by those who are attached to worldly life and who wish to remain in the World in this life and the next.

The Yoga, whereby one visualises oneself as infinite, eternally blissful and beyond the Physical World, is known as Abhava Yoga (the Yoga of Non-Being). It leads to the realisation of My Divine Transcendental Self and is higher than the former. Therein all manifested things are absorbed in the Original Source Whence everything comes and Whereto everything does return, even as thoughts come to rest in the emptiness of deep sleep and waves subside in the silence of the Ocean deep. It should be practised only by those who wish to leave the World behind and merge for ever in the Formless Being.

The Yoga, however, wherein one meditates upon oneself as identical at once with My Transcendental and Immanent Being, that I regard as the highest Yoga leading to true God-Realisation. It is called Maha Yoga because it is the Yoga of the Great Life (Maha Satta).

The Great Life is Greater than both Being and Non-Being. It is the Supreme Being (Para Bhava or Para Satta) Itself. It is Higher than, and at the same time contains within Itself, all other forms of being. Therefore the Yoga that leads Thereto is known as Maha Yoga (Greatest Yoga) and Arya Yoga (Higher Yoga). It is also called Shiva Yoga (the Yoga of Shiva) as it leads to Identity with Shiva Who is both God and the World in One. It is called in three ways because it is Three Times the Greatest among all.

This Greatest of all Yogas shall be practised by all who wish to attain Perfection in this very life. Verily, this Yoga is practised even by the Gods. For, thereby one obtains the Joys of Heaven even now.

Those Paths of Yoga one sees being followed by others or one hears about in other Teachings, are not worth as much as one-sixteenth of this Divine Yoga. The Yoga whereby Enlightened Souls directly experience everything as One with God, that Yoga alone shall be known as the greatest of all Yogas. Those who follow it, see God in each other and at the end of their earthly life go to the Supreme Abode.

But those followers of the Yogic Way (that is, of Bhava Yoga), who, even though they have brought their mind under control still consider themselves to be separate or different from the Lord, shall not perceive Me as One without a Second. Thus I, the Lord, declare.

The Soul is The Supreme Spirit, Hence Should Realize He is Beyond All Limitations; Transcending The Three 'Malas' (Stains) – Sri Shiva Rahasya

Now there is another great secret to be known. The Soul, being made of Spirit, nay, *being* the Supreme Spirit Itself and Identical with Me, is eternally happy, all-wise and free. Yet as he descends at My Divine Command into this Material World, as he must in order to participate in My Creation, he passes through the dark veil of Maya, My Cosmic Magic. In the course of his descent, he becomes tainted by the Threefold Impurity called Mala.

Anava Mala, the Impurity of Imperfection, is the first product of Maya. Thereby, as in a dream, the Soul though being Identical with Shiva deems himself and everything else to be limited and imperfect. Impelled by this impurity, he desires limited and imperfect things. O you who are endowed with Wisdom! Know this to be the seed of worldly existence.

The second, Maiya Mala, is the Impurity of Delusion that develops from the first even as a plant sprouts forth from a seed. It causes the Self to see all things as different and separate both from each other and itself.

Karma Mala, the third, is the Impurity of Limited Action. Growing from the previous two, it is their fruit, as it were. Having been rendered imperfect and endowed with limited knowledge, the Soul acts in limited and imperfect ways. Having performed such action, the latent seed thereof comes alive in due course, binding him to this World and its endless cycle of death and rebirth. Thus the Soul is forced to enjoy the fruit of his imperfect actions, both bad and good.

Yoga And Dharma (Righteousness) Are One And The Same; Among The Five Castes Of Man, The Yogi Is The Head Who Spreads My Word Of Truth

The Farmer, the Merchant, the Warrior, the Priest and the Yogi in their midst: these five are supporting My Law. They are the five fingers of My Divine Hand whereby I establish the Holy Dharma on Earth. Know that Yoga and Dharma are one and the same. He, who sees the two as one, sees things as they are and does not go astray. Let every man keep within his own fold and not overstep his lawful boundaries. Let him ever keep to the path of his duty according to My Command. The Farmer shall till and tend the earth; the Merchant shall trade in the fruits of the Farmer's labour; the Warrior shall protect the land; the Priest shall conduct the holy prayers; and the Yogi shall spread My Word of Truth. This is My Eternal Law.

The Five Castes are like unto one man. The Yogi is the head; the Priest is the mouth; the Warrior is the arms; the Merchant is the thighs; and the Farmer is the feet. Together they are like unto one body that forms the whole of Humankind. Therefore let every man conduct himself according to his duty as established at the beginning of time. And let living in unity with one another be the duty of them all. He who lives in unity with Mankind lives in unity with Me. And he alone who lives in Unity with Me is a Yogi and a True Man. Let no part of the whole swerve from its duty. Let the five parts of Mankind ever work in unity for the welfare of the whole. And let the whole work for the good of each part. This is My Divine Command.

The Soul Drinks The Milk Of Heaven Which Is Attained By Renunciation And Not Attachment; The Yogi Who Learnt The Art Of Letting-go By Watching The Wise Heron

The body delights in physical food; the mind delights in beautiful sensations, beautiful feelings and beautiful thoughts. But the Soul delights in Truth. All things that are true, beautiful and good shall be deemed to be the Soul's own food. But the Bliss of Heaven is the highest delight of all. As an infant drinks the mother's milk even so the Soul drinks the bliss-bestowing Milk of Heaven whereby one is endowed with illustrious wisdom and power. That Bliss is not attained through worldly food but through detachment from the World. My devotee shall not be too attached to possessions, kinsfolk and other worldly things for they tie him down to the World. And a bound Soul knows not the Joys of Heaven even as the captive elephant knows not the joys of his free-roaming kin.

Verily, it is detachment from the objects of the senses that relieves man from the burdens of this World. Therefore, detachment shall be cultivated at all times. He who masters the art of detachment evades the troubles of the World even as the wise Heron evaded the Crows. A Heron while fishing in the river made a big catch. Two voracious Crows at once descended upon him, wishing to snatch away the fish. The Heron flew this way and that way seeking to escape the Crows. Perceiving that he was no match for them, the Heron at last let go of the fish and alighted upon a tree where he could repose in peace. A Yogi who was sitting on the riverbank saw this and with great wonder exclaimed: Adoration be to Shiva! to Him, Who this day in the form of a wise Heron has taught me the art of letting-go.

The World wherein man lives is like unto a great Tree and man's body like unto a bird's nest. Through detachment from both body and the World, the Soul who is like a bird rises up into the Sky and joins himself to the Most High. He unites himself with the One and becomes equal to the Radiant Gods in this very lifetime. Verily, of all things the Unmeasured alone lives on for all times; but that which is measured is born and in due course dies. He who abides upon the lofty Peak of Unity with the Immeasurable One falls not over the stumbling-block of limitation. He is not hunted by the hounds of Discord. His eye is not blinded by the Cloud of Delusion. His heart is not pierced by the arrows of Death. He is above Limitation, above Delusion, above Discord and above Death, who ever abides in the sunlight of Unity with Truth.

Therefore, do not be attached to the things of this World, for this World is a mere wave in the Ocean of Life and a passing reflection of My Everlasting Light. What is a passing wave like as a wave shall pass; but That Which is Abiding shall stand for all time: even when the World has come to an end. Verily, in this World, some laugh and others cry. But the follower of Dharma is ever serene and content. For he knows things which men who are devoid of knowledge fail to understand. As the Moon is not attached to mountains, forests and the Sea as she travels on her path across the Sky, so the wise Yogi abides ever unattached to the things of worldly life. Detachment is of two kinds. Firstly, observing all things calmly and as if from afar. And secondly, seeing all things for what they are, namely, emanations of the Most High. Through detachment from the things of the World, the veil of delusion falls off from the Yogi's eyes and he at once begins to see My Signs. O noble ones! I did not create the World for nothing but that it might be an example and guidance to all Souls. All things in this World have a meaning and are a Sign from On High: a message to be understood and followed.

God's Signs Of Two Kinds, The Enduring Ones Like The Sun And Moon And Passing Ones Like Visions And Dreams – Sri Shiva Rahasya

My Signs are of two kinds, those that endure and those that pass away. The enduring ones are the Sky, the Earth, the Sun, the Moon, the Stars, the Mountains and the Sea. The passing ones are of three kinds. Things that come to pass in daily life, visions and dreams. Some are a guidance to be followed, some are a good tiding and some are an ill omen or a warning. A human form of handsome features, a Radiant One (a God), a holy man, a King or Queen; the Sun's or one's own clear reflection in water, a bright cloud, a rainbow or a sky-blue light; riding upon a horse, white bull or elephant; women, children and wild beasts being kind towards each other and to oneself; dwelling in a sheltered place or a well-kept house; eating pure food, wearing pure apparel in the day and resting in a pure bed at night; flying into the bright Sky, being in beautiful surroundings, being in the company of good friends or Gods; lying down with the head towards the South; casting a clear, unbroken and unshaken shadow; a growing plant; a running stream or lotus pond; a pleasant scent. These are auspicious Signs (Sulakshana) to be sought whilst waking, dreaming or seeing a vision. For they all are boding well.

But a hideous form, an evil Spirit, an unrighteous man, one afflicted by his own sins or a lifeless corpse; the Sun's or one's own hazy reflection in water, a dark cloud, an ill-shaped lightning or a blood-red light; riding upon a dog, a black bull or a donkey; women, children and wild beasts being hostile to each other or to oneself; dwelling in a wind-swept place or a dilapidated house; eating impure food, wearing polluted clothes in the day or sleeping in a polluted bed at night; falling into a dark pit, being in a repugnant place, being in the company of enemies or demons; sleeping with the head towards other directions than South; casting a fading, broken and shaking shadow; a withering plant; a stagnant pool; a foul smell. These are Signs that bode no good (Durlakshana), whether seen while awake, in a dream or perceived in a vision; whether seen from afar or from anear.

Know that if a single ill-boding Sign is seen, it is a warning. If it be accompanied by others of its kind, the time has come for him who has seen them to depart from this World. But if good and bad omens are seen together, there shall be a loss and a gain to him who has perceived them. Having perceived ill-boding omens, the wise Yogi shall at once immerse himself in contemplation and abide in that state with one-pointed concentration upon My Supreme Self. If then he should desire to live on, his wish shall be assuredly granted. If he should desire to forsake his mortal body, he shall exit the same by the crown of the head and rise heavenwards without delay.

The People of India Alone Remained Faithful To My Law; The Holy Land of India, the Abode of Light (Bharat) which shines like unto a jewel on this Earth – Sri Shiva Rahasya

Verily at the beginning of Time I established One Law for all of Mankind. But of all

nations upon Earth, the People of India alone have stayed faithful to My Law. The others have changed their faith many times over, like a woman who gives herself to many men. Don't they know that I have eyes everywhere and ever watch them from close by? Let them do as they please, the day of reckoning is never far! But of you I have made a nation of righteous men that you might lead the others to the True Faith.

The Holy Land of India, the Abode of Light (Bharat) which shines like unto a jewel on this Earth was given by Me to My devotees that they might lovingly tend her like a precious garden and make her an example and a guidance unto others. Those who neglect My Holy Gift shall not only lose their possession but suffer a dreadful fate as a reward for their sin. Verily, I say unto you, I did not create the Earth for her to be ruled by miscreants but by righteous men who abide in Unity with Me. If the unfaithful prevail, it is not because I Myself will thus, but because the righteous having become weak and corrupt, neglect their holy duty: which is to uphold Righteousness upon Earth.

Therefore, desist from suffering unbelievers in your midst. For they are a devious lot. They will rob you of your possessions and drive you out of your own homes. They will defile your womenfolk and take your children as slaves. They will brand the mark of servitude upon the brow of free men. Verily, strangers are not to be trusted. Do not make friends with them. It was far better to live alone than join oneself to the enemies of My Law. But those amongst the sons and daughters of the Holy Land who stray from the Path of Dharma are the worst by far. For they betray their own people and are the greatest sinners of all. An evil fate awaits them all.

The total discarding of the mind is alone victory, achievement, bliss, yoga, wisdom and liberation. The sacrifice of the mind is, in fact, the totality of all sacred sacrifices – Ribu Gita

The firm denial of the existence of the mind and the firm belief in the existence of Brahman-Self, is the sure way to the conquest of mind, leading to the experience of the sole effulgent Self.

If one gives the slightest room for the thought that the mind exists, pure Awareness itself will vibrate as the ruffled mind, which is the parent of all trouble and illusions. Therefore, one should ever abide in the conviction that there is no mind, and that the pure Awareness-Self is the sole Existence. This is the easy way to conquer the mind with all its vagaries. (Ch.15, v.12)

There is no such thing as the troublesome mind, no world of names and forms, not the least bit of ego. All these are nothing but the perfect Brahman-Self, which I am. In this conviction one should abide firmly, **until one achieves the state of sleepless-sleep which is alert-peace-eternal**.

Having realised that the world picture on the screen-Self is evanescent and essentially non-existent, one should ever remain still and blissful in the firm conviction of ever being the sole Brahman-Self only. This conviction should be maintained even while functioning as an individual in the world of name and form. This matured state of abidance in the Self is called Sahaja Nishta (the Natural State). In that blissful Self wherein there is no action of body, speech and mind, no virtuous or sinful karma (action) and the fruits thereof, **one should remain still, eschewing the least trace of thought**.

Totality of all Knowledge attained in the Blissful-state of 'no-mind' – Ribu Gita:

In that Self wherein there is neither conceiver nor conception of the world of names and forms, one should remain blissfully still, eschewing the least trace of thought.

In that Self wherein desire, anger, covetousness, confusion, bigotry and envy are all absent; in that Self wherein there is no thought of bondage or release, one should abide blissfully still, eschewing the least ripple of thought.

Firmly abiding in the Self one acquires the totality of all knowledge and achieves the successful completion of all endeavours and duties. In that state one should abide blissful and still, eschewing the least ripple of thought.

"One is absolved of all his sins and remains established in Brahman-Self" – Ribu Gita

Mind merged completely in the Self, one becomes a lord without rival-steeped in bliss beyond compare. In that state one should abide still, free from the least trace of thought.

I am that Self which is integral existence awareness-bliss, the sole impartite Brahman-Self. Firm in the conviction born of this experience, one should abide still, free from the least trace of thought.

In the conviction that 'I am the Self' in which no thought, ego, desire, mind or confusion can exist one should abide still, free from trace of thought.

The firm faith of being the Self is sufficient to dispel all thought and establish one in Brahman-Self. In due course of this practice, even the thought involved in that faith fades away leading to the spontaneous effulgence of the Self. If a person hearkens to this teaching and practises the faith, even if he is a great sinner, he is washed clean of all his sins and is established in Brahman-Self.

There is certainly no such thing as mind with its constituents of thought and thought forms of objects. In this conviction one should ever abide still and at peace, in the state of thought-free alert Awareness-Self which endures after all sadhanas and its rigours have exhausted themselves in Brahman-Self. Having gained the experience that there is no creator, no maya, no duality, and no objects at all, and that pure Awareness-Self alone exists, one should ever remain still and peaceful in that state of Selfhood.

If a person gives heed to these teachings he would certainly gain the grace of Lord Siva and attain the state of Selfhood even though he is immersed in the dense darkness of nescience which could not be banished by the glare of a million suns.

Why waste words? This is the truth in a nutshell. Only those who have earned the Grace of our Lord Siva by long devotional worship will get the rare opportunity of reading this scriptural text which leads to the bliss of peace everlasting in Brahman-Self.

The True World Guru (Teacher) is the one who teaches that one is the Absolutely Thought-Free, Blissful, Infinite Self – Ribu Gita:

Only that Jnani who teaches 'Thou art the thought-free, alertly aware, absolutely still, ever blissful, intensely peaceful, unqualified Brahman-Self', is the true Sat Guru, and others are not.

Unbroken abidance in the state of alert awareness, unruffled by thoughts, is Self-realization. That is at once the spotless jivan mukti and the magnificent videha mukti. This state is easily attainable only for those who have earned the divine Grace of Siva by deep devotion to Him, and not for others. What is stated here is the import in a nutshell of the message of that charming crest jewel of the Vedas known as the Upanishads.

Those who give heed to this message and abide in accordance with it will forthwith attain mukti (liberation). They will not suffer from the least particle of affliction; they **will enjoy a bliss far greater than the bliss attained from this and all other worlds;** they and their environments will be filled with the plenitude of auspicious events. Totally free from all trace of fear, they will never again enter the cycle of births and deaths. They will become the immutable Brahman-Self. All this we swear is the truth beyond doubt. By our Lord Siva, again and again we swear that this is the fundamental truth.

That state of still, pure, effulgent awareness is moksha, the state beyond compare. Those who maintain an unbroken abidance in that supreme state will never more be touched by suffering or confusion, and will be absolved from all duties. Such duties if any will somehow be completed without any volition on their part. They will eternally abide as the sole supreme. Self.

True Liberation (Moksha) is steady abidance in the pure thought-free Alert-Awareness-Self only – Ribu Gita:

The non-dual sole being existing in deep sleep conjures up a world in the dream state. Even so, the shadow world conjured up in the waking state is the work of the power, inherent in one's own Brahman-Self. Abiding firmly in the experience of pure Brahman-Self, one finds that the mind and all its confabulations are lost for ever.

One should remain firm in the conviction 'I am the Self' and reject all thoughts like 'I am this body' and 'This world is real'. If one maintains this habit unremittingly, this false belief will drop away even as a flower held in the hand slips away when one falls into deep slumber.

One is solely responsible for one's own liberation or bondage, since the choice of destroying the restless mind or allowing it to roam at large rests with that one only. Therefore, one should conquer the restless mind by steady abidance in the pure thought-free Alert-Awareness-Self only. This steady abidance is moksha.

The Three-fold impurities of Maya the dark Veil of ignorance has to be Transcended to reveal one's Divinity and thus lead from agony to ecstasy – Sri Shiva Rahasya

Now there is another great secret to be known. The Soul, being made of Spirit, nay, *being* the Supreme Spirit Itself and Identical with Me, is eternally happy, all-wise and free. Yet as he descends at My Divine Command into this Material World, as he must in order to participate in My Creation, he passes through the dark veil of Maya, My Cosmic Magic. In the course of his descent, he becomes tainted by the Threefold Impurity called Mala.

Anava Mala, the Impurity of Imperfection, is the first product of Maya. Thereby, as in a dream, the Soul though being Identical with Shiva deems himself and everything else to be limited and imperfect. Impelled by this impurity, he desires limited and imperfect things. O you who are endowed with Wisdom! know this to be the seed of worldly existence.

The second, Maiya Mala, is the Impurity of Delusion that develops from the first even as a plant sprouts forth from a seed. It causes the Self to see all things as different and separate both from each other and itself.

Karma Mala, the third, is the Impurity of Limited Action. Growing from the previous two, it is their fruit, as it were. Having been rendered imperfect and endowed with limited knowledge, the Soul acts in limited and imperfect ways. Having performed such action, the latent seed thereof comes alive in due course, binding him to this World and its endless cycle of death and rebirth. Thus the Soul is forced to enjoy the fruit of his imperfect actions, both bad and good.

The Faithful Yogi conquers old age and death and becomes Master of his own life and becomes a 'Siddha' a Perfect One attains Divine Wisdom, the Eight Great Supernatural Powers, attain celestial bodies of radiance and enjoys the fruits of heaven here and now –Sri Shiva Rahasya

Yet even before attaining Union with Me, My devotee shall enjoy the Bliss of Heaven. For he who practises Yoga diligently in a secret place, conquers Old Age and Death, and becomes Master of his own life. He becomes a Perfect One (Siddha). He can understand the secret tongue of wild beasts, Spirits and Gods. He can traverse the Sky at will and congress with the Deathless Ones. He obtains the Eightfold Supernatural Power called Ashta Siddhi and becomes one of the Gods.

Verily and without doubt, by the Power of Anima, the Yogi makes himself small as an atom and perceives the inner workings of Matter; by the Power of Laghima, he makes himself weightless or rises up in the air; by the Power of Garima, he makes himself exceedingly heavy or impossible to move; by the Power of Mahima, he can stretch himself forth in space and see or touch even the remotest of things like the Sun, the Moon or the Stars.

By the Power of Prakamya, the Yogi acquires irresistible will-power; by the Power of Ishitva, he gains absolute power over body and mind; by the Power of Vashitva, he has control over all creatures and elements; and by the Power of Kama-Vasayitva, he can fulfil all his desires.

Endowed with Yogic Powers, My devotees shall ascend to the Celestial Regions wherein they shall enjoy all the pleasures known unto the Immortal Gods.

Provided with Celestial bodies, translucent, shining and imperishable like the best of gems, the Enlightened Yogis shall hear the most beautiful sounds. They shall enjoy the most exquisite tactile sensations, sights, flavours and scents.

All this they shall enjoy in the company of Celestial Beings of Light whose unsurpassed beauty is beyond what mortal man has ever seen; who shine like corals, diamonds and pearls; who are ever blissful, radiant and fragrant; and who gladden the hearts of all. Thus they shall abide in My Glorious Heaven to their heart's content for countless Ages.

With Souls resonant with Divine Sound, with hearts satisfied to the brim and overflowing with Celestial Delight, they shall be fit to drink of My Infinite Ocean of Bliss Supreme. For otherwise, they would be overwhelmed and drown like flies in a milk jar. Verily, they only shall enjoy Celestial Delight that have emptied their heart of worldly pleasures. And they only shall relish My Bliss Supreme who has fortified their senses in the Joys of Heaven.

But My devotee shall attain the Bliss of Heaven even in this lifetime. Turning his gaze within, entering the secret cave of his heart, he shall find the Luminous Path that leads to My Celestial Abode (Arya-Laya) wherein the Noble Ones reside.

But those who are not My devotees, who follow other paths, who are not thus guided by My Inward Light, shall go astray and wander in the dark recesses of their own mind. Verily, for countless Ages they shall wander in that darkness like travellers on a moonless night.

O Sages! I accept all who approach Me with a pure heart and reward them according to their sincere effort.

Erasing the imprints (karma) on the Soul and renunciation makes one to ascend to the higher and the Highest of Planes – Sri Shiva Rahasya

Every experience leaves an Imprint upon the Soul. The more actions man performs in the pursuit of desired objects the more Imprints will be left upon the Soul. The more an Imprint of the same kind is repeated the deeper it will sink into the Soul. As the seed of corn springs to life when the season has come, so the Imprints, the seed of one's actions, come alive each at their appointed time. As they come alive, they give rise to a field of desires which man spends a lifetime to fulfil.

At the end of this life, if only man had no desires, he could easily ascend to the Higher Worlds above. But as he fulfils only a fraction of the total sum of desires, a great many remain to be fulfilled. Thus he is forced to descend back upon Earth by the force of his desires. This repeats itself again and again. Only when he rises above worldly desires, can man ascend to the Higher Worlds and not otherwise. This is the Eternal Law.

O noble ones! man acts to fulfil his desires, both bad and good. As the desires, so his works too, may be right or wrong. And as his works, so his rewards are pleasant or painful. Righteous works that are done in unity with My Law and for the sake of good desires, result in good rewards. But evil works, done in disobedience to My Law and for the sake of sinful desires, result in painful rewards. This is the Law of Cause and Effect, called Karma by the Wise. Every creature, whether on Earth or in the Otherworld is justly rewarded according to its works. I am Ever Compassionate and Wise.

I gave man the Day, that he might wake and Night that he might rest. I gave him fruit-giving trees and rich fields of golden grain. I gave him milk-yielding cows and cool waters full of fish. I gave him forests and caves for shelter, the Moon that he might measure time, the Great Stars for direction and the light-bestowing Sun. And I gave him the Law whereby he might live in abundance and peace. Know that all these are My Signs (Lakshana).

As a King speaks to some of his subjects face to face but to others through his ministers, envoys or messengers and to still others through signs, so I, the Lord, at appointed times reveal My Law unto the World either in Person or through My faithful devotees. They roam the Earth and bring My Word of Truth to those that wish to hear; who having heard, have the power to understand; and who having understood are moved to follow that which is True. And I also reveal My Law through certain signs that are known to the Wise.

The Wise see how the Moon follows the Sun and the Sun is stationed in the Great Sky. They see how the young calf follows the mother cow and how the herd follows the leading bull. They see how one season follows another, Night follows upon Day and Death follows Life. They see how parched fields become green again and how dense jungle turns to dust. In all this there is a sign of guidance and of warning. To some I reveal My Law overtly and to some covertly. And to still others by clear signs that are seen by all but understood only by a few. Let the Wise take heed. For he who follows My signs shall be rightly guided. As for the others, assuredly, indeed, they shall go astray.

Thus My Law is made known unto every nation in the World. Amongst these there are some that deny My Revelation and stubbornly adhere to their own law. Others accept My Law but then forget It and follow any false prophet that may come their way. Others again will seek to change the Truth. As if Truth could be changed like unto a painting on the wall! Verily, only a few hold fast unto My Truth. They shall ever be an Eternal Lamp unto the World and an Abode of Righteousness on Earth. Amongst the Righteous Nations the Holy Land of India shall ever be the first. For, amongst her noble sons and daughters dwell the most faithful followers of Truth. They ever abide by My Law even if the World were to fall to pieces or be drowned by a great flood.

Verily, My Law is heard by every Soul according to his own Karma. The righteous ones that on account of their good Karma are born amongst the Righteous Nations receive My Law in full. But those that on account of their evil Karma are born amongst the unfaithful, must content themselves with whatever fragments of My Law they may come by. For, having done a work for the sake of obtaining an end, man must reap a reward according to the nature of his intentions. Thus every man is born in the land that he deserves on his merits or sins. This is the Eternal Law. I am Ever Compassionate and Just and so is My Law.

Tripura Rahasya, chp. ----XVIII, Lord Dattatreya: *"Parasuram, try to understand that **what appears as space is the pervasive consciousness** for each soul within it. The space appearing in someone else's body and yours as well is blissful self-essence. When one limits it by his own limited self-consciousness, it is known as the mind. As such, it is nothing but the self".*

The sight of the third-eye of Wisdom alone reveals Truth as it is; he sees not the multitude but as the one; When he realises the whole diversity of living things as existing in the One and as born of that One, he attains the Highest; When he sees the Absolute Self as a real experience, and the entire Universe as immaterial like an illusion, he experiences the Highest Bliss (Paramananda); there is nothing in the Three Worlds save God, Soul and Mind. When the Mind has been stilled, Soul and God alone remain, when Soul is no longer distracted by Mind, he sees God face to face; Enlightened Ones in Heaven names are established among the Radiant Stars. – Sri Shiva Rahasya

The Sleeping Soul is like the Moon and the Waking Soul like the Sun. The Moon which is the left eye shines by Night, far off from the Sun; and when the Sun, the right eye, rises, the Moon is gone. But when the Fire of Knowledge which is the Third Eye of Wisdom burns away both night and day, then Sun and Moon become one and are seen by no one. When neither Moon nor Sun are seen then the eye is not two-sided but one. By means of that Single Sight he who is one sees the True Man in the Sky. He, verily, beholds Truth as It Is.

Knowledge is the Light whereby Truth reveals Itself. Without Knowledge there is no Truth and no Life. For those that are devoid of Knowledge are as if asleep. And who can tell a sleeping man from a lifeless stone? But he who sleeps not, is ever awake. He is an Awakened and Wise One (Buddha).

Truly, those who know the Truth declare that the Self is the All-Witness, beyond the Sphere of Matter. It is the Universal Enjoyer, deathless, omnipresent, perfect and ever-free.

Hence, all embodied beings remain subject to worldly existence as a result of ignorance (avidya), which is not knowing the Truth. Due to ignorance and wrong knowledge, Reality is confused with Matter.

Although It is One, It appears as Many through Its Magic Power and not due to Its inherent nature. For this reason, the Knowers of Truth bear witness that the Truth is One (Satyam Ekam).

As the Sky does not become soiled through contact with clouds and the Sun is ever untouched by darkness, even so the various activities of the mind such as thoughts, feelings or sense perceptions, do not affect the Perfect Self. Only the mind and the body, being by nature imperfect, are affected thereby.

As a pure crystal shines by virtue of its own lustre, as the Sun shines unaided by any lamp, as the Lightning blazes across the Sky independently of man-made fire, even so does the pure Self shine independently of any conditioning cause.

Having realised the Highest, the Soul abides in the state of Unified Consciousness (Samadhi), wherein he perceives not the multitude of living beings but only the One. Then he is One with the Supreme Self and has attained the state of Absolute Being.

When the Soul has perceived the Truth, all the passions that cleave to the heart drop off, and having become pure, he attains Perfection. Verily, he acquires a living body of light and becomes an Immortal in this very life. When he realises the whole diversity of living things as existing in the One and as born of that One, he attains the Highest.

When he sees the Absolute Self as a real experience, and the entire Universe as immaterial like an illusion, he experiences the Highest Bliss (Paramananda).

When one attains Perfect Knowledge of the Supreme Being (Para Satta), the Sole Remedy for the sorrows of birth, old age and all kinds of ailments, he becomes One with Shiva, the Lord of those who are Perfect.

Just as rivers large and small merge with the Ocean and become one with it, even so the Soul becomes one with the Deathless and Unblemished Reality.

As the diverse sweet juices are extracted from different flowers and mingled into honey by a bee, even so the Souls human and Divine are indistinguishably United with each other: as a Cloud joining another Cloud, as Water joining Water, and a Flame joining another Flame.

Verily, there is nothing in the Three Worlds save God, Soul and Mind. When the Mind has been stilled, Soul and God alone remain. When Soul is no longer distracted by Mind, he sees God face to face and is lost in His Infinite Embrace.

Therefore, Knowledge of the Supreme alone exists. Neither the World nor its existence is real by comparison. This fact is known to the Enlightened Ones in Heaven whose names are established among the Radiant Stars.

However, in this World, Perfect Knowledge lies in a shroud of ignorance as a lump of gold is covered in dirt and as the Sun is shrouded in clouds. Those who possess not the Perfect Knowledge of Yoga, are deluded and led astray by ignorance which is knowledge imperfect, defective and false.

Perfect Knowledge is without defect, subtle, free from doubts and ever-changeless. Everything else is imperfect knowledge (Ajnana). The thorough realisation of this is called Perfect Knowledge (Vijnana).

This, O noble ones! is the Teaching of the Insight into Reality which is called Excellent Knowledge. It is the essence of all Spiritual Teachings. The practice of Yoga is the single-minded concentration upon this Knowledge.

Knowledge is born of Yoga and Yoga is established by means of Knowledge. There is nothing that cannot be accomplished by one who is endowed with both Yoga and Knowledge.

That which is attained by means of Yoga is also attained through Spiritual Knowledge. Therefore, he who sees Spiritual Knowledge and Yoga as one, sees things as they really are.

For this reason it has been rightly said that the Self alone exists. The Self is indeed the All-Knowing and All-Powerful Reality That contains everything within Its sphere of awareness. By Its power everything comes into being, endures for a while and before long passes away. He who by means of Yoga knows this, attains Unity with Me, the Only Existing, the Perfect, Ever-Living One.

Cycles of Creation, Sustenance and Destruction as waves united in eternal continuum; He who knows this, with concentrated mind, enters My World of Uncreated Light by the secret gateway between two moments and goes to Everlasting Life; man shall strive to become Perfect even as I Myself am The Most Perfect; Verily, man is born to strive for Perfection. For he that seeks Perfection is a Seeker of Truth; He who seeks Truth seeks his True Home. No Soul shall ever find peace till he has found his True Home. Home is that Place where a man finds Peace. Therefore the life of man is a quest for Peace; And Peace is found in Perfection, there is no Peace where there is no Perfection; I grant many lives to a Soul that he may steadily grow in wisdom and become wise. For, no creature that is born imperfect attains Perfection in one lifetime. To expect man to become Perfect after one brief life would be unjust and unwise –Sri Shiva Rahasya

Thus the Cycle of Creation, Maintenance and Dissolution takes place in waves constantly arising, culminating and subsiding, upon the Shining Mirror of My Eternal Self. I, the Supreme Lord, by the Power of Unity (Yoga Bala) unite all into a whole continuum.

As a River, at once ever-the-same according to its long-established banks and ever-new according to the water that freshly runs along its course, so the Stream of Creation though initiated millions of years ago yet is projected every moment anew by Myself.

He who knows this, with concentrated mind, enters My World of Uncreated Light by the secret gateway between two moments and goes to Everlasting Life. Verily, the present moment is the Door to Eternity and the Ford for crossing the River of Time. It is the only appropriate Time for Souls to meet Me, their Creator.

Some realise Me through Meditation (Dhyana), others through the Path of Spiritual Knowledge (Jnana), others through the Path of Devotion (Bhakti) and still others through the Path of Righteous Action (Dharma).

Among the devotees, he who constantly pleases Me through Spiritual Knowledge, is the most dear to Me. For, without Spiritual Knowledge neither right Meditation, nor Devotion, nor yet Righteous Action are possible.

From God all things do come and unto Him they shall return. This is the Eternal Law. Having descended from Heaven down to Earth, the Soul must return to God. And how else is he to return if not by the very same path whereby he came? Verily, let those that follow the Truth not be deceived. God converses not with the imperfect save to call them to the Path of Perfection. When, in due time, they have become Perfect, *then* they shall be called to Him and not a moment before. Therefore, let no man speak things about God that are sinful and wrong.

O noble ones! whatever else in the World stands out through its shining excellence, know that to be a Manifestation of My Radiance Divine. All the things in the Three Worlds were created that My Glory might be made known. But those that are greater than others are My Especial Signs given by Me unto man. For they illumine and uplift the mind of men and set it upon the Path of Truth that leads to the Highest Greatness of all. It is by means of great things that man rises above other creatures.

Therefore, having perceived My Supreme Perfection in those things that outshine all other things, man shall strive to become Perfect even as I Myself am The Most Perfect. Verily, man is born to strive for Perfection. For he that seeks Perfection is a Seeker of Truth.

All things are born of Truth and shall return to Truth. He who seeks Truth seeks his True Home. No Soul shall ever find peace till he has found his True Home. Home is that Place where a man finds Peace. Therefore the life of man is a quest for Peace. And Peace is found in Perfection, there is no Peace where there is no Perfection.

Having been put to sleep at the moment of creation, man begins his worldly life in the form of an inanimate thing made of space, air, fire, water or earth. He abides in that condition for forty-two thousand lifetimes. He then enters a state like that of dream and assumes the form of half-sentient things such as plants or trees. Thus he passes fifteen thousand lifetimes. In the form of insects or worms he abides for twelve thousand lives. Nine thousand in the form of a sentient beast such as land-borne, water-borne or air-borne creatures; and six thousand lifetimes in human form.

Having thus passed through eighty-four thousand lives, man is born only three more times: once as a Yogi and twice as a God. Then, having attained the Supreme Perfection of Heaven (Para Siddhi), he is born no more.

O Sages! I grant many lives to a Soul that he may steadily grow in wisdom and become wise. For, no creature that is born imperfect attains Perfection in one lifetime. To expect man to become Perfect after one brief life would be unjust and unwise. I, the Lord, am Ever Just and All-Wise, and so is My Work.

In the Beginning, I created the Upper World, the World of Light wherein abide all Beings Bright. I am the Eternal Ruler of that World. I then created the Lower World wherein abide the dwellers upon Earth. That World is ruled by the Radiant Ones who are the Rays of My Own Light and who rule over the World by the Power of Yoga and in accord with My Command.

Yoga is living in Unity with Truth. He who abides in Unity with Truth shall know neither fear nor grief; nor pain, nor yet disappointment shall he know but he shall ever rejoice in Heavenly Bliss. And rejoicing Therein he shall bring Joy unto the World even as the Sun brings joy to the flowers in the field.

Verily, the Yogis who have attained Perfection and have risen above earthly life are equal to the Gods. They are the Jewels of My Creation and rule the World together with the Gods.

The Yogis' task is to make My Will known unto the World. They shall ever work for the establishment of Righteousness on Earth. They shall live a holy life and ever be an example of Divine Perfection unto all men. They shall sit in the Assembly of Holy Sages and be a guiding light unto the King. For they are My Messengers and I am their True Sovereign. This was ordained by Me for the welfare of all. I am Compassionate and All-Wise.

That land shall be known as Land of Righteousness (Dharmabhumi) wherein Yogis are honoured by all. For he that honours a Yogi who is ever immersed in Unity with Me, he honours none other but Me. This is My Eternal Law.

Those who live in harmony with Creation (Nature) live in Unity with the Lord; Thus, from Wish, to Thought, to Word, the World came into being at My Divine Command. Everything is born of That Supreme Sound. Even the Divine Form you are now beholding with your eyes is a Manifestation of That; I Am That Supreme Reality. I am Boundless Freedom and Might and My Powers are Five: Omnipotence,

Omniscience, Infinite Fullness-and-Satisfaction, Omnipresence and Eternity. These are My Five Powers Divine. When obscured by My Mighty Magic they become limited and the being who holds them is known as Soul. Thus the Soul is born as the sixth in the midst of the five. He is the power-holder and their master even as I am the Holder of the Five Powers Divine; The Awakened Ones, the Buddhas, they alone know that Maya is the Mother and I Alone am the Father of the multitude of creatures born in this World.

O Sages! the World is My Own Creation and a Manifestation of Truth. Therefore, righteous men honour and revere My Creation and live in Harmony with it. Verily, he who lives in Harmony with My Creation lives in Unity with Me. He who honours a work, honours the workman too. I and My Work are One and the Same.

It is out of Love that I created the World. Out of Love for My Creation I set the World in Order and I established My Law. I created the Day, that man might wake and Night that he might rest. I created fruit-bearing trees and rich fields of golden grain. I created milk-yielding cows and cool waters full of fish. I made forests and caves for shelter, the Moon that man might measure time, the Great Stars for direction and the light-bestowing Sun. And I gave him the Law whereby he might live in abundance and peace.

Verily, My Love for man manifests itself in that I give him life of my Own Life and that I offer him sustenance, guidance and protection. And man's love of Me shall be seen in his following of My Law. By the following thereof he abides in Unity with Me. Therefore, he who desires a long and happy life in this World and the next, shall ever abide by the Law of Unity. He who abides not thereby goes the Path of Separation which is the Path of Sin and Discord.

The Farmer tends and tills the earth. The Merchant trades the fruits of the Farmer's labour. The Warrior protects the land. And the Priest conducts the holy prayers. In the midst of the above four, the Yogi proclaims my Word of Guidance for the welfare of all. In this way, Righteousness is upheld upon Earth. This is My Eternal Law.

Let Earth be honoured at Sowing Time with festive song and fair dress. For, it is Earth that bears the seed, that it may grow and yield fruit. But

Heaven shall be honoured at Harvest Time. For it is from Heaven that the life in all seeds comes and Heaven it is that sows the seed.

But I the Lord shall be honoured at all times. For I am both Heaven and Earth: I Create, I Make Grow, and I set the Harvest Time too. I set the Wheel of Time in motion. I determine the beginning and end of a day, the seasons, the year and the age of many years. I ordain both life and death. Therefore, let all Souls worship Me with devotion in temples, holy places, in their homes and in their heart. In every fortnight, they shall set aside the eighth and the fourteenth for My Devotion. Likewise, when the Moon is Full. But that worship which is done upon a Moonless Night shall be regarded as the best of all. These four shall be My Holy Days.

Verily, O noble ones! I rule the Universe through My Highest Power of Yoga (Yoga Bala). He who realises That, becomes immortal.

For this reason, the Wise Ones have called Him Shiva which means, That in Whom everything rests (Shi) and by Whose Power everything moves (Va). I Am that Shiva, the Original Ever-Living One; the Unseen and Uncreated Who Ever Is before everything that is seen and created is born or dies.

From the Stillness of My Heart a Wish was first heard and then brought to Light. The Wish was made firm in the form of Thought. The Thought was made audible as a Word. And the Word was made visible as the World.

Thus, from Wish, to Thought, to Word, the World came into being at My Divine Command. Everything is born of That Supreme Sound. Even the Divine Form you are now beholding with your eyes is a Manifestation of That.

I Am That Supreme Reality. I am Boundless Freedom and Might and My Powers are Five: Omnipotence, Omniscience, Infinite Fullness-and-Satisfaction, Omnipresence and Eternity. These are My Five Powers Divine. When obscured by My Mighty Magic they become limited and the being who holds them is known as Soul. Thus the Soul is born as the sixth in the midst of the five. He is the power-holder and their master even as I am the Holder of the Five Powers Divine.

He who understands that everything is made of consciousness knows everything;

He who understands that everything is made of Consciousness, knows everything. He who understands that Consciousness Alone exists, knows the Highest Truth. He knows both himself and all other things. He becomes the All-Knowing Truth. Such a one is the One who Sees and is Awake while all others are asleep. Verily, when Consciousness is asleep, It knows not Itself. Therefore, know that Sleep is a form of Ignorance and the greatest impediment on the Path. For he who sleeps can never be Awake and he who is Awake sleeps not. Beware therefore of Sleep for Sleep is like unto Death.

The Soul having become imperfect on his descent to Earth must become Perfect again to return unto the Perfect One. For only that which is Perfect can join Perfection. The imperfect is doomed to ever abide in separation from Supreme Perfection. Yoga is the means whereby a Soul is made Perfect and pleasing to the Lord; When other faiths have passed away, Yoga will prevail. Then Perfection shall rule over the World.

Having descended down into the earthly World from the Abode of Life, the once-Watchful Soul is overcome by the multitude of worldly things and falls prey to the slumber of nescience. In that state he deems himself Awake and calls his condition Waking. Yet in that state he is neither Awake nor truly Alive. He who knows this, enters upon the Path of Awakening. He is like unto a man who first stirs in his sleep, then awakens and opens his eyes to the clear light of day.

In My Abode of Spirit, neither Sun, Moon, Stars nor Lightning shine, nor yet physical fire. All being Identical with Me, the Immaculate Supreme Radiance, everything therein shines by the Light of My Own Conscious Self. That Which is called the All, Which is Indivisible, Immutable, Pure and Great, That Alone Shines by Its Own Self-Luminous Light. That Immovable Reality which the Enlightened Ones permanently see within themselves, is the Universal Consciousness, My Own Self.

All Scriptures declare that I, the Supreme Self, am Pure, Sweet, Perpetually Blissful and the Embodiment of Truth. Those who have understood this by hearing My Revelation, meditate upon Me, the Lord, by means of the sacred Sound OM, as their true Self. Neither Earth, nor Water, Fire, Wind nor Ether; neither Mind, nor Intellect, nor Vital Breath, nor indeed anything else shines in the Firmament. Verily, I, Lord Shiva, shine Alone in the Great Sky of Reality.

O you who are worthy of My Grace! know that those teachings that deny My Truth are false. They are the mind-created aberrations of the mad and the deluded who seek to lead the righteous astray. Do not listen to what they preach but watch their evil deeds: you will see how they transgress My Law. Verily, in this World, some are mad and others are sane. One who is mad with delusion will lead many a Soul astray. Therefore, beware! do not follow false teachings that promise an easy way to Salvation. The wise know well that everything is for a price. If gold and precious stones do not come cheap, is Heaven going to be free?

Just think! had I only wanted, I should have granted Salvation to all. Know that the faithful following of My Law, and a pure heart, *that* is the price for a dwelling-place Above. Therefore, be patient and forbearing for this is the sign of a truly wise man. Follow not the falsehoods of the misguided, for their works shall come to naught. Follow the Path of Perfection and you shall not be harmed by grief.

The Soul having become imperfect on his descent to Earth must become Perfect again to return unto the Perfect One. For only that which is Perfect can join Perfection. The imperfect is doomed to ever abide in separation from Supreme Perfection. Yoga is the means whereby a Soul is made Perfect and pleasing to the Lord. The Lord will not embrace those Souls that make themselves repugnant and unpleasant to behold. By following the Path of Righteous Unity, Perfection is attained even in this lifetime. There is no other way. He who seeks another way to Heaven is like the man who digs a well on the banks of the River Ganges instead of drinking straight from its holy water.

O you who are the first among noble Souls! My Revelation is the Mightiest and Most Great. There is no other one like It. It is Truth Itself. It shall bring to pass the destruction of false teachings even as the Rising Sun destroys the dark. Those that dread My Revelation will seek to corrupt It and debar the faithful from following It. Therefore, It shall first be kept secret. But when the time has come It shall be openly revealed to all. When other faiths have passed away, Yoga will prevail. Then Perfection shall rule over the World.

The Alpha and Omega of Yoga explained in one line in the 49th Sutra of Sage Patanjali's Yoga

Sutras: *"prayadna saydilananda smabaktipyam"* - by stilling the thought-waves that arise of their own accord and by meditating on the vast expanse of space, asana or yogic-posture, the seat of a firm and harmonious nature is attained. The mind should be made to expand or mushroom into the limitless space. To achieve such a state, a firm and steady but relaxed asana is a necessity. A calm and tranquil state of the mind itself means it is a state of vast emptiness (space).

Evolution - Sage Patanjali:

The physical body changes in accordance to the changes that take place in the mind. When one advances from a lower life-form to a higher form of life over various births, that process in known as evolution (*parinama*). Man along with the three gunas took to countless births and evolved from the lowest form of life. When he realizes that he is the Self (Soul) not attached to anything material but at the same time existing in everything and is the Divine Ecstasy he is in search of, requires no more births. The gunas (characters) are non-existent.

Sage Patanjali on Pranayama (art of regulating the Pranic-energy through the vital-breath:

"bahyapyantrasthampa vrittirdesa kala sankyabi bhartirushto theerkasasukshma" Pranayama is of three types which could be shortened or lengthened by their placement, duration and timing. Regulated-intake is one method, regulated-exhalation is another and retention of air within or

outside the body is the third method. The *placement* of prana (along with one's consciousness) over particular spots within or over the body signifies *place*. *Time* is determined by the duration or passage of the time prana is held over a particular spot in the body.

Sage Patanjali on restraining the breathing-process for extended and un-limited period of time:

When we are given a sudden shock or are frightened or anticipate a critical move like trying to outwit the stare of a fierce lion or even when watching the final serve at championship-point at Wimbledon, without being aware, will hold our breath. This also happens when we go into deep-contemplation and this is known as Kumbaka. An accomplished Yogi after much practice is able to attain such a state at will, and he can maintain that state for duration of time as he pleases.

Patanjali on attainment of Divine-Wisdom through pranayama:

"thatha sheeyathae prakasavaranam" By performing the pranayama mentioned above the veil of ignorance that clouds our mind is lifted. In the depths of our mind worldly as well as Divine-knowledge lies buried. That Jnana or Wisdom is in sattvic-form (soft-natured, harmonious, brisk, alert, intelligent). Apart from sattvic, the other two characters or type of moods which are present in varying degrees in man are rajas (violent) and tamas (lethargic, ignorant) which conceal this wisdom. Through pranayama this *avarna* or veil is lifted whereby wisdom is revealed.

The three levels of meditation - pratyahara, dharana, dhyana - Sage Patanjali:

The five sense and five motor-organs (indriyas) in their original pure-state without blemishes of their past experiences aligned with the mind is pratyahara. The mind fixed on any object (*desa bandaschittasya dharana*)is dharana. When dharana fixed on an object becomes prolonged and is un-interrupted spontaneous knowledge (*jnana vritti*) is the outcome which is known as dhyana.

Total recall of all past-life memories of one's own and of other people's minds - Patanjali:

The memories of all previous experiences exist as subtle and ultra-subtle (sukshma, adi-sukshma) vibrations in the depths of the mind. These vibrations of all previous births never ever stop. The Yogi performing Samyama (dharana, dhyana and Samadhi coalesced) on the subtle and ultra-subtle vibrations can at Will bring back memories of previous births. By performing samyama over identification spots on bodies of other persons, the yogi is able to attain knowledge of person's minds. When further samyama is performed on another person's mind, all the knowledge contained in the person's mind is revealed in totallity to the yogi.

Acquiring the prowess of an elephant and understanding the languages of beasts and birds - Patanjali:

To gain the strength of an elephant or an equally powerful creature, the yogi performs samyama on its prowess thereby acquiring it (*balaeshoo hastibhalathini*). When one at first practices samyama, he fixes his mind in all totality on the object. The mind is fixed in such concentration for a prolonged period of time. After much mastery, he does not see the physical-part, only the memory of it lingers in his mind. In a perfected state the physical as well as the image vanishes. The effect is no more, only the cause or reason remains clearly in the mind. (*Sapthartha...*) - In general, the word, its meaning and its cause are coalesced together. When samyama is performed on them independently, the sounds emanated by animals are understood in their totality. When a word is uttered, vibrations are created in the atmosphere which causes vibrations in the hearing-organs which are carried to the brain. The newly-aroused vibrations cause previous identical-vibrations that exist in the brain as memory to vibrate in a similar manner. By such high-speed comparison a word or words are identified. So to identify a word, there is an outside-vibration, inner-vibration and an opposite-vibration caused due to memories. So an yogi by performing samyama on a sound, within *no-time* is able to gain full knowledge of the sound caused. The sound or sounds, be it of any language, man, bird or beast, everything in their totality is understood to the yogi in an instant.

David and Solomon had Knowledge of the beasts and birds – Holy Qu'ran; sura XXVII.15,16:

"We gave (in the past)
Knowledge to David and
                    Solomon;
And they both said:
"Praise be to God, who
Has favoured us over many
Of His servants who believe!
And Solomon was David's heir.
He said: "o ye people !
We have been taught the speech
Of birds, and on us
Has been bestowed (a little)
Of all things; this is
Indeed Grace manifest (from God)."

When past and present are compressed into a single-point, realm of timelessness result – Patanjali:

"santhotithela tulyapratyaela chittasyay kakrate parinama" When the past and the present are treated on par, evolution is attained. We could determine that mental concentration is achieved when thoughts of time and its passage disappear. The growth in concentration of the mind can be judged by the

prolonged passage of time. Even in our everyday life this phenomenon takes place when we are reading an interesting book or engaged in a favorite hobby, the passage of a couple of hours seem to be that of a few minutes. In such a state of mind, the past and the present are not differentiated and exists as the present moment, thus it could be said that concentration of mind had been achieved. A concentrated mind is fit to go into the realm of timelessness.

Swami Vivekananda on Time-Phenomena (1890's); Thomas Mann (1924):

Swami Vivekananda in 'Jnana Yoga':" The Present-time is only the gap or interval found inbetween the past and the future; so it is not intellectually correct to select only the present. For there is no space for the present-time to exist contrary to the past and the future. All three are an indivisible whole; The time-phenomena is a myth, a burden, a state thrust on us, defined in a way acceptable to us."

Thomas Mann in the 'Magic Mountain':

"Time has no divisions to mark its passage,
There is never a thunderstorm or blare of
Trumpets to announce
The beginning of a new month or year.
Even when a new century begins it is only
We mortals who ring bells and fire off pistols."

Hunger and thirst can be transcended and sight of Siddhars (perfected beings) could be attained – Patanjali:

When samyama is performed on the throat-chakra hunger and thirst are not felt. And to gain sight and get the blessings of the Siddhars who possess bodies of radiant-light, samyama should be performed on the glorious-light that emanates from the crown-chakra (*"moordhajyodishi siddhadarsana"*).

Practice of Yoga at dawn, noon and dusk gets rid of the 3 'poisons', hence turns one young; Thirumandiram 727:

"As body wax-like suppleness attains,
Practicing yoga at dusk the phlegm leaves;
Practicing at noon, the wind that is treacherous leaves;
Practing at dawn, the bile leaves;
Thus all poison from body is expelled
And you shall know no greyness or wrinkles."

The human body is an amazing storehouse of magical qualities. According to the Ayurvedic and Siddha science, the human body is affected by three main 'humours' or poisons:'vada' – wind(concerns all joint-movements and arthiritis in one of main problems),'pitha' – fire(concerns digestion and metabolism) and 'kapha' – phlegm(concerns mucus and moisture). These three are further divided into five each, a combination of them expand into all diseases totaling 3000 in number. Practicing yoga at dusk, one is relieved of phlegm; when yoga is practiced at noon, the treacherous wind is expelled; when yoga is performed at dawn, bile is expelled. When one is no more affected by the three poisons, there is no more graying of hair nor shrinkage of skin, there is everlasting youth.

Control of seminal ejaculation and dieting prolongs life; you become the Lord; Thirumandiram 735:

"If the seminal seed thickens by sexual abstention
It shall never be destroyed;
If the body is lightened by austere discipline
Long shall the life be;
If food is consumed sparingly, many the good flow;
You may verily become the Lord of dark-hued throat."

By not ejaculating the seminal fluid, the body not only becomes light but also radiates light caused due to suffused energy. When food is eaten sparingly, life too is prolonged and tremendous psychic powers are attained and the person virtually becomes the Lord who quaffed the deadly poison (that emanated when the 'milky-seas' were churned during the process of Creation) to save the worlds and all life-forms and hence became known as the "Lord with the blue color-throat" – Lord Shiva.

Man can vision the past, present and future (trikala jnana), ambrosia flows hence beyond clutches of hunger and thirst; Thirumandiram 875:

"They traverse spheres of sun and moon
And see vision of past, present and future earth;
And in that full-moon day the nectar ripens
Until the moon drops back from Kundalini,
Time stands to a stop."

When one with sheer concentration and will-power is able to take along with the Pranic-force, the Kundalini or 'Cosmic-energy' lying at slumber at the muladhara chakra at the base of the spine upto the 'Chandra mandala' or moon's sphere which is above the forehead, he sees visions of the past, present and future as well as realizing its causes and reasons. When he crosses the moon's sphere, he becomes part of the Whole so that time stops still and ambrosia flows in abundance (the 'Siddhars' or perfected-beings have a continuous flow of this nectar which they say tastes sweeter than sweetened sugarcane-juice) so that he is never in need of food or water, hunger and thirst never trouble him again.

Man 'turns' young by 'internal-breathing', attains immortality when ambrosia flows down through secret mystic-opening; Thirumandiram 805:

"If you can send the breath twain
Into the internal tounge's upper-cavity
You shall not be bound by time;
And the gates of nectar will open be;

Graying and wrinkling (of skin) will disappear
For all to see; youthfull will the person be
This is the word of the Lord Nandhi."

The Prana which is actually the vital, dynamic sum of all forces is breathed in, it acts and functions as "ten vital vacuum-forces" known as 'dasa vayus' which govern all vital functions of the body like digestion, reproduction upto decimation of the body after death, they are: prana, apana, samana, udhana, vyana, naga, kurma, krikara, devadatta and dhanamjaya. When one is able to bring up the descending 'apana' to the mouth's upper-cavity and merge it with prana through the secret mystic opening that is connected to the 'tenth-opening' at the crown of the head known as 'Brahmarandra' (in Sanskrit) and 'Brahma puzhai' (in Tamil) which means "gateway of God", ambrosia flows. The person hence conquers death, hair does not turn grey and he becomes young to the astonishment of all. Unlike ordinary man, the Yogi forcibly sends the Prana inhaled along with the air through the 'Sushumna nadi' (most important astral-nerve that flows within the spinal-column from the muladhara chakra at the base of the spine upto the sahasra chakra at the crown of the head). When one starts to breathe through the Sushumna, air need not be inhaled anymore through the nostrils, Prana the vital energy can like fish and frogs, can be obtained even under water or buried under the earth!

Beautiful maiden are attracted when Kundalini rises to the cranium-top; Thirumandiram 736:

"If Kundalini that is in muladhara
Is sent upward often to reach the space in cranium,
Comely your body becomes;
A desire-object for damsels bedecked with flower s
Around which bees swarm humming."

Kundalini Yoga practiced regularly, confers comeliness and youthfulness and the Yogi will frisk like a tender fawn. Beautiful women would throw themselves against the Yogi who would be most charming and irresistible.

Saint Ramalingam who de-materialized in 1872, like the 'King' as Elvis Presley was known, used to be sought after by beautiful women who would throw gold and diamonds at the Saint's feet to entice him, which he of course politely deterred.

The realized person and the omni-present state – Adi Sankara's Viveka Chudamani, sloka 338:

The one who realizes that he exists within and without moveable and immoveable objects in the form of knowledge (*jnanathmana*) which is his basic-nature and who is not bound to anything, who is in a form that cannot be segregated (*ahanda rupa*) in a perfect-state (*paripurnanai*) is the liberated person (*muktha*).

Cessation of thoughts brings about state of no-mind, result being spontaneous-state of Divine-Bliss - Adi Sankara's Viveka Chudamani, slk.368:

Solitude brings about control of the sense (*indriya upara-manae*) – 5 motor and 5 sense-organs; control of the senses is the cause for controlling the mind (*sedhasa samrodhe*). Controlling of the mind brings about obliteration of the strong ego-centeredness (*aham vasana vilayam*). Therefore the Yogi attains the continuous and spontaneous-state of Divine-Bliss (*sadha asala Brahmi ananda rasa anubudhi*). Thus cessation of thoughts (*chitta nirodha eva*) should always be striven for with effort (*prayathnath kaarya*).

Stand apart from the body, be a witness and realize that you are the Supreme - Adi Sankara's Viveka Chudamani, slk.377:

Negate all desirious-activities that are poisonous in nature for it is these desires that leads us to the death of forgetfulness of our soul (*aesha aeva mrutyo sruti*). Negate any bindings to caste, race or school of thoughts (jadhi – kula – ashramaeshu) and any activities that follow due to those bindings should be left far behind. The false things like the body and the 'I' consciousness should be left behind. Fix your mind on the supreme Lord, for really you can stand apart from your body and be a witness to it (yath vasthutha thvam dhrashtha asi); You are without any blemish (amala asi); You are the indivisible Supreme (nirthvaya – param brahma asi).

Meditate on the Self as the vast expanse of space – Adi Sankara's Viveka Chudamani, slk.384:

After discarding the body, senses, vital vacuum-forces, mind, ego and other faculties (deha-indriya-prana-mano-aham-ahibi) which were out of ignorance wrongly presumed to be his true self, the soul which is indivisible and truly omni-present in nature (ahanda rupa-purna-atmanam) should be seen in the expanded state like the vast expanse of space (maha-akasa avalokaeth).

Omnipresence of the soul - Adi Sankara's Viveka Chudamani, slk.386: From Lord Brahma to the atom-like tiny insect (Brahmathi – sthamba – baryandha) all creations are merely false (mrushamatra). Hence one should witness his soul as that which extends, expands and pervades everything and everywhere as a single-entity (thata purnam svatmanam pachyae – dehatmana sthikam).

The Perfected-being is in a constant state of ecstasy - Adi Sankara's Viveka Chudamani, slk.418: Even when a person is alive in the physical-body and had attained liberation(from the endless cycle of death and re-birth)as well as perfected-beings who had achieved their life's purpose(samsiddhasya) and Yogis on their own, externally and internally (bahi-ananda)always exist experiencing spontaneous Divine-Bliss(sadhananda-rasasvadhana), this is the purpose (balam) of life.

Sins no more (salvation) when one realizes that he, the soul is none other than God - Adi Sankara's Viveka Chudamani, slk.447: When I realize that I am the soul which is none other than God (aham brahma *idhi vijjnanadh*) the sins accumulated over ten billion (*kalpakodi-sadha arjitham*) kalpas (kalpa is 4.32 billion years being the day-time of Brahma the Creator) –over countless births are due to the awakening, dissipiate like the deeds committed in the dream-state dissipiate after waking up from slumber (*swapna karmavath vilayam yadi*).

Realize your Perfection - Adi Sankara's Viveka Chudamani, slk.472: You also should through spiritual discernment realize the glorious state of the soul (*atmana paratattva*) which is in the form of Divine-bliss and realize its true state (*swarupa*) and by deep study and analysis, the evil of ignorance that you had constructed out of false-belief in your mind (*swamana pragal pidham*), delusion should be cast out. You should be a liberated one (*muktha*) who had attained the purpose of this life and should be one who had woken up from ignorance totally (*praputha pavadhu*).

I am in all animals (life-forms) - Adi Sankara's Viveka Chudamani, slk.495:

Among all animals (*sarvae shu bhoodaeshu*) in the form of knowledge – all knowing, omniscient (*jnana atmana*) permeating and extending within and without (*anda bahi achraya sun*) as the one who experiences and the object that is experienced, exist. Whatever that maybe, that was seen before as quite different from this is all nothing but me (*yathyadha pura idhandhaya prudakh dhrushtam sarvam svayam aeva*).

After realization of the Self, nothing more to know - Adi Sankara's Viveka Chudamani, slk.393: Like space, without any blemish, as a single-form (nirvikalpa), infinite, motionless, changeless, that doesn't have an inside or an outside (andhar-bahi sunya), that doesn't have another, that which is indivisible, you that exist a yourself (svayam) are that Brahman (Parabrahma). After realizing That (bhodyam) – what else is there to realize?

Realized person in an expanded-state is Brahman (God) - Adi Sankara's Viveka Chudamani, slk.394: What more needs to be said here, in an expanded manner the soul in its true form is Brahman (*svayam Brahma* *aeva).* All these worlds in their expansiveness are Brahman. From the Vedas it is clear that God is without a second (*srudhae Brahma advhidhiyam*). Enlightened persons who realize – "I am the Brahmam" (I am God), totally renounce the outside-world and in clear super-consciousness are in a constant state of and form of wisdom and bliss (*sandhadam chit-ananda, atmana aeva*), this state that they live in is for sure.

Glorification of the body leads to misery, self-realization brings purity and divinity - Adi Sankara's Viveka Chudamani, slk.396:

As long as this corpse-like body is glorified by man, he is unclean; he is prone to misries created by his enemies (*paraipya klaesa syat*); he is caught up in the whirlpool of birth, death, disease and hell (*janana – marana – vyathi – nirya*). When he realizes that he is the soul that is pure (*suddham*) that is divine in nature (*sivakaram*), motionless (*asalam*), he is released from the misries mentioned above. Do not the Vedas also say this (*tat ruti abhi aaha hi*)?

Advaita (God, cosmos and man are one) – the truth through sushupthi (deep sleep-state) - Adi Sankara's Viveka Chudamani, slk.405:

This dvaita cosmos – viewing the worlds and God as two different entities (*idam dvaitam*) is an empty illusion only, the Brahmam without a second exists truly say the Vedas (*paramarthata idi sruti sakshath prudhae*). In the deep sleep-state of sushupthi this can be experienced – the other two states being jagrat – woken-state and swapna – the dream-state (*suhupthela anubhuyadey*).

Through self-experience realize the expansiveness of the soul and siddhis (supernatural powers), oneness and Bliss – remain entrenched in that state – Adi Sankara's Viveka Chudamani, slk.477:

One should through self-experience (*sva anubutya*) see himself in the expansive-state of the soul (*atmanam ahantitam*) as one who had attained siddhis (supernatural powers) attained when one attains perfection (*samsiddha*) as one who does not see the world with its innumerable beings and himself as two separate entities (*nirvikalpatmana*) in total bliss (*susukam*) remain firmly entrenched in his soul (*atmani disdaith*).

The soul possesses infinite-energy, the realized person of Divine-Wisdom is greatest among great - Adi Sankara's Viveka Chudamani, slk.535:

This Soul is radiant of its own, possesses infinite-energy (*anandha shakti*), cannot be studied or analysed (*apramaye*) but is in the form that can be experienced by everyone. As soon as it is realized, this God-realized person of Wisdom (*ayam Brahmavidh*) is one who is free of all hindrances and bonds that bind him (*vimuktha bandha*) is the greatest among the great (*uttamothama*) and thrives in victory (*jayathi*).

Creation as was in existence in previous-cycle – Srimad Bhagavatam. bk. II, dis. II:" Sri Suka continued: It was through such concentration that Brahma (the self-born) propitiated that Lord and got from Him at the dawn of creation the knowledge (about creation), which he had forgotten (during the last pralaya or universal destruction). Having thus acquired unfailing vision and a conclusive understanding, he created this universe even as it existed before the universal dissolution."

Not the least difference between the individual soul and God – Srimad Bhagavatam, bk. XI; dis. XXII: "The glorious Lord replied: ...9. Self-realization in the case of the jiva (individual soul), who is characterized by ignorance that has no beginning, cannot take place by itself, there must be another who knows the truth and is able to impart his knowledge. 10. There is not the least difference in this body between the individual soul and God. The assumption that they are distinct from one another is meaningless..."

Vedas transcend time and space and taught by the Lord to men and various beings of other evolutionary-cycles existing in other global-constellations in other dimensions according to Srimad Bhagavatam, book XI, dis. XIV, "Glory of the path of devotion and the process of meditation described": "2. The glorious Lord replied: In course of time this Word bearing the name Veda, in which stands described the course of conduct helping one to fix one's mind on Me, disappeared during pralaya (the great deluge of final-dissolution). At the beginning of the next creation it was delivered by Me to Brahma (the Creator). 3. By Brahma again it was taught to his eldest son, Manu (Swayambhuva); and the seven great Seers associated with the creation of the universe, Bhrgu and others received it from Manu. 4. From them, the fathers of creation, their progeny, the gods (Angels), the Danavas and the Guhyakas (yaksas), human beings, siddhas and gandharvas, including vidyadharas and caranas as well as men of other dwipas (other lands than India), kinnarvas, nagas, raksasas, kimpuruas and others received it."

The Supreme Lord born as Kapila expounding the true nature of self-realization which is immortality and supreme joy – Srimad Bhagavatam, dis. XXIV, "Descent of Lord Kapila":

"34. The Lord replied: Whatever I say is an authority to the world in matters secular as well as sacred. Therefore, it is only to redeem what I said to you that I have been born as your son, O sage. 35. My present birth in this world is meant only for expounding the true nature of the categories so helpful in self-realization to those seeking release from their subtle body. 36. This mysterious path of self-knowledge had been obscurbed through long ages. Know that this personality has been assumed by Me in order to revive that path. 37. Allowed by Me, go wherever you like and, *conquering death, which is exceedingly difficult to conquer*, through actions dedicated to Me, adore Me with a view to attaining immortality. 38. Beholding Me – the supreme Self-effulgent Spirit dwelling in the heart of all beings – in your own heart through your intellect you will be freed from all sorrow and attain the fearless state (viz. final beatitude). 39. To My mother (Devahuti) as well I shall impart that spiritual knowledge, which frees one from the bondage of all actions and by virtue of which she will get over the fear of transmigration and attain supreme joy."

The Perfected-person, Kardama, who had forsaken ego and transcended pair of opposites attains the omni-present state – Srimad Bhagavatam, bk. III, dis. XXIV, 'Descent of Lord Kapila':"

40. Maitreya resumed: Thus addressed by the celebrated Kapila, Kardama went round the Lord (his own son, Kapila), as a mark of respect and straightaway withdrew to the forest, full of joy. 41. Observing a vow of non-violence practiced by hermits and exclusively depending on Sri Hari (the Supreme Spirit), the sage renounced the sacrificial-fire as well as a permanent dwelling and roamed about the globe, free from attachment. 42. He fixed his mind on the infinite-Lord who is beyond both cause and effect, who though devoid of the three gunas (characters), yet brings them to light, and who can be realized through exclusive devotion. 43. Free from egotism and the sense of mineness, indifferent to pairs of opposites (such a heat and cold, pleasure and pain, joy and sorrow etc.,), and viewing all with the same eye, **Kardama perceived his own self everywhere.** His mind had inward and was perfectly composed, and the self-posessed sage looked like an ocean without waves. 44. His mind being fixed through Supreme-devotion on the all knowing Lord Vasudeva, the self (inner-controller) of all embodied souls, he was now free from the bondages of ignorance. 45. *He perceived the Lord, his own Self as present in all living beings, and all living beings in the Lord, His own Self.* 46. In this way Kardama, who had no desire and was free from malice, who was even-minded towards all, and who had developed devotion to the Lord, attained union with the Lord."

The body and mind get purified, becomes disease free, salvation and immortality through pranayama and process of the eight-fold Yoga – Srimad Bhagavatam, bk. III, dis. XXVIII.' The process of eight-fold Yoga':

"2-7: The Lord replied: Having controlled one's posture, one should spread a seat (consisting of kusa-grass, deer-skin and so on) in an undefiled-spot. And sitting therein an easy posture, keeping the body erect, one should practice control of breath. 8. At the very outset the striver should clear the passage of the breath by first inhaling the air to his utmost capacity, then holding the breath and finally exhaling it, or by reversing the process, that is, by exhaling the air in the first instance, then holding the breath outside the body and finally inhaling it so that the mind may become steady and free from distraction. 9. Even as gold throws off its dross when heated and melted by the force of air and fire, so the mind of the striver who has controlled his breath gets purified before long. 10. A striver should therefore eradicate the disorders of the three humours of the body (wind, bile and phlegm) by the aforesaid three processes of breath control, his sins by concentrating his mind, contacts (with sense-objects) by withdrawing the senses from their objects and the characteristics which are contrary to the Lord's Divine-nature (such as attachment and aversion etc.,) by means of meditation. 11. When the mind gets purified and concentrated by the practice of Yoga, he should meditate on the form of the Lord (as indicated hereafter) with his gaze fixed on the tip of his nose."

The full-blown Yogi attains the Supremely blissful-state and the 8 great supernatural powers and finally the immortal-state of the Lord – Srimad Bhagavatam, bk. III, dis. XXVII.' How to attain liberation through the differentiation of matter and spirit':

"25-26. The Lord replied: When a man who is given to contemplation remains absorbed (as aforesaid) in meditation on the Self for a period extending over many births, he develops a distaste for everything as far as (the enjoyments of) Brahmaloka (the highest heaven and home of Brahma the Creator). 27. Having realized the Self by My abundant Grace, that strong-minded devotee of Mine has all his doubts resolved by self-vision and, when freed from his astral-body, easily attains in that very life the **Supremely blissful-state** known by the **name of final beatitude, which is his essential character and rests on Me**, and having attained which a yogi never returns to (the cycle of) birth and death. 28-29. If the mind of the accomplished Yogi, O beloved mother, does not get attached to the **eight kinds of superhuman powers** (such as faculty of reducing one's body to the size of an atom and so on, which are products of Maya, developed through Yoga, which is the only means of acquiring them, **he is sure to attain My immortal state, where death has no power**."

The enlightened person attains serenity, tranquility and power - The Holy Qu'ran; sura IX.26:

"But God did pour His calm
On the Apostle and on the believers,
And sent down forces which ye
Saw not: He punished
The unbelievers: thus doth He
Reward those without faith."

Comments by A.Yusuf Ali:" Sakin: calm, peace, security, tranquility. The Apostle never approved of over-weening confidence, or reliance merely upon human strength, or human resources or numbers. In the hour of danger and seeming disaster, he was perfectly calm, and with cool courage relied upon the help of God, whose standard he carried. His calmness inspired all around him, and stopped the rout of those who had turned their backs ...."

Acquiring the 5 states of the Lord through Bhakti (Devotion) – Srimad Bhagavatam, bk. III, dis. XXIX.

'True meaning of devotion and the glory of Time': "6. The Lord said: The discipline of devotion, O noble lady, is recognized as manifold according to our ways of approach (latitudes of mind with regard) to it; and men's attitude of mind varies according to the diversity of their natural characteristics. 7. A man who is given up to anger and views me as distinct from himself, and who practices devotion to Me with a mind full of violence, hypocrisy and jealousy is a devotee of the Tamasic-type. 8. He who worships Me through an image etc., as distinct from himself with a view to acquiring objects of senses, fame and power is a devotee of the Rajasika-type. 9. And he who adores Me as distinct from himself, aiming at the eradication of his sins or with the intention of offering his actions to the Supreme or again with the feeling that it his duty to worship Me is a devotee of the Sattvika-type. 10. The un-interrupted flow of the mind-stream towards Me, dwelling in the hearts of all – like the waters of the Ganga towards the ocean – at the mere mention of My virtues, combined with motiveless and un-remitting love to Me, the Supreme Person, is spoken of as the distinguishing character of un-qualified Bhakti Yoga. 11-12. My devotees accept not, in exchange for My service (the 5 forms of final beatitude, viz.) '*Salokya*' (residence in My divine realm),'*Sarsti*' (enjoying My Powers),'*Samipya*' (living in My Presence),'*Sarupya*' (poessign a form similar to Mine) and '*Sayujya*' (absorption into My Being) even when they are offered to him (by Me). 13. The aforesaid Bakti Yoga has been declared as the highest (final) goal; for transcending the realm of the three Gunas (modes of Prakrti) the devotee thereby becomes **qualified for My State (without any effort)**."

Idol and image-worship only until one realizes that God exists in his as well as in other living-beings – Srimad Bhagavatam, bk. III: "15-19:

The Lord said: Just as odour wafted from its source through the vehicle of a breeze catches the olfactory sense, so an equipoised mind engaged in the pursuit of Yoga (devotion) embraces Me. 20. I am ever present in all beings as the very self (inner controller). A man therefore who worships Me through an idol, showing disrespect to Me (as abiding in all creatures), makes a travesty of worship. 21. Ignoring Me, the Supreme Ruler, the Self present in all living beings, he who **stupidly resorts to idol worship alone** throws oblations into the ashes. 22. The mind of a man who, full of pride, hates Me, abiding in the body of another, views Me as distinct from himself and **bares deep-rooted malice to living creatures can never find peace**. 23. I am not pleased, even though adored through an image by means of formal worship carried on with costly or cheap materials, O sinless mother, by a man slighting other creatures. 24. Performing his allotted duties a man should worship Me, the Supreme Ruler, through images etc., only so long as he does not realize Me as present in his own heart as well as other living beings. 25. Figuring as Death, I cause great feat to him who makes the least discrimination between himself and another because of his differential outlook. 26. Therefore, through charitable gifts and attentions as well as through friendly behavior and by viewing all alike, one should propitiate Me, abiding in **all creatures as their very Self**."

Utkala saw his own Self projected through the universe and the universe as existing in his own self – Srimad Bhagavatam, bk. IV, dis. XIII: "5. Maitreya said: When his father retired to the woods, Utkala, Druva's eldest son, felt no inclination to accept the imperial fortune and the imperial throne of his father. 6. Congenitally possessed of a tranquil mind, free from attachment and viewing everything with an equal eye, *he saw his own self projected through the universe and the universe existing in his own self.* 7. The impurities still lurking in his mind, in the form of impressions of actions done in the past having been burnt by the fire of uninterrupted practice of Yoga (meditation), he looked upon his individual soul as none other than the tranquil Brahman (Infinite) – wherein all differences are set at rest forever, and which is one's real Self – and hence *identical with the joy of consciousness, all-blissful and extending everywhere*, and no longer perceived anything apart from his own Self."

Ali Shariati An Iranian Philosopher on His Experience On 'Oneness' With The Universe

"As you circumambulate and move closer to the Kaaba, you feel like a small stream merging with a big river. Carried by a wave you lose touch with the ground. Suddenly you are floating, carried on by the flood. As you approach the centre, the pressure of the crowd squeezes you so hard that you are given a new life. The Kaaba is the world's sun whose face attracts you into its orbit. You have become part of this universal system. Circumambulating around Allah you will soon forget yourself. You have been transformed into a particle that is gradually melting and disappearing. This is absolute love at its peak."

Charles Lindberg on his personal experiences of 'oneness' and 'omnipresence':

"On the equatorial plateau of Kenya and Tanzania there are nights when the stars shine with extraordinary brightness, when the dark mystery between them seems as potent as a womb. Lying on my back in dry grass and staring skywards, I would sometimes lose my sense of individuality and seem to expand through space, as though the universe and I were one awareness, one existence. Then I would retract into myself again, a man bound by gravity's inexplicable force to the surface of planet earth. It was like a waking dream in which time telescoped. My fantasy of seconds compressed what had taken place through eons in actuality. Had I not descended from universe and star in about this way? Modern scientific theory postulates particles of matter forming from energy that interlaces space, condenses them to galaxies in which suns and planets spiral, organizes them into molecules that become the elements of life, evolves life from single cells to the awareness and biological complexity of man."

Barbara Cartland on "One with the universe" in 'The Enchanted Moment':

'The Enchanted Moment', page 152:" ... She could feel a glow of warmth reaching out to her, possessing her whole being. For a moment she was lost to time and space – past and present, it was all hers and all immeasurably clear. She was no longer alone, but one with the whole universe."

William Wordsworth

"... For oft, when on my couch I lie
In vacant or in pensive mood,
They flash upon the inward eye
Which is the bliss of solitude;
And then my heart with pleasure
Fills
And dances with the daffodils."

'Kailash' the realm of Lord Shiva filled with celestial earth-like living forms as well as extinct ones and one-footed and eight-footed

animals – Srimad Bhagavatam, bk. IV, dis. VI – 'Brahma and the other Gods proceed to Kailash and appease Lord Shiva:

"12-13. Maitreya went on: The mountain is adorned with celestial trees such as mandaras, parijatas as well as saralas (a species of pine), tamalas, salas and palmyras, kovidaras, asanas and arjunas. 14. It is further beautified with mango trees, kadambas and nipas, nagas, punnagas and champakas, patalas (trees bearing the trumpet flowers), asokas and bakulas, kundas (a species of jasmine) as well as kurabakas (trees bearing the red amaranth flower), golden lotuses, creepers bearing cardamoms, malatis, kubjas, mallikas and madhavis. 15-16. Nay, its beauty is enhanced by bread-fruit trees. Udumbaras, the holy fig trees, plakas (the waved-leaf fig trees), banyans and bdelliums, birches, annual trees (such as the banana), betel-nut trees, amras (a species of mango trees) and so on, priyalas, madhukas and soap-nut trees and other varieties of trees, and clusters of bamboo – both of the hollow and solid types. 17-18. It is further graced with swarms of birds sweetly warbling on the margin of its ponds rich in their bed of lilies and lotuses of various kinds. 19. It is infested with deer, monkeys, bears and porcupines, gayals, sarabhas (a species of eight-footed animals), tigers, rurus (a species of black antelopes), wild buffaloes and other wild beasts as well as with karnantras, ekapadas (a species of one-footed animals), aswamukhas, wolves and musk-deer; and the strands of its ponds look charming with the cluster of banana trees surrounding them. 20-21. It is hemmed in by the river Nanda (the holy Ganga), whose water have been hallowed by the touch of Sati (the deceased consort of Lord Shiva), who bathed in it. The gods felt astonished to see the beauty of mount Kailash, the abode of Lord Shiva (the Lord of the ghosts)."

Stephen Hawking on interstellar travel:

"I am afraid that however clever we may become we will never be able to travel faster than light. If we could travel than light we could go back in time. We have not seen any tourists from the future, that means that travel to other stars is going to be a slow and tedious business. Using rockets rather than warp drives. A

100,000 year round trip to the center of the galaxy. In that time the human race will have changed beyond recognition, if it has not wiped itself out."

Travelling at the speed of light or even going beyond it doesn't seem possible or even plausible for we would then be going on a journey with infinite-time on our hand or travel into the past or even the future. The only possible and practical solution would be to break the dimension-barrier whereby great distances could be traversed like cutting across the *'hairpin-bends'* that we find on roads that zigzag over mountains. The idea may seem farfetched right now but there was a time when man thought that travelling faster than a horse would blow our brains out and running a mile under four minutes was thought as impossible until Roger Bannister broke the barrier and Chuck Yaegar broke the sound-barrier paving the way for our supersonic jets to make it an ordinary affair. Research is going on and theoretically it is said that spaceships could travel through *'wormholes'* in space and that *'blackholes'* could be those gateways to other universes in even other dimensions.

There are many multitude of references to such type of interstellar travel in ancient Indian texts that could be found nowhere else in such detail. There is mention of a flying-craft that flew *"as swift as the sun"* that belonged to Priyavrata in the Srimad Bhagavatam, bk. V. There are many references to crafts that resembled *'rotating firebrands'* that sound like the *'flying-saucer'* UFO's we talk about presently. Lord Vishnu had in his *'boar-craft','tunnelled'* his way traversing our plane (or worlds or dimension) and going beyond even the lower seven planes which seem much like travelling through wormholes in space.

After the 'Kandha Puranam' war that took place on earth about 30 million years ago, it is mentioned that all the Gods and Angels flew down to earth in their individual *'Vimanas'* or flying-crafts and after the marriage of Lord Muruga with Devayanai the daughter of Indra the Lord of the Angels, everyone boarded their vimanas and flew to 'Amaravathi' the capital city of the Devas (Angels) in the third plane and reached their destination in *'no-time'* for they flew at *'mano veham'* or *'thought-speed'*.

In the epic Ramayana, Ravana the King of Lanka abducts Sita the wife of Lord Rama in the forests of Northern India and flies with her in the Pushpaka vimana Lanka. Again while the battle between Ravana's and Lord Rama's forces rages on, Sita is flown to a vantage height over the battlefield for her to see in person the utter hopelessness of her position. After vanquishing Ravana, Rama takes along Sita, his brother Lakshmana, Sage Vishvamitra and Vibishana the newly crowned King of Lanka in the celestial car back to his Kingdom in Northern India.

In a race between Lord Vinayaka (who rides the mouse-craft) and Lord Muruga to see who would circumvent "all the worlds", Lord Muruga riding his 'Peacock-craft' circumvented a "hundred billion universes" (Thirupugazh: "ayiram kodi andangal") within a second and to stress on to the fact that the peacock is not just a bird, in 'Kandhar Alankaram':" the hero who gets on and rides around in the red burnished-golden peacock that is a craft" ("sempon mayil yenum theril yeri ulavi varum veerarae") and again in Thirupugazh; Muthu Tamil:" When will you come riding the golden-red peacock-craft?"

Four holy-men who are the mind-born sons of Lord Brahma the Creator, flew from 'Sathya loka' in the fifth-plane or fifth-heaven (the realm of the Creator)down to earth in 'Fiery-chariots' (agni rathas), landed on a great mass of land that covered most of the Indian ocean and existed right up to Australia in the south, Africa in the east and the American continent in the west. They stayed here on earth for 400,000 years and speeded up the evolutionary process as a whole. Among the four brothers, Lord Sanarkumara is said to be forever 16 years old! One very similar incident is mentioned in the Holy Bible; Ezekiel: One day late in june, when I was thirty years old, the heavens were suddenly opened to me and I saw visions from God. I saw, in this vision, a great storm coming towards me from the north, driving before it a huge cloud glowing with fire, with a mass of fire inside that flashed continually; and in the fire there was something that shone like polished brass. Then from the centre of the cloud, four strange forms appeared that looked like men, except that each had four faces and two pairs of wings. Their legs were like those of men, but their feet were cloven like calves feet and shone like brass. And beneath each of their wings I could see human hands...

Deadly missiles,'stealth-warfare', aerial-cars, stun-weapons and 'life-giving' medicines and herbs in the Ramayana War – 'Sri Shiva Gita' & Ramayana:

1. Rama, upon the advice of the sage Agasthya (in brief as mentioned in the 'Sri Shiva Gita'), entered into a the 'Pasupadha viradha' (a very powerful fast and penance) whereby he smeared Holy-Ash all over his body, sat on it and even slept on it for four months. In the first month, Rama ate only the wild fruits collected by his brother Lakshmana in the forests on the banks of the river Sarayu; in the second month he consumed only green leaves; in the third month he drank only water; in the fourth month he was nourished by Prana (breathing) alone. After the completion of the fasting and penance, one day accompanied by deadly ear-shattering thunderous-sounds and brilliant lights, a great vimana landed on the banks of the Sarayu river, the wheels of it even got sullied by sinking into the soft river-sands. When Rama went for a closer inspection, he saw Lord Shiva who looked like transparent crystal, seated upon the 'Rishaba Vahana' (bull-craft) and all the gods, goddesses and angels and the 18 heavenly-hosts assembled there having landed there in their own individual flying-crafts. Lord Shiva at first presented His divine 'Pasupadhastra' and his blessings, following which he received the 'Narayanastra' from Lord Vishnu, the 'Brahmastra' from Lord Brahma and all other divine-missiles and their blessings from the divine-beings assembled there.

2. In Ramayana's 'yudh kanda', Indrajit son of Ravana the Lankan King, performed 'Tantric-rites'before the Sacred sacrificial holy fire-pit (homa gunda) whereby he became invisible and he then entered the battlefield.

3. Rama activated the 'Ghandarva astra' whose activation was known only by Lord Shiva and Rama. On activation, countless number of Ramas were seen without the real Rama not to be perceived.

4. While Ravana had in possession the divine aerial-craft 'Pushpaka Vimana' captured by him from Lord Kubera the Lord of riches, Lord Indra's (the Lord of the devas or angels) vimana of Divine powers and Divine weapons was sent along with his pilot Maatali to help Rama.

5. In 'Yudh Kanda' when Rama, Lakshmana and countless were knocked down in a death-like state by Indrajit's 'Brahmastra' (mightiest of weapons), presented by Lord Brahma the Creator. Jambavan requested Hanuman to collect four radiant herbs found only on a mountain-peak near mount kailash in the Himalayas. The four very rare herbs are: a. 'Mryta-sanjivini' which brings the dead back to life. b. 'Visalya-karani' which cures a wound in an instant. c. 'Savarnya-karani' which brings to life only the close and related ones. d. 'Sandhana-karani' which in an instant restores mutilated parts of the body.

Rotating firebrand aerial (stealth) craft that was amphibious and as big as a miniature-city – Srimad Bhagavatam, bk. X, dis. LXXVI. 'Salva's encounter with the Yadavas': "Sri Suka began: 5. Salva requested the Lord to confer on him an aerial-car which could be taken wherever he liked, and which could not be broken by the gods, asuras, men, ghandarvas and raksasas and which would be a terror to the Yadus. 6. Sankara said, "be it so!" Under His command, the demon Maya (Titans), constructed an aerial-car called Saubha, which was made of steel, and handed it over to Salva. *It was not a car, but a city in miniature.* 7. Full of darkness within it, it was inaccessible. It could be taken wherever one liked. 19…. The aerial-car of Salva constructed by Maya contained such magical contrivances that *now it appeared as many and now only as one, now it appeared in the sky, and now disappeared altogether…* 20-21. Now it descended on the ground, now flew into the air, now perched on the summit of a hill, *now began to float on water. Like a rotating firebrand it went round and round* hardly stopping at any point.

Celestial-cars crammed in the skies – Srimad Bhagavatam, bk. VIII, dis. VIII, 'Lord Narasimha extolled on the death of the demon-king': "Prahrada replied: 34. Hearing that the celebrated (tyrant-king) Hiranyakasipu the headache of the 3 worlds (upper, our solar-system being in the midst of the middle and lower worlds), had been killed in a combat by Lord Sri Hari, celestial women, whose faces were blooming with an outburst of joy, sent down showers of flowers upon Him again and again.

35. At that time the sky was crammed with rows of aerial cars of heavenly beings eager to have a look at the Lord …"

Effulgent car as swift as the sun, the tracks of which dug up the seven oceans – Srimad Bhagavatam, bk. V, dis. I, ' The story of Priyavrata': Sri Suka continued: 29. Once Priyavrata observed that evento the extent the glorious Sun-god lights the earth's surface in the course of his circuit round mount Sumeru (the mountain of the gods), he shines only on one-half of that portion and leaves the other half shrouded in darkness. He did not like this. His superhuman glory having been enhanced by virtue of his adoration of the Lord, he therefore like another sun made seven circuits (round the earth) after the sun, in his effulgent-car, as swift as the sun, determined to turn night as well into day. 30. *The tracks that were sunk by their fellies of the wheels of his chariot came to be the most celebrated seven oceans*, which divided the earth into (what are known as) the seven Dwipas (or main divisions)."

Sooran the Asura, Titan-King ruled over 1008 universes, ultimately defeated by Lord Muruga in the Kandha Puranam war in the 1st Yuga (eon) more than 30 million years ago in Southern India and the Lost continent of Kumari Nadu; Adi Sankara's 'Subramanya Bhujanga'; 'kandhar Alankaram':

There existed a great mass of land below the Southern tip of India which eventually sank into the ocean-depths about twenty million years ago. Four great Cyclic-Yugas or eons are quoted frequently in all the great Indian epics, the present one being 'Kali Yuga' which began about 5000 years ago with the advent of Lord Krishna and the Mahabharata war took place eventually, this present Yuga lasts for a period of 432,000 (four hundred and thirty two thousand years). The previous one is the 'Dwapara Yuga' and is double or 864,000 years and the Ramayana war took place in that era. The one preceding it was the 'Treta Yuga' which again is double that of its preceding one and its period is 1728,000 years(a little more than 17 million years). The first one is the 'Kreta Yuga' and is for a period of more than 34 million years. These four yugas are cyclic in nature and are contained in

14 'manvantras' each extending for a period of 308 around million years, totaling 4.32 billion years which is the day-time of the Creator Lord Brahma. There are great upheavals and deluges after every 308 million years, with the following 308 million years being 'rest-periods' for the souls. After the completion of a day-time of the Creatore of 4.32 billion years, the entire earth is destroyed, the night-time of another 4.32 billion years being a great rest-period and creation is again resumed when dawn heralds a fresh-day for the Creator! After a hundred such years for the Creator had passed, all the planets and stars of the lower three planes which also contains our solar system is destroyed and after hundred such years have passed, Creation on a grand scale is resumed under a new Creator, a new Brahma.

That Lord Muruga the hero of the Kandha Puranam war that took place in the 1st Yuga, preceded Lord Rama is mentioned in the Ramayana. The Sage Viswamitra while leading the young princes Rama and Lakshmana into the forests to help protect him while performing his religious rites, tells Rama that he should be as brave Lord Skanda or Muruga. In the Mahabharata war also, Bishma the war-hero and general tells that as a brave warrior, he would be on par with that of Lord Skanda. And in the Bhagavad Gita which is a part of the Mahabharata Epic, Lord Krishna says:" *Senaneena maham Skanda*" – "*among generals I am Skanda.*"

1008 Universes ruled by Sooran – Sri Adi Sankara in 'Sri Subramanya Bhujanga'; sloka 23:

"*Sahasrandabogdha dhvaya sooranamha*
Sadasdharaha: Simhavakthracha daitya:/
Mmantharhridistham mana: Klasameham
Na hamsi prabho kim karomi kiva yami //"

Meaning: "*A thousand and eight universes was ruled by Sooran, he along with his brothers 'Singhamukan' (the lion-faced one) and 'Tharagan' and Asuras (the Titians are the nemesis of the Devas or Angels) - were destroyed to let the Devas live by your Holy Grace! Who else but You will wipe out the grief and turmoil in the depths of my heart and if not so, what would I do? To whom else could I go and plead kindness? My Lord! Please shower your love on me!*"

The Kandha Puranam war lasted for ten days and at first the sons of Sooran, Banugopan, Agni-muka Sooran and his brothers Singha-mukan and

Tharakan were killed. Singha-mukan's flying-craft the 'Indra-jnala-ther' (the craft of Indra, the Lord of the Angels that possessed magical-contrivances) was destroyed along with Singha-mukan's flying-craft, the 'Singha vahana'. Sooran's warriors had come from a 1008 universes and surrounded Lord Muruga, who had on the request of the devas come to rescue them from their traditional foes the asuras or Titans. The devas upon seeing the sea-like swarm of asura warriors were stunned beyond belief and wondered whether it it was the day of reckoning usually caused by tumultuous floods of water or a hail of fire and mighty stones followed by the mighty claps of thunder and lightning or the rain of deadly poison! Deva warriors ran helter skelter in frightened confusion, to add to the confusion as if all the clouds bearing the waters of the seven seas burst at a single moment, the asuras aimed their missiles at Lord Muruga. Missiles in the millions were let loose so that the sky and earth couldn't be distinguished. Fire erupted everywhere, the clash of the missiles was deafening so that it sounded like continuous thunder. Battle elephants shrieked in terror. The deafening sounds turned the devas deaf. Mighty warriors turned to their heels in sheer terror. Lord Muruga angry on seeing the utter helplessness of the devas and not wanting to see the massive destruction go on, opened his third-eye a little, "The Lord who is the embodiment of flame opened his third-eye and the flames that roared out within a moment turned the asura forces into ashes" – Kandha Puranam.

During the Kandha Puranam war (30 million years ago)the entire world was enveloped in darkness (nuclear winter?) caused by the Asura (Titan) King Sooran, who then stood in the form of a 'mighty tree' in the midst of the ocean that measured a million miles high; Sooran eventually destroyed by Lord Muruga's 'Nedunchudar Vel' ("missile with the lengthy flame"):

Sooran the Asura (Titan) King, enraged that the devas (Angels) were the cause of Lord Muruga entering the battle, intended to destroy the devas at first and after a brief respite which would bring down his temper, planned to engage Lord Muruga directly. He then by chanting a mantra, enveloped the entire world in darkness (nuclear winter? – there are three plausible and possible scenarios that could be imagined by our limited-minds: 1. By detonating a thermo nuclear device about 200 miles above the earth, an 'electro-magnetic pulse' or EMP of great magnitude could cause all gadgets to blow-out; 2. Stephen King in one of his sci-fi novels says that extraterrestrials could place a large object in the sky synchronized with the earths revolution which would cut off the sun's rays;3. After a nuclear war, the intense heat which could cause great fires and the explosion itself would cause huge amounts of dust, ash and smoke to entirely fill the sky which would cause what is known as a 'nuclear winter' that would envelope the entire globe in darkness for not less than six months.). Lord Muruga 'asked' his missile the 'Vel' to destroy the web of gloom and darkness and evil that had descended on earth, roared out as if a thousand billion suns had united, gushing a rain of fire and in a flash lifted the veil of darkness caused by Sooran.

The enraged Sooran on the intention of destroying all life-forms from 'Baathala loka', the lowest among the "lower seven planes" upto 'Sathya loka'(the realm of Lord Brahma, the Creator), the fifth plane among the "upper seven planes", the lowest of them being our own universe,'boo loka', took on Lord Muruga head on. The battle between Sooran and Lord Muruga lasted for three days beneath the seas off the Tiruchendur-coast in Southern India and in the skies also for Sooran could disappear and appear again at many places at a given particular time. He finally stood in the guise of a mighty inverted-tree in the midst of the ocean that had 'fiery-shoots','smoke-like leaves', branches like huge 'cloud formations', unripe fruits like 'emeralds', fruits like 'huge rubies' and with roots of 'huge dimensions' measuring a million miles high and making all the worlds in all the planes trembled fought on with Lord Muruga.

Sooran who stood in the form of a mighty tree in the midst of the ocean, made his shadow fall on the thousand and eight universes and when he shook his leaves which were as strong as iron, caused intense pain and grief on all forms of life. When the mighty tree moved a little, all the planes shook, mountains and hills were crushed to dust, the axis of the worlds were drastically altered, stars fell from the skies. All the universes trembled and were shaken from their foundations. when eventually Lord Muruga's 'Vel' or missile with the 'lengthy-flame' ("**nedunjchudar Vel**" as stated in 'Kandhar Alankaram') annihilated him. The Vel that had the radiance of all the fires of the "hundred billion universes", split into two the mighty tree (the form of Sooran) that caused havoc among all the worlds" – Thirupugazh.

The mighty missile the 'Vel' that blasted a massive mountain into dust in the Kandha Puranam War 30 million years ago:

The Asura (Titan) King Sooran's general was 'Tharaka Sooran' and his leutineant was 'Khraunjan'. Khraunjan the wicked was black-magic exponent who killed Devas (Angels) and 'Munivars' (a pious and holy people of another evolutionary cycle) in the millions. Khraunjan took on the form of a mighty mountain and brought about hardship on many and once blocked the way of the venerated Sage Agasthya who was on his way to the 'Pothigai Mountain' in Southern India from the Himalayas to set right the balance of the world which had sunk in the north and had risen up in the south. Khraunjan not only obstructed Agasthya's path, but also ridiculed him for being of a short-stature and so was cursed by the Sage to be turned into dust by Lord Muruga's mighty missile, the Vel.

Much later, on his way to destroy Sooran, Khraunjan once more obstructed the path of Lord Muruga who stood in the form of the mighty mountain to weaken the mighty onslaught that was to follow. Lord Muruga duly ordered his mighty missile the Vel to blast the mighty mountain into smitherens and come back to him. The Vel, the missile with the "lengthy-flame" in an instant turned the mighty mountain into dust and duly came back to once more settle into Lord Muruga's hands.

The 'Peacock-Craft' that could circumvent the 14 planes and beyond within a micro-second:

When Apollo 11 landed on the moon, the successful venture was proudly announced to the world with the words:" the eagle has landed!" 'Eagle' being the code name of the space craft. Likewise, Lord Muruga's Peacock Craft is affectionately called the 'Peacock' by one and all. Thirupugazh's 'Muthu Tamil' says:" When will you come here riding your "red-gold Peacock that is a Craft?" ("Sempon mayil yenum theril"). Another sentence in Thirupugazh:" The hero who rides the fast-flying chariot that is the Peacock-bird!"

In a race between Lord Muruga and his elder brother Lord Vinayaka (who rides the 'mouse-Craft') for the "fruit of Wisdom", Lord Muruga in his Peacock-Craft circumvented the 7 lower planes: 'athala loka','Suthala loka','Mahathala loka','Tharathala loka','Rasathala loka' and 'Baathala loka', then 'Kanitam' which is eight million miles above it which is another 'Baathala loka'; then 7 upper planes with the world with its seven seas and hills (our planet), then the planets and the stars; then 'Bhuvar loka' which is above and around us which has the 'Dhurva' star; then 'Suvar loka' which houses the Devas (Angels) and their Lord 'Indra'; then 'Jana loka' which houses the 'Munivas' such as 'Markandeya' who had transcended the 'Kala tattva' (time concept); then 'Thaba loka' of the 'Pithirs'; 'Mahar loka' that houses the "mind-born sons of Lord Brahma the Creator:'Sanaka','Sanan thana','Sanathana' and 'Sanarkumara'; then 'Sathya loka' of Lord Brahma; 'Vaikuntha loka' of Lord Vishnu, the Sustainer; then 1008 universes and finally all the 100 billion universes in the span of a micro-second!

Chariot of Fire with horses of fire takes Elijah – The Holy Bible,2 Kings; ch.2:

1. And it came to pass, when the Lord was about to take up Elijah into heaven by a whirlwind, that Elijah went with Elisha from Gigal. 11. Then in happened, as they continued on and talked, then suddenly a chariot of fire appeared with horses of fire, and separated the two of them; and Elijah went up by a whirlwind into heaven.

Thunder, fire, smoke, trumpet-blast and violent shaking on Mount Sinai, The Holy Bible, Exodus 19;16 to 20:

On the morning of the third day there was a terrific thunder and lightning storm, and a huge cloud came down upon the mountain, and there was a long, loud blast as from a ram's horn; and all the people trembled. Moses led them out from the camp to meet God, and as they stood at the foot of the mountain, all Mount Sinai was covered with smoke because Jehovah descended upon it in the form of fire; the smoke billowed into the sky as from a furnace, and the whole mountain shook with a violent earthquake. As the trumpet blast grew louder and louder, Moses spoke and God thundered his reply. So the Lord came down upon the top of Mount Sinai and called Moses up to the top of the mountain, and Moses ascended to God.

The Japanese Royal Family are the direct Descendants of the Sun-God; Karna the son of the Sun-God (the Mahabharata warrior); Indians living on shores of Lake Titicaca descendants of Sun-God:

'Amaterasu' the Sun-Godess, grand-mother of the God Niniji who came down from heaven to rule Nippon (Japan) was the great grand-father of the mortal emperor 'Jinmu-Tenno' founder of the imperial dynasty 2500 years ago. The Sun-Godess had landed on Mount Fujiyama,(one of the main reasons of it being considered holy) and the Orb (mirror) and the Sword of the Sun-God was presented to be preserved as royal relics, which are still being held in deep reverence in the Imperial Palace of the Royal Family.

More than 5000 years ago, Karna the son of the Sun-God was born with the '*kavacha Kundala*' (armour and ear-ornaments) which grew along with him as he grew up, that would protect him against the harmful-effects of any weapon.

South American legend says that the Indians who live on the shores of Lake Titicaca descended from the Sun-God, who sent his son and daughter to 'Sun-Island' (still having the same name), the largest Island in the lake which in turn is the highest lake in the world, lying at a height of four kilometers in the Andes, measuring 224 kilometers in length,111 kilometers in width and 224 meters in depth. The native Indians still hold ceremonies and celebrate the event.

The ancestors of the Dogon tribes of South Mali came from Sirius the Star:

The Dogon tribes of South Mali in West Africa have literature and customs dating back to antiquity and lost in the mists of time, but emphatically state that their fore-fathers had come from Sirius and that they had travelled in a great ship. To celebrate their arrival here on earth, they don helmet-like masks and dance. This celebration is done once in every fifty-two years not realizing the significance of the act. It has only recently been determined that Sirius lies on a straight line with our own planet on its celestial travel, once in every fifty-two years!

The Brahmastra – a retractable missile that scorched the upper, middle and lower worlds – Srimad Bhagavatam; Ist canto; part I; txt.31:

"drstvastra – tejas tu tayos
tril lokan pradahan mahat
dahyamanah prajah sarvah
samvartakam amamsata"

The brahmastra released from planet earth produced tremendous heat, it is said comparable to the *'Samvartaka fire'* – the fire that would annihilate all life-forms on judgement-day – which scorched all planets in the first three planes. The previous text further says that to counteract a brahmastra released by the son of Drona – 'Drona putrasys' – Arjuna on the advice of Lord Krishna released another brahmastra since he was an expert in military-science, and subdued it; Txt.28:

"Na hy asyanyatamam kincid
Astram pratyavakarsanam
Jahy astra – teja unnaddham
Astra – jno hy astra – tejasa"

When the rays of the two brahmastras combined, a great circle of fire, like the disc of the sun, covered all outer space and the whole firmament of planets.

'Stun weapons' in the Ramayana war (1.7 million years ago)

Indrajit the son of the Lankan Emperor Ravana, who after turning himself invisible by chanting a special mantra, unleashed serpent-missiles (naga panam) on Rama and Lakshmana. The power rendered the brothers immobile and made them fall to the earth as if dead. Vibishana consoled the grief stricken warriors and said that they were only stunned for though they were in a comatose-state, they did not loose their radiance. Hanuman was chosen to bring the necessary herbs to revive the fallen princes. Hanuman rode the mighty-bird Garuda, flew to the Himalayas from Srilanka and successfully accomplished the mission whereby the princes were saved and ultimately Ravana and his armies were decimated.

Atom bomb in the Mahabharata war (3500 B.C.); Dr.J.Robert Oppenheimer remembered a passage from the Mahabharata after seeing the first atom bomb explode at Alamogordo, U.S.A. in 1945:

Mahabharata's Drona Parva tells of the "iron thunder-bolt", a bomb of immense destructive capabilities. The bomb is said to have bursted with the brightness of ten thousand suns and killed people in the tens of thousands. When the bomb burst, clouds which 'sucked-out' the lives of people, shot up and formed a huge mushroom-shaped cloud which filled the entire sky. In its vortex was sucked in thousands of men, chariots, horses and elephants. Those who were close by were killed instantaneously and their bodies disfigured and burnt completely. Those at a distance too were burnt beyond recognition. The eyes, nails, hair and skin burnt and fell off from their bodies. Those who escaped had to constantly wash and scrub their bodies and belongings in running stream waters.

A passage from Mahabharata came to the mind of Robert Oppenheimer considered as the father of the atomic bomb after witnessing the first bomb explode at Alamogordo, U.S.A. in 1945:

"If the radiance of a thousand suns
Were to burst at once in the sky,
That would be like the splendor

Of the mighty one …
I am become Death
The destroyers of worlds."

Guru Dronacharya presented Druyodhana a body-armour that could not be pierced by any weapon – Mahabharata,'Drona parva' – Arjuna & Karna presented with similar armour:

Drona presented Druyodhana the Kaurava Prince, a body-armour that could not be pierced by any weapon available on the seven upper and seven lower planes and their worlds including all the heavens. The particular armour was previously obtained by Drona from Lord Agni (Lord of Fire) which was presented to him by Lord Brihaspati (Guru of the devas or angels), which was presented to him by his father Agnirasa, presented to him again by Lord Indra (Lord of the angels), presented earlier to him by Lord Shiva to help him fight and destroy the invincible Vriturasooran who was a great menace to all the angels. Lord Indra the Lord of the angels, presented Arjuna the Pandava Prince with an un-breakable armour and helmet. The Sun-God presented Karna with an armour and 'ear-protecters' (kavacha kundala) to help protect him against the deadly heat of powerful weapons.

Cloning performed by Sage Vyasa 5500 years ago:

It is mentioned in the great epic Mahabharata that Sage Vyasa took a piece of flesh from queen Ghandhari, cut it into a hundred and one equal pieces and placed them in jars. After the stipulated period, ninety nine princes and one princess 'Dhushala' of the 'Gaurava' clan were born. King Duryodhana was born one month after the rest.

Suka sated in Self-Realization, a master of Yoga, is forever 16 years old – Srimad Bhagavatam, bk. I, dis. VI.: "76. Suta continued: While Narada, the foremost of the votaries of Lord Vishnu, was speaking in this strain, there actually came wandering about at the moment Sri Suka, a master of Yoga. 77. Presently there appeared on the scene at the end of the exposition, slowly and fondly reciting rimad Bhagavata, Sri Suka (the son of Veda Vyasa), a (veritable) moon that occasions a rise in the ocean of Spiritual Wisdom, who is sated with Self-Realization and (ever) looks like a youth of sixteen summers."

Only Wise men experience Supreme Bliss – Srimad Bhagavatam, bk.1, dis. V,' Glory of singing the Lor's praises and an account of Devarsi Narada's previous life': "15. Narada only some wise man can by withdrawing from worldly enjoyments experience the Supreme Bliss which forms the essential character of the eternal and infinite Lord. Therefore, kindly narrate the exploits of the Lord for the good of those who are working under the impulse of the three Gunas (modes of prakrti or matter) and lack the Spiritual sense."

Gains of 'Uttama Pranayama' – becomes master of lions, tigers and elephants; gets resolved of all sins; advanced Spiritual-advancement – Sanatkumara (the mind-born son of Brahma the Creator) to Vyasa in 'Shiva Maha Purana': "Sri Vyasa! I am going to tell you what Lord Shiva told Nandi Deva a long time back. *Pranayama, pratyahara, dharana, dhyana yoga* are the five divisions spoken of (the preceding three of 'Ashtanga Yoga' or eight-limbed yoga being *Yama, Niyama and Asana* are said to be related more to the physical and the other five to the Spiritual).

Pranayama is the art of getting hold of the *Prana vayus* and holding it firmly at a place. It is broadly termed as *Uttama* – exalted-state, *Madhyama* – fair-state and 'Adhama – lower or inferior-state. Each of those three states is again further classified in three sub-grades according to their degree of utility and quality. When the prana vayus are retained for a timing of twelve *matras* (time taken to count 12 letters slowly), it is known as the inferior-state (adhama or mandha) say the yogic-texts. When the prana vayus are retained for a period of 24 matras, it is of a fair-state (madhyama) and when it is done for a period of 36 matras, it is of the exalted-state (*uttama* or *tirukatha* state). It is harmful to practice the aforesaid types of pranayama in excess, it is said. It is good to practice in moderation.

The person, who masters the art of breath-control, literally is the master of lions, tigers, elephants, deers, birds, crocodiles – all life-forms come under his control. This mastery of all life-forms is known as *Vasitvam* (one among the ashtanga Siddhis or eight great supernatural powers). Performing the aforesaid Uttama Pranayama even once would resolve a person of all the sins he had committed since his birth.

The Spiritual advancement gained by performing Yagas (Holy Sacrifical-fire rites) such as '*Agnisthoma*', taking purification-baths in holy-rivers such as the Ganga and the Seven Seas, performing penances, leading a righteous way of life, all acts of generosity – cannot be compared to the gains attained by persons performing the aforesaid Pranayama.

Resolving all sins committed through the practice of Pranayama, harnessing the mind through Dharana, controlling the internal and external sense-organs through Pratyahara and by meditaing through Dhyana continuously on the Infinite on who is the Purna (whole, Absolute), on who is the Source and in the Form of all radiance – is Yoga."

"*Like the snake sheds its wasted-skin, man is resolved of all his sins when he meditates on Me*" – Lord Shiva to Dhurvasa in 'Shiva Maha Purana':

At one time in Kailash (the realm of Lord Shiva), when the Infinite One, Lord Shiva, out of love and compassion was blessing all those assembled there. The one person who is considered to be the highest of the devotees of Lord Shiva,'Dhurvasa' stood humbly before the Lord with folded hands and prayed: "*Lord! The sinners among the four class of people in the world, the meat-eaters, those who torture and harm cows, birds and various form of lives, the ungrateful ones, the sex-maniacs, the ones' who against the sayings of religious-texts, rapists, those who spurn their parents, those who had killed Just-Kings and rulers, those who had robbed the properties of others, those born in the 'Kshatriya' class (warrior class) who instead of facing the enemy had in cowardice and terror run-away from their duty and all other sinners, if they are to be absolved of their sins, I humbly request you to explain to me in detail the ways and means to do so.*"

Lord Shiva replied: "*Dhurvasa Muni! Even the greatest of sinners, if he meditates on Me in utter devotion, like the snake sheds its skin, he would be absolved of all his sins. Firmly meditating on Me within one's heart (spiritual-centre) is 'dharana yoga'. Only through this process can one attain the state of renunciation known as Sannyasathva. Renunciation without dhyana – meditation, would serve no purpose.*

So only by praying to Me and meditating on Me and whose mind, speech and body is always utilized in service to Me, would reach heaven – Me, or after attaining the worlds (heavens) of Indra, Chandra, Kubera, Brahma, Vishnu and other Devas, he would come to Me."

Man can quit the physical body (without dying) – Srimad Bhagavatam, first canto – part I; txt.28:

"*prayujyamane mayi tam*
Suddham bhagavatim tanum
Arabdha – karma - nirvano
Nyapatat panca – bhantikah"

Swami Prabhupada's translation and explanation: "Informed by the Personality of Godhead that he would be awarded a transcendental body befitting the Lord's association, Narada got his Spiritual body as soon as he quitted his material body. This transcendental body is free from material affinity and invested with three primary transcendental qualities, namely eternity, freedom from material modes and freedom from reactions of fruitive activities. The material body is always afflicted with the lack of these three qualities. A devotee's body becomes at once surcharged with the transcendental qualities as soon as he is engaged in the devotional service of the Lord. It acts like the magnetic influence of a touchstone upon iron. The influence of transcendental devotional service is like that. Therefore change of the body means stoppage of the reaction of the three qualitative modes of material nature upon the pure devotee. There are many instances of this in the revealed Scriptures. Dhurva Maharaja and Prahlada Maharaja and many other devotees were able to see the Personality of Godhead face to face apparently in the same body. This means that the quality of a devotee's body changes from material to transcendence. That is the opinion of the authorized Goswamis via the authentic Scriptures. In the Brahma – Samhita it is said that beginning from the Indra-gopa germ up to the great Indra, king of heaven, all living beings are subjected to the law of karma and are bound to suffer and enjoy the fruitive results of their own work. Only the devotee is exempt from such reactions, by the causeless mercy of the Supreme Authority, the Presonality of Godhead."

The Lord is in the Form and Formless state – Srimad Bhagavatam, first canto – part I; txt.18:
Original Sanskrit Text:

"Rupam bhagavato yat tan
Manah – kantam sucapaham
Apasyan sahasottasthe
Vaiklavyad durmana iva"

His Divine Grace, A.C.Bhaktivedanta Swami Prabhupada's (Founder of ISKCON) translation and explanation: "That the Lord is not formless is experienced by Narada Muni. But His form is completely different from all forms of our material experience. For the whole duration of our life we go see different forms in the material world, but none of them is just apt to satisfy the mind, nor can any of them vanish all perturbance of the mind. These are the special features of the transcendental form of the Lord, and one who has once seen that form is not satisfied with anything else; no form in the material world can any longer satisfy the seer. That the Lord is formless or impersonal means that He has nothing like a material form and is not like any material personality.

As Spiritual beings, having eternal relations with that transcendental form of the Lord, we are life after life, searching after that form of the Lord, and we are not satisfied by any other form of material appeasement. Narada Muni got a glimpse of this, but having not seeing it again, he became perturbed and stood up all of a sudden to search it out. What we desire life after life was obtained by Narada Muni, and losing sight of Him was certainly a great shock for him."

In an ancient civilization that predated the Vedic and Chaldean, there is mention of the Glorious body – The Mother (of Pondicherry) in 'Questions and Answers,1957'; radiant-luminous body – the Jyotirmaya

deha of Vaishnavites; transformation of body into gold – Tamil Siddhar Thirumoolar:

"... In the very, very old traditions – there was a tradition more ancient than the Vedic and the Chaldean which must have been the source of both – in that ancient tradition there is already mention of a *glorious body* which would be plastic enough to be transformed at every moment by the deeper consciousness: it would express that consciousness, it would have fixity of form. It mentioned *luminousity*; the constituent matter could become luminous at will. It mentioned a sort of possibility of weightlessness which would allow the body to move about in the air only by action of will-power and by certain processes of control of the inner energy, and so on. Much has been said about these things."

The Vaishnavites (those who worship Lord Vishnu as the Primal-Lord) also speak of a *spiritualized conscious body* (chinmaya deha) and of a radiant or *luminous body* (Jyotirmaya deha) that they attain before entering *Vaikunta* the realm of Lord Vishnu.

The Tamil Siddhar Thirumoolar in his Thirumandiram 1511:

"All things, living and non-living, As they reach the Golden Mount of Meru,
Are themselves transformed into gold;
Even so, They that reach the world to Master Divine,
Attain the Form of Light Divine, His of the King of Kailash."

When through Yogic-meditation, one with full-consciousness and sheer will-power coaxes the Kundali or cosmic-energy that lies in slumber and in a subtle-form at the base or root-chakra at the base of the spinal column along with the dynamic Prana (vital breath) up towards the chakra at the crown of the head, the Sahasra chakra, he is instantly transformed into a body of golden-radiance whereby he can travel to any world in any dimension and be back in a jiffy!

Perfection is the true aim of all culture... - **Sri Aurobindo in,'The Supramental Manifestation'; Thirumandiram – attainment of perfection**

through self-analysis of the body and Realization of the Self; body the microcosm, universe the macrocosm, all of interdimensional-space can be traversed:

The Supramental Manifestation, pg.5.: "Perfection is the true aim of all culture, the Spiritual and the Psychic, the mental, the Vital and it must be the aim of our physical culture also. If our seeking is for a total perfection of the being, the physical part cannot be left aside; for the body is the material basis, the body is the instrument which we have to use. *"Sariram Khalu dharma sadhanam"*, says the old Sanskrit adage,- the body is the means of fulfillment of dharma, and dharma means every ideal which we can propose to ourselves and the law of its working out and its action. A total perfection is the ultimate aim which we set before us, for our ideal is the Divine life which we wish to create here, the life of the Spirit fulfilled on earth, life accomplishing its own Spiritual transformation even here on earth in the conditions of the material universe. That cannot be unless the body too undergoes a transformation, unless its action and functioning attain to a supreme capacity and the perfection which is possible to it or which can be made possible."

Physical transformation is a necessity for physically we are no way superior to animals, birds, fish, insects …plants and trees even rivers, lakes, sand, rocks (all have life)! In brute strength the carnivores like lions and tigers are superior to us, herbivorous ones like the elephant, bull and deer are stronger and swifter than us. Fish can swim faster than us, the penguin beats us even in diving for they can dive up to a depth of two thousand feet! Birds of course can fly without any external aid. The python can do without food for months at a time, which we cannot. Trees live for hundreds and even thousands of years providing food and shelter without any selfish attitude. Stones stand the test of time and provide a visual treat as an art and spiritually as images of gods (yes, stones do have life, Michelangelo realized it and in ancient India, by tapping a stone they knew which was male and which was female and the female-stone was selected for sculpting for it yields to the gentle tap of a chisel) and in a utilitarian manner also by providing us with shelter. Rivers, lakes and the seas are the home and nourish numerous forms of life. Mountains and hills help to hold down the earth's crust, provide mineral wealth and break down the moisture bearing clouds and let flow down its gradient the nourishing streams to make mighty rivers. Taking into account our own simian cousins, leaving the rest, the gorilla is eight to fourteen times stronger than an equal sized man! The average orangutan could easily bend an iron bar which only a circus stunt-man could do, may be with a bit of cheating on the side!

So to transform the physical body, we apart from performing exercises and eating sensibly, which we usually don't, have to tap various latent powers lying within and without the body, which is possible for only us humans to do. Deep concentration, awareness,'I' consciousness and discrimination and the sheer will-power have all to be focused and channelized to reap the results, which animals and other life –forms aren't capable nor provided with the higher-thinking to do so. Many think of the physical body as unclean and a hindrance to achieving spiritual progress as even the great Siddhar or perfected-being Thirumoolar thought so initially; Thirumandiram 724:

> "When the body wastes away, Prana (vital energy, life) too departs
> Nor will the Light of Truth be reached;
> I learned the way of preserving of my body
> And by doing so, my Life too."
> Thirumandiram 725:
> "Time was when I despised the body;
> But when I saw the God within
> And the body, I realized, is the Lord's Temple
> And so I began preserving it, with care infinite."

Vedanta and the Saiva Siddhanta philosophies very clearly state that what exists in the Anda (universe, macrocosm), exists in the Pinda (human body, microcosm). In fact the body is the exact miniature of the universe, each and every vital organ has a corresponding star or a planet. The right-eye is related to the Sun while the left-one to the moon, the kidney, lungs, heart each of them are related and affected by their corresponding heavenly-body. In the astrological-science these relationships are known and when the influence of a particular star or planet is on the negative-side, the corresponding organ in the body is affected and manifests as a disease. These bad-effects can be rectified. The human body is also connected in a multi-dimensional manner with billions upon billions of universes influencing us and vice versa! The seven vital chakras existing from the base of the spinal column right up to the crown of the head, have the tattva or the principles of the seven upper worlds and there are seven lower chakras from the hip down to the feet, which have the principles of the seven lower worlds. A **Purna Yogi** or a **full-blown Yogi** is a person who would have realized the full potentialities of the body, would have activated each of those chakras which apart from being vortexes of energy, are also wisdom-centres, transcended them, gone beyond the highest chakra at the crown of the head and finally crossed the '**Anda-Kosa Yellai**' or '**Universe-body limit**' or border (which exists about 12 inches above the head) and hence all the dimensions have been literally crossed, and he can be at any place in space and be back here in no-time! Thirumandiram 1571:

"The Universes seven,
The cosmic space beyond,
The life - animate and inanimate –
The gunas (moods, characters) three,
The ancient Vedas,
The Gods that create and preserve
And their Primal Lord that is Siva
-   All they are but in me."

Thirumandiram 1572:

"Baffling indeed is the mystery of life's goal
Baffling it is, why into the six systems was it made;
A baffling mystery far,
How into the shedding sheaths of this body micrococsm
God imprinted a veritable macrocosm."

Transition of the Physical body from imperfection to Perfection could take a thousand years! – Sri Aurobindo, The Mother:

When the Mother put the question, "how long would it take to transform the body?" Sri Aurobindo answered:" *oh! Something like three hundred years!*"

Someone else asked the mother, "three hundred years from when?" She answered:" three hundred years from the time one has the consciousness I was just speaking about." "… No, the conclusion, what you must succeed in doing, is to be able to prolong life at will: not to leave the body until one wants to. So, if one has resolved to transform the body, well, one must wait with all the necessary patience – three hundred years, five hundred years, a thousand years, it does not matter – the time needed for the change. As for me, I see that three hundred years is a minimum. To tell you the truth, with the experience I have of things, I think it is truly a minimum."

To transform the physical body, one should first understand that the physical is the '*shadow*' and the Vital the '*real*' for the physical is the effect and the vital is the cause and not vice versa as we generally presume. And it is so with the universe – unlike the western concept which say that matter holds energy, the eastern philosophies say that it is *energy that manifests as matter*. In fact, there are planets and other heavenly-bodies that are in the process of manifestation, they have taken shape in the Vital that cannot be seen and are yet to manifest into the physical, and this process could take billions of years, which of course means nothing in terms of the cosmic calendar.

Ayn Rand on Human Perfection in 'Atlas Shrugged','The Fountainhead'; Ayn Rand:" My philosophy, in essence is the concept of man as a heroic being, with his own happiness as the moral purpose of his life…" Roark – "the truth remains that he exists in everyone – the Self sufficient ego":

Ayn Rand in 'Atlas Shrugged':" *Philosophical knowledge is necessary in order to define human perfection. But I do not care to stop at the definition. I want to use it, to apply it…*" Again in pg.974:" *Discard that unlimited license to evil which consists of claiming that man is imperfect. By what standard do you damn him when you claim it? Accept the fact that in the realm of morality nothing less than perfection will do. But perfection is not to be gauged by mystic commandments to practice the impossible, and your moral stature is not to be gauged by matters not open to your choice. Man has a single basic choice: to think or not, and that is the gauge of his virtue.*

Moral perfection is an unbreached rationality – not the degree of your intelligence, but the full and relentless use of your mind, not the extent of your knowledge, but the acceptance of reason as an absolute."

In 'The Fountainhead', presents her hero 'Howard Roark' the architect depicted as the ideal man, *"man as he could be and ought to be"*. *"My purpose, first cause and prime mover is the portrayal of Howard Roark or John Galt or Hank Reardan or Francisco d'Anconia as an end in himself …"*

Most ideas, thought-provocations and diseases originate in the Spiritual or finer bodies of man; We are in the midst of a sea of tremendous vibrations – The Mother, Micheangelo, Thiruvalluvar:

Michelangelo: *"I don't know from where ideas come from, perhaps from God!"* The Mother in 'Questions and Answers 1956': "Ideas have a higher origin than the mind. There is a region of them mind, higher than the ordinary mind, in which there are ideas, really prototypes; and these ideas descend and are clothed in mental substance. So, in accordance with – how to put it? – the quality of the receiver, they either keep all their own qualities and original nature or become distorted, colored, transformed in the individual consciousness. But the idea goes far beyond the mind; the idea has an origin much higher than the mind. So, the functioning is the same from both the universal and the individual point of view, the individual movement is only representative of the universal one…"

We are in the midst of a sea of tremendous vibrations and are constantly bombarded by the thought-waves of others not necessarily of human nature. Though we seem not to be affected physically by them, the finer bodies accept or deter them depending upon the strength of the will-power and purity of mind. Persons who possess the sight of the *third-eye* classified generally as *extra sensory perception* or ESP are able to *see* the *thought-waves* of particularly drunkards and drug-addicts spreading out in great multitudes and latching or hooking on to the finer bodies (utilizing their deadly hooks) of like-minded people in the shape of weird-looking tiny scorpions, bats and spider-like creatures(known generally as magnetic-impurities). These persons are induced and the frenzy in them grows manifold and only after getting high and drunk to a level of stupor do these deadly creatures let go to seek others of the same nature. Rapists and serial-killers too are haunted and affected by such thought-forms radiated from like-minded people and spirits of dead persons and/or spirits that live in worlds of other dimensions. Even simple day to day thoughts have a form, for example when we think of a flower or a car, the shape of the object floats in front of our third eye-centre in between the eyebrows, which can be seen after much practice.

Diseases also at first manifest in the finer bodies and perhaps month or even years later only manifest in the physical. Some deadly diseases like blood cancer are said to be of karmic causes which are the result of bad acts committed during past-lives. In fact everything we enjoy, good or bad is due to karma, some are earned or gained shortly while others take years or even several lives to be gained and have to be exhausted one way or the other. People who for example choke, suffocate and kill kittens and other such innocent animals are said to suffer from chronic asthma and other breathing related diseases in their next lives. Those who loot, plunder and hoard wealth that would benefit thousands of people would pile up their bad-karma too and would have to suffer in various ways in many following harrowing-lives. The Tamil Siddhar Thiruvalluvar has said:" *Those who perform penance (meditation) make their karma, all others would commit bad-acts (and wallow in sufferings ultimately) getting ensnared in desires.*"

Mother in her,'Questions and Answers,1953', says that once she dreamt of receiving blows on her face and on the next day there were bruises to be seen on the very same places on her face, on her fore-head, the cheek…! Mother also tells of a person who dreamt that one of her eyes was hurt and in a few days the person lost the corresponding eye. She adds:" *It was in the Vital that I was beaten. It is from within that this comes. Nothing, nobody touched anything from the outside. If you receive a blow. If you receive a blow in the vital, the body suffers the consequence. More than half of our illnesses are the result of blows of this kind, and this happens much oftener than one believes. Only, men are not conscious of the vital, and as they are not conscious they don't know that fifty percent of their illnesses are the result of what happens in the vital: shocks, accidents, fighting, ill-will … externally this is transferred as an illness. If one knows how it reacts on the physical, one goes to its source and cure oneself in a few hours.*"

Again, Mother in 'Questions and Answers,1929':" *Each spot of the body is symbolized of an inner movement; there is there a world of subtle correspondences. … The particular place in the body affected by an illness is an index to the nature of the inner disharmony that has taken place. It points to the origin, it is a sign of the cause of the ailment. It reveals too the nature of the resistance that prevents the whole being from advancing at the same high speed. It indicates the treatment and the cure."*

"There exists an underground reservoir of aggregated memories through which minds may communicate" – Carl Jung, Arthur Koestler, Adrian Dobbs, The Mother, Dr.Ramamurti:

Carl Jung (the psycho analyst and therapist), assigns everything that could not be ascribed to cause-and-effect relationships to the influence of the 'unconscious' – an underground reservoir of aggregated memories through which minds may communicate.

Arthur Koestler in 'The Roots of Coincidence', *"we are surrounded by phenomena whose existence we ignore, if they cannot be ignored, we dismiss them as superstitions. For centuries man did not realize that he was surrounded by magnetic forces."*

The Mother of Pondicherry:" *… you are all in a sea of tremendous vibrations, and you are not all aware of it because you are not receptive."*

British Physicist and Mathematician Adrian Dobbs suggests that hypothetical messenger-forces which he calls Psitrons, sweep out like a sort of radar into a second time dimension, sampling future probabilities and conveying them back into the here and now. Dobbs speculates that his positron bypasses the senses and triggers a sort of illumination directly into the brain.

Prominent neuro-surgeon Ramamurti when asked whether it was possible for a person to telepathically contact with another person located thousands of miles away, replied that it was certainly possible for there are as many neurons in the human brain as there are people in the entire world.

"Two of the most advanced fields of modern science, higher mathematics and particle physics are sliding into the fantastic world of phenomena such

as 'anti-matter', "the four-dimensional universe",'imaginary-masses' and electrons which "move backward in time" – **Sir Cyril Burt:**

The late Sir Cyril Burt, professor Emeritus of Psychology at the London University:" *It would be easy to compile a long list of eminent psysicists, biologists and neurophysicists who take an active interest in Parasychology; in universities in many countries there are now departments regularly engaged in Psychical research.*"

Two of the most advanced fields of modern science, higher mathematics and particle physics are sliding into the fantastic world of phenomenon such as 'anti-matter', "the five-dimensional universe",'imaginary masses' and electrons which "move backward in time." Hans Bender, psychologist at the 'Institute of Freiburg', an acknowledged leader in this field, has shown evidence of another reality:" *This other reality is not supernatural, it is natural, but we cant fully explain it yet." The* aspect of para-psychology that interests Bender most is Psychokinesis – PK, the study of abnormal motion in objects."

Just as we haven't yet fathomed the depths or the vastness of space and the infinite-power held within even an atom, we have yet to fathom the depth and vastness of our intelligence leaving alone the intelligence that exist elsewhere. Neurologists and modern research now determine that we utilize less than ten percent of our brain's capacities and a major portion of the brains utilization is yet to be determined. For example, involuntary actions like the breathing-process and the heart-beat have their orders originate from the medulla oblongata generally known as the animal or serpentine-brain. But Yogis know that as the breathing-process grows deeper and slower, orders actually originate from the higher reaches of the brain which passes currents to the rib-cage to stimulate the spasms needed to expand and contract to simultaneously draw in and expel Prana the outward vehicle being air. Yogis also are aware that the current needed to stimulate the heart to pump has its source at a higher point than even the brain and so are even able to functioning of the heart when and if necessary. Moreover apart from the brain, there are many other whirlpools or vortexes of energy over the body which are energy as well as wisdom-centers. These Centers or Chakras expand according to the good, noble and spiritual growth of the concerned person and draws in energy and is influenced and inspired by intelligence from multi-dimensions.

Carl Jung, psycho-analyst and pupil of Sigmund Freud says that we possess *"blocked-off memories"* that contain memories of our pre-historic past, even that of animals.

Carl Jung further claims that no one is born a *'tabula rasa'*, that is with a blank state of mind. As the body carries features specifically human yet individually varied, so does the psychic organism. The psyche preserves an unconscious stratum of elements going back to the invertebrates and ultimately the protozoa. Jung speaks of a hypothetical peeling of the collective unconscious, layer by layer, down to the psychology of the amoeba. The full-blown Yogi who has un-ravelled the depth of his mind, has total recollection and thus is able to remember all acts committed in all the thousands of births he had taken in all forms of life. Lord Buddha in a second recollected four hundred of his previous births – the life of an eagle, snake, hare, deer – everything flashed before him in no-time at the moment he attained enlightenment. In fact in an expanded state of consciousness all the knowledge of everyone and everything surrounding the person becomes his knowledge. Further when total realization dawns in him, from the mini-computer that gets connected to many computers possessing greater data, ultimately he becomes the super-computer that possess all knowledge. Adi Sankara defines this simply and beautifully in the 'Viveka Chudamani' when he says that the space within a pot (*gada akasa*) seems to merge with the space 'outside' when the pot is broken, the mind of a person seems to merge with the cosmic-mind after the head is broken (death), in fact there is only the cosmic-mind and it is the ego that separates or causes the idea of a separation.

A recent global study on AIDS conducted by WHO found that prostitutes in Nigeria were immune to the HIV virus and after further study it was found that their DNA were naturally programmed to resist the aforesaid virus just as the DNA of the mongoose is programmed to resist the venom of snakes. Research is going on to identify and isolate each gene that causes a particular disease and in future scientists say that man could be programmed to become immune to the 3000 known diseases. The Yogic-science says that all diseases could be avoided by practicing Yoga three times a day and by proper breathing alone more than eighty percent of the toxins within the body are flushed out.

Many a saint and a Yogi were able to neutralize the deadly effects of poisons like cobra-bites – Saint Thirunavukarassar brought back to life a little boy who been killed by the bite of a deadly black-cobra; The poet Kamban also performed a similar miracle by chanting the 'naga ...' from the Ramayana; The Lord Jesus in The Bible, Luke;10;19 That he gave the authority to his apostles to trample over serpents and scorpions and power over the enemy and nothing could ever hurt them. And again in Mark 16;17,18 he tells his apostles who believe in his authority that he gave them the power to cast out demons, to speak new languages, to handle snakes with safety and no poison would hurt them and the power to heal the sick by placing their hands on them.

A couple of years back a man in Moscow who was out jogging in the morning was knocked out into a comatose-state by a snow-block that had melted and fallen off a roof-top which happens often. He recoverd after a few days in a hospital but what was surprising was, he started speaking in an unknown language. A linguist was able to confirm that he was speaking perfect Turkish language though he had never been to Turkey. It was later speculated by doctors that since his forefathers had migrated from Turkey 250 years earlier, the language could have been imprinted in his genes and the blow to his head could have brought about the recollection! The Yogic-science says that we already know all known languages, even that of the beasts and birds! All letters (all sounds) of all languages are contained in 50 vowel-consonants (though the Chinese language has literally thousands of letters, it also contains 50 vowel-consonants). These 50 letters exist as 50 distinct sound-vibrations in the six chakras that exist in the subtle-bodies of man, for example the base chakra or the muladhara chakra at the base of the spine has 4 letters, starting from there the other chakras have 16,10 etc. and the ajna chakra at the third-eye or eyebrow-centre has 2 letters, totaling 50 letters. When the Kundalini or Cosmic-energy that lies at slumber in the base chakra is aroused through Pranayama and meditation, coaxed to rise gently, activate each of the other 6 chakras, rise even further and flow into the Sahasra chakra at the crown of the head, the person becomes a full-blown Yogi who possesses Divine-Wisdom, he comes to know all languages and their texts, this is confirmed by many perfected beings like Thirumoolar, who in his Thirumandiram writes:

Fifty letters alone contain all Vedas, Fifty letters contain all Agamas...."
And Vedas means every text ever written or uttered for the fifty letters contain within them the entire gamut of sounds possible.

Regarding programming of the DNA of man, it has already been programmed billions of years ago as it is said in the Vedas that man was programmed to live for 100,000 years in the first era, the Kreta Yuga,10,000 years in the Treta Yuga,1000 years in the Dwapara Yuga and 100 years in the Present era, the Kali Yuga. Man's height also has been programmed to come down to around six feet from probably 100 feet for the average height in the first era was 30 feet! Regarding intelligence also the Vedanta and Saiva Siddhanta of the Tamils says that we contain the 'tattvas' or principles of 'lower-knowledge' (*apara vidya*) and of higher or 'Divine-knowledge' (*Para vidya*) and one among the seven vidya tattvas being the '*Kalai*' or 'Arts-principle' which contain the '64 arts' or branches of knowledge that include music, dance, poetry, prose, painting, sculpting, astronomy, astrology, medicine … – everything! And there is also the '*Kala*' or 'Time-principle', which when transcended, man becomes immortal!

There have been artists like Michelangelo and his contemporary Leonardo Da vinci who were masters in several fields, but only full-blown Yogis like Kalidasa, Markandeya, Chaitanya and Saint Ramalingam who de-materialized in 1872 were masters in all subjects, had turned 'eternally-young' and attained Divine-Wisdom and merged with God.

When Lord Rama was asked to explain this transition and realization of one's divinity, he requested his primal-devotee, Anjenaya (Hanuman) to do so, for he had transcended them, and Anjenaya said:" *As long as I am governed by my body and its senses (sensual pleasures), You are the Lord and I am your loyal and humble servant; when knowledge of the Soul (Jivatma bodham) dawns in me, You are the Whole, the Perfect, while I am an exact replica of You, possessing Your qualities (Amsa); When I realize the Soul in its entirety (Suddha chaitanya bodham), there is absolutely no difference between You and Me, We are One.*"

Cycle of death and birth – Plato, Socrates, Zen Master Daito, Lord Krishna:

Plato:" *Life in the universe would have gone out of existence if there were no succeeding births.*"

Socrates:" *If death had been only the end of all, the wicked would have had a bargain in dying; for they would have been quit not only of these bodies but of their own evil, together with their souls. But now in as much as the soul is manifestly immortal there is no release or salvation from evil, except attainment of the highest virtues and Wisdom."*

When the Zen Master Daito saw the emperor Godaigo who was a student of Zen, the master said:" we were parted many kalpas (a day-time for Lord Brahma,4.32 billion years) ago, yet we have not been separated even for a moment. We are facing each other all day long, yet we have never met."

Lord Krishna to Arjuna the warrior-prince in the Bhagavad Gita II,12.13.:" It is not wise to think that I, You, these kings and rulers were not here before (in past lives) and that we would not be here again. We all were here before, we will exist hereafter. The enlightened ones realize this truth and so are not affected by the birth death cycle. Arjuna: How can this be explained intellectually? Krishna: My dear brother Arjuna! Just as this body transcends through childhood, adulthood and old age, the soul transits from body to body. The realized person doesn't grieve on the subject."

Reply to Sadhu Sundar Singh's (Christian Preacher) criticism on Yogic-meditation and the Yoga-System; Essenes of Judaism, Sufism, Islam, Pythagaros, Ch'an, Zen, Buddhism; Holy Bible, Thirumandiram:

Sadhu Sundar Singh a Christian Preacher (converted from Sikhism) of late 19th and early 20th century:" *Then among ascetics and devotees the yogi is considered to be worthy of the highest honor of all. But it is the defect of the yoga system that is Samadhi (meditation), as the yogi sits in a set posture, with breath restrained and eyes fixed on the tip of his nose (Gita,613), he frequently falls into a state of trance, in which he sees a topsy turvy world, in which, instead of his being able to find the truth, he is in danger of being deceived. Would it not be better for him to fix his attention on God rather than on the tip of his own nose?"*

Without deeply studying and experiencing a Scientific-system personally it is not proper to pass judgement on it. Tenets of the Yoga system existed in the Jewish sect of the Essenes (in which Jesus Christ was born); Sufi Muslims knew Yoga as 'Saluk' and Pranayama as 'Habs-e-dam'(they would often attain an ecstatic-state by restraining their breath and even faint in the process) and some accomplished Sufis acquired the power of arresting persons by the power of their sight known as 'Habs I nazr'; Pythagaros had learnt the Yogic-techniques in India and ancient Egypt,500 years before Christ and established a mystic school of thought in ancient Greece. Pythagaros also knew of the power of music and that it had positive influences on man and nature; In the east, Buddhist monks took along the tenets of Yoga from India and Tibet and became known as 'Ch'an' (derived from the Sanskrit word 'Dhyan' for dhyana or meditation) and in Japan became known as 'Zen' and from there spread worldwide.

The human body is not something to be scorned at for it houses the Lord; Holy Bible, Acts7:48 says that God dwells not in the house built by hands but by hearts. Thirumoolar in his Thirumandiram says that like everybody, out of ignorance, he too at first scorned the body as something full of waste and dirt, but later when he realized that it was the House of God, nurtured it with great care; Thirumandiram 725:

"Time was when I despised the body;
But when I saw the God within
And the body, I realized, is the Lord's temple
And so I began preserving it
With infinite care."

Sundar Singh criticizes the Gita statement of fixing one's concentration at the tip of one's nose, but he doesn't seem to realize that there are many vital as well as psychic and energy-centres that are store-houses of wisdom and the best and safest way to connect with these and the Spirit is by aligning with and contolling the breath that is twelve inches long; Thirumandiram 2546:

"At the tip of the nose
Is the breath, twelve finger-breadth long;
At its peak is the Sahasra (cranium) Chakra,

That verily is the Lord's abode;
None know this;
The Vedas that in expansiveness truths expound,
Of this was hesitant to speak;
Such indeed is Lord's greatness."

The real heart (of love and compassion) is in the subtle bodies that permeate the physical body and this exists within and without the body. There are many techniques to cross over from the gross to the subtle (it is actually breaking the dimension-barrier and crossing over for the finer bodies are constructed of atoms of other dimension) and one vital-centre is the 'Kandam' or throat-centre and the mantra or power-packed sound utilized is 'Aum' (it is also 'Amen' of Judaism and Christianity;'Amin' of Islam;'Hum' of Buddhism) and the sound-vibration 'M' originates at the throat-centre. Beyond the three words A, U and M, which are its gross aspect,'bindu' and 'nada'(the eternal sound-light vibrations or the "sound-light continuum) are its subtle-aspect or nature. When at a time a person crosses or transcends the gross and reaches the subtle nada-vindu, the light that is the soul merges with the Infinite Light, and 'Jiva' the individual soul and 'Siva' the Eternal Soul, become One. The human body is thus a marvelous and brilliant vehicle used to realize and become one with the Lord; Thirumandiram 1823:

"This subtle-heart is the holy Sanctum
For the bounteous Lord,
The body of flesh is the vast temple
The mouth is the tower-gate;
To them that discern,
Jiva is Sivalinga;
The deceptive senses but the lights that illumine."

By realizing the Holy Compasssionate Light within (one's body), one becomes One with the Lord, like Him omniscient and omnipresent; Thirumandiram 3027:

"There is no one place where I can seek
That object I have known;

Taking to the astral way,
There as perfection, will it appear;
Seeking within the body,
There a Living Light will it be;
You then become omniscient and omnipresent."

Swami Vivekananda ('Bhakti Yoga'): ".... One's love and knowledge of one's own religion should be deep and the knowledge and acceptance of other religions should also be broad":

"There are people who say that they respect all religions, but they really do not love nor study in depth nor follow their own religion neither do they know much about other religions.

Another set of people are narrow-minded who follow their own religion fanatically. The more they fanatically follow their religion, they in turn hate all other religions.

Both set of people are useless. Like when a river keeps on widening, at a point, the water is more stagnant than at a move. It starts to turn dirty. That very same river, when runs through a deepn inclined-ravine, its flow is terrifying. It is again useless to anyone. The so-called broad-minded person who talks incessantly is like the stagnant river. The religious fanatic is like the fast flowing rapid waters!

One should be like the vast deep ocean. The ocean is deep as well as vast. Likewise one's love and knowledge of one's own religion should be deep and the knowledge and acceptance of other religions should also be broad.

Persons who possess both these qualities are indeed rare, they are the men of high caliber. Increase in their numbers would bring good to the world. Let us pray to the Lord that more of such persons would emerge."

"If we profess these high qualities, there would be more of such persons who would know and love all religions."

Dr.Carl Jung - Yoga superior to gymnastics and breathing-exercises; Yoga is the perfect and appropriate method of fusing body and mind; a psychological disposition which makes possible intuitions that transcend consciousness:

Carl Jung the Swiss Psychologist:" *Every religious or philosophical practice means a psychological discipline, that is, a method of mental hygiene. The manifold, purely bodily procedures of Yoga (Hatha Yoga) also means a physiological hygiene which is superior to ordinary gymnastics and breathing exercises, inasmuch as it is not merely mechanistic and scientific, but also philosophical; in its training of the parts of the body, it unites them with the whole of the Spirit, as it is quite clear, for instance, in the Pranayama exercises where Prana is both the breath and the universal dynamics of the cosmos ....*

Yoga practice would be ineffectual without the concepts on which yoga is based. It combines the bodily *and the* spiritual *with each other in an extraordinarily complete way.*

In the East, where these ideas and practices have developed, and where for several thousand years an unbroken tradition has created the necessary spiritual foundations, Yoga is, as I can readily believe, the perfect *and appropriate method of* fusing body *and* mind together *so that they form a unity which is scarcely to be questioned. This unity creates a psychological disposition which makes possible* intuitions *that transcend consciousness."*

Recognition of Superconsciousness which in its grandeur is the exact opposite of the subconscious mind conceived by Sigmund Freud (From 'Autobiography of a Yogi' by Paramahansa Yogananda):

Professor Jules-Bois of Sorbonne said in 1928 that French psychologists have investigated and accorded recognition to the superconsciousness, which in its grandeur, "is the exact opposite of the subconscious mind as conceived by Freud; and which comprises the faculties that make man really man and not just a Super-animal. The French savant explained that the awakening of the higher consciousness is "not to be confused with coueism or hypnotism. The existence of a superconscious mind has long been recognized philosophically, being in reality the Over-Soul spoken of by Emerson, but only recently has it been recognized scientifically."

Emerson wrote:" In the Over-Soul, the man is the façade of a temple wherein all wisdom and all good abide. What we commonly call man, the eating, drinking, planting, counting man, does not, as we know him represent himself, but misrepresenting himself. Him we do not respect; but the soul whose organ he is, would be let it appear through his actions, and would make our knees bend … We lie open to one side to the depths of spiritual nature, to all the attributes of God."

Sir jagadis Chandra Bose:"...*to my amazement, I found boundary lines vanishing, and points of contact emerging between the realms of the living and the non-living."*

"In the pursuit of my investigations I was unconsciously led into the border region of physics and physiology. To my amazement, I found lines vanishing, and points of contact emerging between the realms of the living and the non-living. Inorganic matter was perceived as anything but inert; it was athrill under the action of multitudinon forces.

A universal reaction seemed to bring metal, plant and animal under a common law. They all exhibited essentially the same phenomena of fatigue and depression, with possibilities of recovery and exaltation, as well as the permanent unresponsiveness associated with death …."

Sadhu Sundar Singh's criticism of Lord Krishna's statement that He is born again and again to save the good:

Sundar Singh:" Krishna said, "To save the good and destroy sinners I am born from age to age" (Gita,4:8). Jesus, on the other hand, came to save sinners (Matt. 9:13; Luke 19:10).

What need was there to save the good and righteous, for already they had ensured salvation for themselves by their works (karma)? But there certainly was a great need of saving sinners; for all mankind are sinners. It is useless, therefore, to look to Krishna for salvation, for he has declared that in all appearances in the world, he comes to destroy sinners rather than save them. This shows the necessity of seeking salvation from Christ, who came into the world to save sinners (1 Tim. 1:15)."

It is the One Lord only who incarnates from age to age, either directly or through empowerment to save the good and by temporarily punishing the sinners for them to redeem themselves in their future births for like a student who has to go through many a test and many a class before attaining a Masters or a Doctorate-degree, we have to evolve though thousands of births. And this evolutionary-process is going on in numerous worlds in various planes and dimensions. In fact there are precisely 18 evolutionary cycles like that of the Angels (devas), Titans (asuras), kinnarvas and Ghandarvas (celestial bards, singers and dancers) etc., that are taking place in 224 'bhuvanas' or global-constellations and in all these, life-forms evolve over countless births form the lowest form of life to the highest which is the state of the Lord. And this resolve in attaining the Perfect-state of the Lord is stressed upon by the Lord Jesus himself; Matt.5.48:" be ye perfect therefore as your heavenly father is perfect."

One should not have a warped-view by differentiating between the various Gods like Krishna and Jesus, for just as Krishna is an 'avatar' or an aspect of God, Jesus too accepts to that when he says; John 5:30:" I can do nothing on my own initiative" and again in John 6:57 "I live because of the Father.". That the One Lord alone manifests as the Holy Trinity, the worlds and multitude of lives is explained beautifully by Thirumandiram:

"One alone creates the worlds (planes) seven,
One alone sustains the worlds seven,
One alone destroys the worlds seven,
One alone is all worlds and lives too."

Lord Krishna emphasizes on the path of devotion (bhakti yoga or marga – the path, way) whereby the soul seeks liberation from the endless cycle of the soul's transmigration and ultimately seeks absorption by God by love and devotion; And of the way of knowledge or Wisdom (jnana yoga) whereby the soul attains enlightenment by realizing the nature of the Self; And by taking to the way of action or work (karma yoga) Krishna asks Arjuna of the Kshatriya class (warrior clan) to perform his duty which is to fight when necessary to save the country's and one's honor, and that certainly everyone should do his duty, whatever it maybe – with total commitment without expecting or yearning for rewards, for every one would be justly rewarded ultimately, so one should not shirk off his responsibilities; Bhagavad Gita II.31:

"Arjuna! You being of the Kshatriya clan (like the Samurais of Japan) should be without fear. The reason being the kshatriyas are heroes and it is their duty to fight and no other action can bring them good.

32. Arjuna: If that is so, should the Kshatriyas always be waging war?

Krishna: No my brother, but it is the duty of the Kshatriya to fight when a war is imposed. War is the gateway to heaven. Blessed are those who have a chance to go to battle, truly they attain great laurels and happiness.

38. Arjuna: Wont I be a sinner my Lord if I wage battle?

Krishna: You do your duty with a balanced state of mind. Do not worry about victory and defeat, gain or loss, pain and pleasure. Accept what you get graciously. If, in that, balanced state of mind, you wage war and kill your enemy, you won't be declared a sinner."

The Samurai warriors of Japan too deemed it a great honor to die at the battlefield and Heraclitus said:" war is the father of all things" and Nei:" The ideal man is a warrior."

In the Holy Bible in Gen.19;24, Deut.2:31 and Num,31:7 too as in the Holy Quran, there are numerous instances of battles that took place, whole cities being destroyed by God, along with all the men, women and children.

Moreover, heaven that a war-hero attains is not the ultimate-heaven, it, like 'Paradise' is only a transitory place, as it is mentioned that the realm of Indra, the Lord of the Angels is also a temporary haven. One must be born again on earth, evolve, realize oneself and attain the realm of the Lord, the 'Empyrean' as mentioned by Milton in 'Paradise Lost' and Dante of 'Seven heavens' and the 'Premium mobile'.

"...If through being holy and pure, a man gains heaven.... Why is he forced again to be born on earth again?(Bhagavad Gita) – Sadhu Sundar Singh; The Holy Bible, The Holy Quran, John Milton, Dante; Manu (the great Indian reformer), Manes (of Egypt), Minos (of Greece), Moses (of Judaism); Sivajnana Siddhiar; Bhagavad Gita; Vedas & Upanishads Sri Aurobindo in 'The Synthesis of Yoga':

Bhagavad Gita IX,21:" The soul of those who hold the Way of the works (action, karma marga) go either to the heaven of the gods or to the moon-sphere (pitrlok) which is the heaven of the fathers, until the accumulated merit of its good deeds has been exhausted, when it returns to earth, and is again involved in transmigration."

Sundar Singh:" *If, through being holy and pure, a man gains heaven of the gods, then what can happen there to cause all his merits to be swept away, and to force him again to return from heaven? If he is perfect and holy enough to enter heaven, then why is that everything that he has gained, with so much toil and pain, will be trampled in the dust again, and he himself turned out of heaven? Or, having reached that holy place, will he commit sin there that will necessitate his having to come back to earth again?"*

Sundar Singh lacks a clear understanding of the heaven he mentions, for there are many heavens and the heaven of the 'gods' is the one of the 'Devas' or 'Angels' (Angels are known as 'gods' in ancient Indian texts) and that even the devas have to take birth again on earth when the fruits or their merits are exhausted! The Holy Bible reader understands heaven as the place where Lazarus (the poor beggar) lies in comfort at the bosom of Abraham in heaven while the rich man is tormented in the fires of hell. In the Holy Quran, there are many references to the 'seven heavens' in Sura XVII.44 and again in Sura XVIII.107, and of 'Firdaus' which in Persian means "the inner circle of heaven", and of hell – 'Kurrat un nar' – the "sphere of fire", and the Highest heaven being the 'Empyrean' in Sura XXXVII 6,7,8. Milton's 'Paradise Lost' and Dante also speak of the seven heavens and the 'Premum mobile' – "that first moved" and the highest is 'Empyrean'.

People like Sundar Singh have to first understand that most of the world's religious philosophies owe their source to India; Harold Bailey,'The undiscovered Country', pg.182:" **You must know that Egypt, Persia, Greece, Rome, the great Kingdoms of the world, owed their philosophy and Religion very largely to India**. *'Manu', the great Indian reformer and teacher, reappears as the 'Manes' of Egypt, the 'Minos' of Greece, the 'Moses' of Hebrew story – the name is impersonal."*

There are some criteria and norms that determine certain states and positions in life for as we know some are born rich while others wallow in poverty, some are full of good health while others are afflicted by many a disease, some even successful people die young while others lead an ordinary but extended life, fame and defame comes to even the same person in different parts of life, so some aspects are pre determined as this 'Sivajnana Siddhiar' verse 99 points to:

"Fame, defame, pleasure, pain, old age
                              Death,
All these six are decreed before conception.
And fate will be gradually executed through
                              Experience;
One's actions in previous births are responsible
                              For these;
Beware ! your actions in this birth will determine your
Status in the next birth !"

The fate of people as well as nations too are pre determined according to the Bible; Acts 17:26 and God pre determines the events of life in Ecc.3:1 and God pre determines the conditions of Life in Ecc.3:10.

Sundar Singh then says that if one is perfect and holy enough to enter heaven, would that person commit sin again to come back to this wretched place of pains and sorrow. Even the Lord of the Angels, known as 'Indra' and/or 'Devendra' and the hierarchy of Angels are not immune to sensuous-pleasures, acts of adultery and varied acts of sin. Though for sensual-pleasures they are said to 'take' to a physical body like we have for theirs is an astral sort of radiant body, full of light (dejas) and to be more specific,'Jyotir maya deha'. Just as the Bible in Genesis says that giants are "sons of fallen angels" (born out of illicit relationship between angels and humans), ancient Indian texts mention the sins committed by angels and of Indra, the Lord of the angels who himself attracted and infatuated by the beauty of Ahalya, the wife of the Sage Gautama, took to his form in the sage's absence and had an affair with her. He was later cursed by the sage and had to ultimately suffer the consequences. Lord Krishna points out the causes for this liking and yearning for pleasures in the Bhagavad Gita, II,44:" Those who follow the words in the Vedas in a limited and literal sense are motivated by the desire (kama)to dwell in swarga (heaven)which offers enjoyments."

It is a fact that all our past memories committed in numerous past lives lie in latent subtle memory and are veiled by 'maya', the great illusive power of God and this veil is mentioned right at the introduction of the Holy Quran, c.31: "The veil was lifted from the chosen one's eyes,

And his soul for a moment was filled with divine Ecstasy …"

In the Indian epic Mahabharata, Arjuna lost control of himself completely when his son Abhimanyu was killed treacherously in the eighteen day war; to rectify Arjuna's mental state(and to demonstrate the power of maya), Lord Krishna sent him to 'heaven' (not the final and ultimate heaven)to meet his son, who promptly dismissed him for he could not identify his own father!

Our past experiences are also similarly veiled, for we would probably go insane if it were revealed that one's spouse or child was the parent in a past life, or one's own pet dog could be one's child in the present birth!

Worldly as well as Divine Knowledge are mostly revealed in stages so as to not shock a person and make it bearable to him. According to the Holy Quran:" well arranged stages, gradually … to strengthen the heart." And in the Holy Bible:" the apostles were endowed with gifts, some above the others." It is for only God and the full-blown Yogis would be able to understand the cause for varying degrees of enlightenment.

The 'Karma Kandas' of the Vedas speak of various forms of 'Swargas' – heavens. But in the 'Jnana Kandas' of the Upanishads, there is no mention of them. The Upanishads in turn say that yearning for the attainment of the heavens should be done away with. They say that real joy cannot be found in heavens but in the depth and realms of one's soul. A mantra in the Upanishads says that like man dimly views objects in the dream-state, he sees them in a likewise manner in the 'Pitir lokas', the world of our ancestors. The 'Ghandharva loka' is a grade below that of the Pitir loka and there sees the truth in a further suffused-manner like we see our reflection in water; The highest of heavens is 'Brahma loka' or 'Sathya loka', the heaven of the Creator, and there man sees the Truth in "light and in shadow", the view is not absolutely clear.

But when man sees the Truth in his mind clear of all impurities, he gets a crystal-clear view like we see our own image in a clear mirror. **So, among all heavens, the highest is one's own clear mind**. His heart (the mind) is the highest Temple of God. Man cannot view God anywhere else other than in his own mind.

Man should not wander anywhere in search of the Ultimate Truth other than inside himself. Solitude cannot be found in the forests or mountainous caves but only in the depths of his own minds-cave. Only limited benefit can be found in sacred places of worship, so he should get rid of wander-lust as this would only deplete him of his energy. The mind's-mirror should be cleansed, when that foremost duty is accomplished, God is reflected in all true splendor. After his mind becomes pure, the place of his residence matters the least. So a pure mind should be his ultimate goal."

Sri Aurobindo on attainment of enlightenment in 'The Synthesis of Yoga':" ... *He who chooses the Infinite has been chosen by the Infinite. He has received the divine touch without which there is no awakening, no opening of the Spirit; but once it is received, attainment is sure, whether conquered swiftly in the course of one human life or pursued patiently through many stadia of the cycle of existence in the manifested universe.*"

Divine Knowledge is realized in stages – Holy Qu'ran; sura XXV.32,33

"Those who reject the Faith
Say: "why is not the Qu'ran
Revealed to him all at once?

Thus (is it revealed), that We
May strengthen thy heart
Thereby, and we have
Rehearsed it to thee in slow,
Well-arranged stages, gradually.

And no question do they
Bring to thee but we
Reveal to thee the truth
And the best explanation
(thereof)."

A.Yusuf Ali:" The Holy Qu'ran was revealed to Prophet Mohammed over a period of 23 years."

Reward for All Religious Followers – The Holy Qu'ran; The Talmud:

Sura II,62. "Those who believe (in the
                                                Qu'ran),
              And those who follow the Jewish
                                                (Scriptures),
              And the Christians and the
                                                Sabians, -
              And who believe in God
              And the Last Day,
              And work righteousness,
              Shall have their reward
              With their Lord: on them
              Shall be no fear, nor shall they
                                                Grieve."

Again in sura II. 112. "Nay,- whoever submits
                                        His whole Self to God
                                        And is a doer of good,-
                                        He will get his reward

With His Lord;
On such shall be no fear,
Nor shall they grieve."

The Talmud (holy Judaism Scripture):' I call Heaven and Earth to witness, that whether Gentile or Jew, man or woman, slave or maid, according to their deeds, so will the Holy Spirit rest on them."

We are all Named before birth itself – Holy Bible; Vedanta & Saiva Siddhanta; Names and other details written on palm-leaf manuscripts:

Jesus Christ, John the Baptist, one and all are named before birth itself tells the Holy Bible in Ecc.6:10 just as Vedanta and the Saiva Siddhanta of the Tamils tell us.

Likeswise just as Vedanta and Saiva Siddhanta says, the Bible tells us that each person's means of livelihood and his periods of fortune and pitfalls, in fact everything is 'sealed' up in the lines that runs in one's palms in Bible, Job:37,7.

Vedanta and the Saiva Siddhanta very clearly state that each person's entire life could be known by studying the position of the stars at the time of his birth, which determines the ups and downs and by matching a person's palm-prints, Siddhars (perfected beings) like Agasthya, Vasishta, Viswamitra have written in cipher-form on palm-leaves (in Tamil at an indefinite period) everything and anything that is to be known of a person. A person's previous birth, the name in the present birth, names of his wife and children, education-level, occupation etc., can be revealed.

How a person's name is given in cipher-form Tamil in palm-leaf manuscripts:

1. A Roman Catholic person's name – "the combination of the sixth letter and the ninth letter in the series of 'sa' is his name" – the sixth letter in the series of 'sa' is 'soo' and the ninth letter is 'sai', so when combined the name 'Soosai' is derived at, and this was confirmed by the truth-seeker.

2. An Englishman's name was given like this:" half a cubit is his name" – half a cubit in Tamil is known as 'Jahn', and the foreigner acknowledged that his name was indeed 'John'!

Similarly the names of even Muslims and Chinese are given in cipher-form which also include their entire life-history.

The Soul in Transition is known under six names – 'Sarvajnanothra' & 'Taittiriyo Upanishad'

1. The 'Sarvajnanothra' says that when a person identifies himself with his physical body, he or the soul is known as 'boodhanma' or 'dehanma'.
2. When all his actions – likes and dislikes – are guided or controlled by the "four sound-forms" emanating from within – a. 'Vaikhari' – articulated speech, whose source is below the tounge; b. 'Madhyama' – sound as it reaches the throat, its source is between the heart and the throat. Its shape is the letter formed articulately inside; c. 'Pasyanti' – thought-form sound, no letter form, its source is the stomach. Its shape is prana; d. 'Para' – unarticulated sound, its source is the navel. Its shape is intelligence. (Thirumandiram states that there is a fifth sound – 'Sukshami' subtle sound-source whose source is ultra subtle. Its shape is 'Pranava' – 'Aum' – the source of all sounds in the cosmos – the soul is known as 'Antharanma'.
3. When through his mind he is able to realize that the perishable body is constituted of 60 'tatvihas' – elements and that his subtle bodies are of 36 'tattvas' (which totally are known in general as "96 tattvas", he is known as 'Taatvanma'.
4. When, with pride he realizes that he is the master of all the tattvas and that he is 'That' – the Lord, he is bound by the 3 'malas' or stains (a.'anava mala' – arrogance or egotism b.'karma mala' – fruits of past actions c.'maya mala' – veil of ignorance), is known as 'Jivanma'.
5. When with the help of chanting mantras that are potent sound-vibrations that contain the qualities of various gods – he with realization tries to delink the fetters that bind him, like the calf is

bound to its mother, and is yearning to re-unite with God, he is known as 'Mantranma'.

6. When he finally mingles with God, he becomes the One Lord and is therefore known as 'Paramanma', the Supreme Lord.

Hence, the soul in accordance to its intelligence-stature and to the varied properties to which it binds itself to, is known as; 'boodhanma','ana taranma','tattvanma','jivanma','mantaranma', and 'Paramanma'.

The Taittiriyo Upanishad terms these six variants of the soul as: 'annamaya atma','pranamaya atma','manomaya atma','vijnanamaya atma','anandamaya atma' and 'Pratyag atma'.

Answer to Sundar Singh's criticism of Vedanta that claims that 'Maya', illusion rid by means of knowledge experienced through 'Samadhi' (deep contemplation)

Sundar Singh:" *Vedantists maintain that in deep contemplation (Samadhi), the devotee gets rid of illusion (maya) by means of knowledge. The question arises: If everything is illusion, how do we know that the devotee absorbed in Samadhi and his knowledge derived from that state are not illusion?*"

Maya or illusion is the power that veils from us the true permanent nature of everything, that is why the Tamil ancient texts address the Supreme Heaven of the Primal Lord as 'Veedu' (home), for it is the final and only permanent destination, all other existence will go out of existence over a period of time. The state of Self-Realization is also permanent for only when the veil of ignorance is removed one's true nature is realized. The following song of Thirumoolar, the Perfected-Being explains philosophically but at the same time simply on how we do not perceive the true nature of things material and immaterial; Thirumandiram:

"The wood is veiled by the mighty elephant;
Into the wood merges the mighty elephant,
God is veiled by the first five elements;
Into God merge the first five elements."

When one views a wooden-carving of a mighty elephant, one does not see the wood, he see only the elephant; a person who understands the quality of wood, is not bothered of the carving, he studies only the quality of the wood. Similarly, the common person sees only the material things of the world constituted of the five elements (earth, water, fire, air and space); but the realized persons sees God in everything.

A rope lying in darkness appears to be a snake. The rope has not been transformed into a snake. The rope remains a rope, but due to lack of true knowledge or perception, the rope looks like a snake. Likewise, due to lack of true knowledge, God appears to us to be the world, all of creation and individuals comprised therein.

Lord Krishna in the Bhagavad Gita explains 'Yoga' as 'Union' which is beyond thought and intelligence:" When thy intelligence shall cross beyond the whorl of delusion, then shalt thou become indifferent to Scripture heard or that which thou has yet to hear. When thy intelligence which is bewildered by Scriptures, shall stand unmoving and stable in Samadhi, then thou shall attain to Yoga."

Just as one could see only into the depths of placid waters, only when the mind is in a tranquil-state the Divine-nature within oneself can be realized as the very first of the 195 'Yoga Sutras' of Sage Patanjali says:" Yoga is keeping the mind in an unchanged tranquil-state ("yoga citta vritti nirodaha")." And J.Krishnamurti says that when one lets go of his ego and arrogance, his divine-nature is reflected:" when you are not, the other is."

The Zen saying:" empty your cup" is further explained in the Bhagavad Gita:" An understanding without attachment in all things, a soul self-conquered and empty of desire, man attains by renunciation a Supreme Perfection – Siddhi of naiskarmya." That is, inner inactivity brings forth perfection of naiskarmya. Lord Krishna, further in the Gita:" Before the life departs from the body (praak sareera vimokshanat), when living in this world itself (ihaiva), one who controls the forces of passion and anger and becomes steadfast in a state of Yoga (unison with the Primal Lord) enjoys eternal bliss."

The greatest and final state that all Yogis aspire for is reaching the omniscient-state of the Lord, that is, to disappear from this plane at a pre-determined time and permeate all space like Saint Pattinathar, Ramalingam, Andal, Meera, Chaitanya and many others of India had de-materialized in the presence of multitude of people and like Enoch(Holy Bible:" Enoch did not die a natural death because God took him away").

To reach that state, the powerful screen of maya has to be removed. When maya is removed, knowledge worldly and Divine knowledge is revealed, such great personalities are not aware of the mind and body, they could at will disappear; Thirumandiram 2548:

"When maya veils jiva (individual soul),
The Truth (God) of Vedas remains hidden;
When maya leaves,
The Truth of Himself reveals;
Those who can make maya vanish
Merge in God;
No more is body; no more is mind."

One must act and progress from the lower to the higher nature, from the apparent undivine to the conscious Divine – Lord Krishna:

"*I abide in the path of action. The path that all men follow; thou too must abide in action. In the way I act, in that way thou too must act. I am above the necessity of works, for I have nothing to gain by them; I am the Divine who possess all things and all beings in the world and I am myself beyond the world as well as in it and I do not depend upon anything or anyone in all the three worlds for any object; yet I act. This too must be thy manner and spirit of working.*

I the Divine am the rule and the standard; it is I who make the path in which men tread; I am the way and the goal. But I do this largely, universally, visibly in part, but far more invisibly; and men do not really know the way of my workings. Thou, when thy knowest and seest, when thou has become the divinized man, must be the individual power of God, the human yet divine example, even as I am in My Avatars." ... "*The whole range of human action has been decreed by Me with a view to the progress of man from the lower to the higher nature, from the apparent undivine to the conscious Divine.*"

"... To one who has tuned to the Infinite, to that person everything in nature teaches high philosophies, stones and brooks, stars, the sun and the moon radiate high thoughts..." - **Swami Vivekananda in 'Bhakti Yoga's 'Guru sishya lakshana'':**

"A poet eloquently stated:" stones radiate inner-heart philosophies (*hitoupadesa*). Running brooks act as books. All that can be seen are in the form of goodness."

To a person who is not tuned to the infinite, not a bit of any truth could be explained by any person. Even if he were to attain as master 'Viyhalha Bhagavan' – the master of masters, he would not gain anything for his mind is a barren-field. It is also a question as to whom do running brooks act as books and serve good intelligence.

To a person whose heart has blossomed in all purity, whose mind-heart's divinity had started to manifest, whose life has matured and tuned to the infinite, to that person everything in nature teaches high philosophies, and that is a fact. To such a person, not only stones and brooks but also the stars, the sun and the moon radiate high thoughts. To such a person of elevated mind it is a fact that the entire cosmos teaches lessons. He is fit to receive high thoughts from all that he sees in nature. Like a blind person cannot perceive anything, try as he may, one needs the sight of the 'mind's-eye' to experience the excellence of the infinite."

"The earth is enveloped by Spiritual powers of varying degrees";"The myths which centered round the plain truths of revelation, owe their origin to India" - **'The undiscovered Country', Harold Bailey, London, U.K.;** *"There are Gods everywhere on all planes"* – **Sri Aurobindo in 'Letters on Yoga'':**

'The Undiscovered Country' – A sequence of spirit messages, describing death and the after-world, published by Harold Bailey, London in 1918, condensed from 19 books written by various authors from 1874 to 1918:

Page 142:" *All life and all development are consequent on the operation of Spiritual energy, obeying the dictate of the will of the Spiritual beings. This once grasped, blind force disappears, and intention takes its place – intention of intelligent and powerful Spiritual workers, of various grades, operating according to certain fixed laws but within the bounds of those laws, free and mighty."*

Pg.147:" *These beings are of many grades and many species. They are not all of the same order, nor all of the same form. But their work is controlled by those above them, as these are controlled by powers of higher grade and sublimity still."*

Pg.161:" *And so the earth is enveloped by and included and effected by the Spiritual powers of varying degrees and kind, entrusted by the Creator God to all these ministers of all these spheres which are around it."*

Pg.165:" *All these zones, of which we have spoken, are inhabited by beings, according to their degree, who progress from one sphere to a higher, as they accumulate knowledge within themselves."*

Pg.181:" *The myths which centered round the plain truths of revelation, owe their origin to India."*

Sri Aurobindo, in 'Letters on Yoga':" *Of course, the gods exist – that is to say, there are powers that stand above the world and transmit the divine workings. It is the physical mind which believes only what is physical that denies them. There are alo beings of other world – gods and asuras (Titans) etc.,."* … *"There are gods everywhere on all planes."*
… *" The dynamic aspect of the Divine is the Supreme Brahman, not the gods. The gods are personalities and powers of the dynamic Divine."*
… *" Brahma, Vishnu, Shiva are only three powers and personalities of the One Cosmic Godhead."*

Angels protect 3 year old Gage Gabriel in Nova Scotia; Indonesian Youth saved from drowning by a Charming Bearded-figure seen in the depths of the ocean-waters during The 2004 Tsunami; Fir Tree attracts Snowfall and a Gnome in Teclen Valley, Algeria, bordering Morocco

and the Sahara Desert - claims to be 'Snow-King' – The Mother of Pondicherry

Widely read newspaper news:" Three year old Gage Gabriel of Amherst, Nova Scotia says that he was guarded by "two Angels with wings and white dresses stood in the water, smiling at him all night", which helped him keep alive while his mom 24 year old Tobi Gabriel died when their car plunged off a 90 foot cliff into the sea. People now widely believe in guardian Angels."

A newspaper news:" An Indonesina youth was like countless people swept back into the ocean from an Indonesian island by the receding tsunami-tides and he clung on to an uprooted coconut-tree for a couple of days. When he was washed off the tree and was plunging into the ocean-depths, he cried out to god to save him and be reunited with his family. A charming white-bearded figure rose from deep within the ocean that had eyes of compassion, slowly but firmly took him to the surface and was eventually saved by a passing boat."

The Mother mentions of how Fir trees (that are of the Nordic habitat) instead of Pine trees were delivered wrongly to be planted in an entire valley (the Teclen valley) in Algeria near the Morrocan border which is near the Sahara desert, eventually brought about snow-fall to occur which had never occurred before for it lies barely 80 miles from Morocco. Her Occult-master Theon told her that a gnome appeared that was short in stature and attired in a green colored attire and cap and when questioned claimed that it was 'Snow King' and the fir trees attracted him and hence snowfall naturally came along with him…! After a few minutes, the gnome gradually faded away and there in a corner of the room remained a clump of snow which slowly melted into a puddle of water … Mother says that snowfall is appearing year after year without fail!

"India is the oldest country on earth" – 'NASA', the news agency (from Washington) in its May 27,1984 edition:

"About 180 million years ago, there was only one continent,(that is one vast expanse of land) in the whole world, and that was called 'PANGEEYA' or 'PANGEEA', which began to break up as years rolled on.

The land Bharat that is India, about 60 million years ago was a very big island by the side of Africa. Later that island too, moved slowly towards Asia, and, removing China from its place further eastwards, jined itself with Asia. That island is the India of the present day.

About 120 million years ago, another expanse of land which had been joined to India by name 'GONDHWANA', separated itself, and from it South America, Africa, Australia and Antartica were born.

So the present expeditions to Antartica are, so much as to say, only to a part of India.

Only from India, all other continents and countries moved away and formed themselves into separate countries as at present."

Sabbath in ancient and present-day India, Original Sabbath is on saturday; Semitic tribes are Indian people; Babylon is India; Origin is India; India is following the Ten Commandments – Hindus don't kill, don't steal.:

R.P.Lawrie in,'The Firstborn of God', sec. C-pg. 45:" Sabbath is kept by almost all sects in India in some form or other. Muslims changed the day to Friday …. Popes changed it to Sunday. Jews kept it, but they are not real Jews. More than ninety percent of the present day so-called Jews are not of the Semitic tribe. Shem has tents. Japeth will increase but at the end will dwell in tents of Shem. Semitic tribes are the Indian people. Origin is from here. Even Babylon is India. But Babylon is blacked-out by westerners, and India too is similarly blacked-out. Any westerner will never talk high of India. That is why Babylon was sent to destroy Jews and they brought the cream to India.

Branham said to me:" You will get the whole of India." The cream Jews are in India. Without war, standing for <u>justice through non-violence – Satyagraha</u>. God will fight for them and will save them by the Lord their

God – vide Hosea 1:7:" But I will have mercy upon the house of Judah, and will save them by the Lord their God, and will not save them by bow, nor by sword, nor by battle, by horses, nor by horsemen."

When the Jews came to India, they were persecuted. So they kept the Sabbath on Saturday, secretly, by pouring oil on their heads and all over their bodies, and called it 'Oil Bath'. No sexual contact with wife on that day. Without knowing, they were celebrating Sabbath. Special meals on that day. Oil Bath was a symbol to show <u>they got 'Abishekam', ie., the Anointing of the Lord</u>, and got the blessing.

Christians lost the blessing by changing the day to Sunday. India is fulfilling the Ten Commandments of our Lord. The Hindus don't kill, don't steal and don't walk behind another man's wife. They keep the Sabbath, take oil bath and take rest on Saturdays.

"India a Nation Bringing Forth Fruits "; "India the only country with Fruit-Bearing Heritage"

R.P.Lawrie:" India a Nation Bringing Forth Fruits". "I had already indicated that the East and especially India is the Origin of the Semitic Tribes. The countries occupied by the Semitic tribes are poor nations (people mostly living in tents), and Japeth only (the West) will be enlarged as they take their sword and the so-called people now widely known as the Semitic races are not Shems <u>People</u> of the Lord God but people of Japeth <u>tribes</u>. Even though all tribes are scattered, the cream is yet as it began.

Jesus said, "Did you never read in the Scriptures, The stone which the builders rejected, the same is become the head of the corner: this is the Lord's doing, and it is marvelous in our eyes? Therefore say I unto you, the Kingdom of God shall be taken from you and given to a Nation bringing forth fruits thereof" – (Matt.21:42-43).

Yes, the West was enjoying the blessings of the Lord for the last 2000 years and has failed God. The Bible says that the Sceptre shall not depart from Judah until **Shiloh** comes in Gen.49.10 ('Shiloh' is an epithet of the Messiah, it refers to the 2nd advent of Christ). When Shiloh comes, the world order has to change. No wonder, therefore, the Sceptre of the Kingdom of God is taken away from them and is given away to a Nation in the East. That

Nation could only be India, because India is the only country in the East with a Fruit-Bearing Spiritual Heritage, fit to usher in the Kingdom of God, for which there have been ample signs and vindications in the recent past, which are still continuing and will continue till the appointed time arrives."

The founder of 'Scientology', Lafayette Ronald Hubbard – The Christian God is much better characterized in the Vedic Hyms (Hinduism):

"The Christian God is actually much better characterized in the Vedic Hyms (Hinduism) than in any subsequent publication, including the Old Testament."

The God the Christians worshipped is certainly not the Hebrew God. He looks <u>much</u> *more like the One talked about in the Veda."*

Thomas Alva Edison, on the verge of death:" It is very beautiful over there…!"; Norman Vincent Peale; Dr.Kubler Ross; Carl Sagan, on "Life after-death Experiences" in 'Broca's Brain':

Norman Vincent Peale in 'Saty Alive All Your Life':" I myself was with a friend when his time came to die. As the mist of the valley came over him, suddenly he said, speaking to his son who was sitting beside him, "Jim I see beautiful buildings. And in one of them is a light and the light is for me. It is very beautiful." Then he was gone."

The son said to me, "my father was a scientist, and in his work he never reported anything that was not a proven fact. The habit of years could not change. He was reporting what he saw.

Dr.Leslie Weatherhead, a minister at the City Temple, London, on his experience gained while comforting a dying man:" I must have gripped his hand more tightly than I thought for the patient said a strange thing, "Don't pull be back,… it looks so wonderful farther on!"

Lord Buddha, just as he was preparing to willingly leave his body, asked a devotee standing beside him to move aside so that he could have a better view at the heavenly-host who had come to escort him to heaven.

A couple of years back, my friend's grandmother suffered a cardiac-arrest and a doctor who was quickly summoned to her bedside, injected adrilin directly into heart to stimulate it to start functioning again. The lady recovered briefly and the first thing she did to everyone's horror was spat the doctor's face and souted at him with the words:" You fool! Just as I was going to be escorted to heaven in a vimana (flying-craft) surrounded by Devas (Angels), you pulled me back!"

Forty years back, when my great grandma was seriously ill, she 'saw' four messengers of Lord 'Yama', the god of death, nearing her and she shouted at them in a loud voice that she was not the Maniammal that they had come to escort and that another lady bearing the same name who lived on the adjacent street was the right person. Within a few minutes, people heard wailing sounds emanating from the adjacent street for the predetermined person had been separated from her physical body, while my great grandma lived for many more years after that experience!

The reason why even great scientists like Thomas Alva Edison are able to have visions of the *other worlds* only on the verge of death is because there exist veils that obstruct the sights and sounds which would otherwise be available to us commonfolk also. Vital energies and forces are constantly flowing from the cosmos right through us and the vital-centres that draw-in them are the Chakras which are vortexes and whirlpools of energy. These chakras exist over vital and important nerve-plexuses and hormonal-centres in the astral or finer-bodies of man, and inbetween the *five bodies* or sheaths as they are known (physical, astral, mind-body, scientific and causal body) exist a fine rubbery like atom-sheath that act as veils and therefore hinder the free flow of energy-forces. For the common man, the veils dissipiate a little only during the dream-state, meditative-tate and when on the verge of death, to give a poor and partial vision of the other worlds. Ordinarily the chakras would be two to three inches in circumference, would rotate at a slow pace and be of dull colors. But the chakras of kind and noble-hearted people, the chakras would be much larger, whirl at higher speeds and be bright and colorfull. But for the 'Purna' or full-blown Yogi, since all the veils would have been removed, the chakras would resemble like mini-suns and would rotate at tremendous speeds and the free-flow of energies would allow the person to receive the type of information he desired and he would be able to see into mountains, ocean-depths and the earth(he can point out hidden treasures and lost cities and civilizations also), into other's minds and see, hear, vision, experience and go to other worlds also. The Yogi can visit the after-death worlds, talk and converse with dead souls, in both the lower and upper regions and if necessary could even bring back dead persons like Lord Krishna, Jesus Christ, Sage Vyasa, Saint Thirunavukkarasar and Saint Jnanasambhandar did.

Dr.Kubler Ross at The Univerity of Chicago's Billings Hospital, Author of 'On Death and Dying', had interviewed scores of terminally ill patients as well as professional people like doctors, nurses, clergy on death and re-birth: 1. On life after death: ..." I have always felt something significant happens a minute or so after 'clinical' death. Most of my patients got fantastically peaceful expressions, even those who had struggled terribly with death. 2. Positive evidence: "About seven years ago, a patient who had been declared dead despite heroic last-minute resustication efforts spontaneously came alive 3.5 hours later. She shared with me how she felt; she had floated out of her physical body and watched herself being worked on. She described in minute detail the resustication team – who was there, who wanted to give up, who wanted to continue, who told a joke to relieve the tension.

This gave me my first clue.

Since then I have investigated scores of clear-cut causes from all over the world, both religious and non-religious people. One had been 'dead' twelve and a half hours. All had the same basic experience.

3. Experiences of the dying: "They virtually shed their physical bodies as a butterfly comes out of a cocoon. They described a feeling of peace, no pain, no anxiety. And they were perfect – completely whole. A young man whose leg was cut off in an automobile accident floated above the crash scene and observed the rescue effort. They were so content that they resented, sometimes bitterly, the attempts to bring them back to life because they were returning to a dreadful existence – cancerous bodies, amputated limbs. Not one of them was afraid to die again."

4. 'Embrace' death and live a 'fuller' life: "If I were to lose this house and everything in it, I couldn't care less. Because of my work with dying patients, I knew that to see a sunset, or watch a pheasant family on the lawn is infinitely more important. If you listen to dying patients say, "If only I'd

gotten to know my children. If only …" you begin to reflect on your own life."

Carl Sagan, on "life after-death experiences", in 'Broca's Brain':" Similar experiences, now widely documented by physicians and others, have occurred all over the world. These perithanatic, or "near-death", ephiphanies have been experienced not on by people of conventional western religions, but also by Hindus, Buddhists and skeptics. For all I know, these experiences may be just what they seem, a vindication of faith that has taken such a pummelling from science in the past few centuries. Personally, I would be delighted if there were a life after death – especially if it permitted me to continue to learn about this world and others. But Iam also a scientist, so I think about what other explanations are possible. How could it be that people of all ages and cultures have the "same sort" of near-death experiences?

…The only alternative, so far as I can see, is that every human being has already had an experience like that of travelers who return from the land of death; the sensation of flight, and the emergence from darkness into light; an experience in which a heroic figure may be dimly perceived, bathed in radiance and glory. There is only one common experience that matches this description… It is called birth."

Charles Lindberg on the transition that is 'life' and 'death' in 'Lesson of Africa':

"…*Gradually, I entered a different frame of time. I saw the animals as less as mortal individuals than as temporal manifestations of the immortal lifestreams they contained. The lifestream rather than the individual appeared the essence of life.*

Then I sensed immortality in myelf. I became as old as the epochs through which my genetic form was shaped. I felt a penetration of the future that made me question all concepts I had held of what are called 'life' and 'death' and 'time'.

The individual transition between life and death no longer seemed terrible or permanent. Death was but a phase of life continuing, a necessary pulse in the evolving relationship between elements described as life and matter."

The Five types of 'body bags' that veil the brilliance of the Soul, which is pristinely pure, is an infinite source of bliss ... – Adi Sankara's Viveka Chudamani;'Atmanatma Vivekam'; sloka 149:

"The five types of body bags (Panjabi kosa) starting from annamaya, pranamaya, manomaya, vijnanamaya, anandamaya kosa – physical, ethereal, mind, scientific, causal bodies, which were brought forth by one's own power (nija shakti – samuthphanai) shroud the Soul, thus does not radiate brilliance (napadi); like the waters of the lake that brought forth hycanith (saivalapadalai) veil it."

Slk.150,151." Like when the hycanith is removed, the lake waters are fit for consumption ... when the five types of bodies get obliterated, this soul is pristinely pure, is an infinite source of bliss, radiates brilliance of its own accord, is perfect and in the form of inner-light."

'I' Beyond The 5 Body-Bags; Witness To The 3 States of Man; Adi Sankara's Viveka chudamani; slk.125:

"There is a root-cause for the 'I' complex that exists naturally and for eternity (Asti kachithsvayam nityamoham pratyaya-lambana). It is a witness to the three states of wakefulness, dream-state and deep sleep-state (Avasta-thraya-sakshi san) and different from the five body bags (Pancha kosa vilakshana)."

The 'Vital' Body or Pranamaya Kosa Controls The 5 Motor-Organs (Karmendriyas); Adi Sankara's Viveka Chudamani; slk.165:

"This Prana is connected and fused to the five karmendriyas – the tounge, hands, feet, sexual and excretory organs (panchabi karmendriya anjisha ayam prana) and hence this is the vital or ethereal body (pranamayadu kosa). That is why it being completely infused and filled (anae anupurna) and taken to be the Atma (Soul) (Atmavan) acts within all actions of this physical body that is built up of food."

The 5 Motor-Organs And 5 Sense-Organs; Adi Sankara's Viveka chudamani; slk.92:

"Ears, skin, eyes, nose, tounge that can 'sense' experiences are known as jnanendriyas (sense-organs) (buddhi-indriyani); tounge (speech), hands, legs, excretory organ and sexual-organs due to their actions are known as motor-organs."

"There were giants on earth in those days" – **Holy Bible; genesis,'Dakes Annotated Bible':**"*interprets giants as one's who had from a union of the sons of god (fallen angels and daughters of men who had escaped the flood"); "Man was as tall as a fully-grown palmyra tree and lived for 3000 years"* – **Bogar 7000 & Chattai Muni 1200**

Hundreds of millions of years ago there lived on earth man who was nearly 100 feet tall, just as there were gigantic animals, reptiles and birds. Ancient Indian texts say that there lived 'andabahirandam (in Tamil) a huge bird that could lift and fly away carrying a weight equal to that of ten elephants!

Modern science, anthropology and geology talk of only the present cycle, whereas there have been countless cycles in which the earth, man as well as numerous life-forms are continuously being destroyed and created again and again in endless cycles.

According to ancient Indian texts, a day for Lord Brahma is 432 crore or 4.32 billion years measured in our time (each and every plane which has numerous planets in various dimensions has a different time-frame, for example the 'Devas' or Angel's (who live on the 3rd plane, known as 'Suvar loka' or 'Swarga loka' literally meaning 'heaven' among the "7 upper worlds") day-time is one year for us human beings). A night for the Creator would again be another 4.32 billion years. This period of 4.32 billion years known as a 'kalpa', is divided into 14 'manvantras' each comprising of 308 million years or so. Only every alternate manvantra has life-forms functioning on earth in their evolutionary-cycles, that is, the $1^{st}, 3^{rd}, 5^{th}, 7^{th}, 9^{th}, 11^{th}, 13^{th}$ are functioning-periods while the $2^{nd}, 4^{th}, 6^{th}, 8^{th}, 10^{th}, 12^{th}$ and 14th being rest-periods, just as we function during the day and take rest at night.

At the end of every manvantra comprising of 308 million years or so, there is a huge global level catastrophe caused by floods, earthquakes, volcanic-eruptions, meteorite crashes etc.,

The present manvantra is the 7th one and is ruled by 'Vaivasvadha Manu', one among the 14 Manu's who rule over each of the 14 manvantras. It is said to be mid-afternoon for Lord Brahma the Creator and this is the first day of his fifty first year, and he lives for hundred such years! Though there are only 'low' level destructions after every manvantra of 308 million years or so, after the passage of 14 manvantras, that is once in every 4.32 billion, there would be massive catastrophes and the entire world would be destroyed; there would be a hundred years of relentless drought when there would not be a drop of water to be found on earth and everything would be scorched and burnt; there would be then a hundred years of relentless non-stop rain and hence the whole world would be submerged under water; all of mankind and all forms of life would perish and all 'lives' would take refuge and shelter under the care of the Manu; after the rest-period of another 4.32 billion years, creation anew would begin. At the end of Lord Brahma's tenure, all planets and heavenly bodies in the first three planes would be destroyed and it is said that everything would revert back to their former state, that is, even the atoms would all revert back to the original building blocks of nature,'Nada Bindu' or the "Sound-Light Continuum" - imagine the deadly mega big-bang that would bring about!

All over the globe, more and more ancient civilizations are being discovered and recently in the North American Continent layer after layer of excavation have thrown out more ancient civilizations. In the vast deserts of Saudi Arabia there have been recent discoveries of the skeletal remains of ancient man who was 30 to 40 feet tall which is available on the net. There is also the tombs of Caine and Abel, the first two sons of Adam and Eve found in the coastal-town of Rameshwaram in a Muslim Dargha in Southern Tamilnadu which are each fifty to sixty feet long. According to the 'Hadith'(a holy book of Islam which contains anecdotes of Prophet Mohammed and other founders of Islam), Adam when he came down from Paradise to earth, at first landed on a mountain named 'Sarandip' in Srilanka, he was 60 cubits or nearly 100 feet tall, and he walked over the Palk-strait of Adam's bridge to India. The Holy Bible says that Adam lived for 930 years. This must be in one cycle of creation for Bibilical scholars say that the seven days that God took to create need not be according to our time-frame. Ancient Indian texts say that in this present eon known as the 'Kali yuga' (which consists of 432,000 years, out of which only 5500 years or so have passed), man is 'programmed' to live for 100 years; in the previous eon known as 'Dwapara yuga' (double that of the present one, hence 864,000 years) man was programmed to live for a 1000 years; the preceding one was 'Treta yuga' (1728000 years) man was programmed to live for 10,000 years; the first among the four cyclic eons is the 'Kreta yuga' (3456000 years) man was programmed to live for 100,000 (hundred thousand years).

That there have been many previous cycles of creation in which man existed in a much different shape and size than what we now possess and that Adam is only the father of 'modern' or should we say 'present-day' man is mentioned by an Islamic scholar and holy man: The celebrated Shaikh, Muhyi-ud-Din al-'Arabi, regarding to the *insila* (a state of contemplation, when it is held the soul of man leaves the body and wanders about without regard to time or space), once when he was in the vicinity of the holy and reverend Ka'ba (Caaba), it happened that, absorbed in mental reflections on the four great jurisconsults of Islamism, he 'saw' three very tall persons engaged in 'tawaf' or circumbulating the holy Ka'ba and they were as tall as the revered structure (which is about 38 feet tall). When he arrested them by the power of his sight (known as "habs-i-nazr"), the leader pleaded with him to release them, and he told them that on the name of Allah the merciful, he should tell him who they were, and he replied that they too were men who lived forty thousand years ago on earth. When the Shaikh asked him how that could be when it was only six thousand years since the advent of Adam, the stranger replied:" **The Adam you speak of was the father of the human race, and though since his time only six thousand** *years have elapsed, thirty other worlds preceded him*. In the Traditions of the Pride of all Beings (the Prophet), and the Sovereign ('Ali), it is said,' Certainly God created the Adam (Man) you know of, **after the creation of an hundred thousand others**, and I am one of those."

The Bible, Genesis 6,4 says that there were giants on earth in those days, and also afterward, when the sons of god came into the daughters of men and they bore children to them. Those were the mighty men who were of old, men of reknown. And in num. 13,32-33 says all the people whom they saw in it were men of great stature. There they saw the giants (the descendants of Anak came from the giants); and we were like grasshoppers in their sight, and so were they in their sight. – The Open Bible (The New King James Version). 'Dakes Annotated Reference Bible' in Genesis – 'giants and sons of God' – 6:4 very clearly interprets that the Hebrew word 'Nephilim' derives from the word 'nephil' which literally means 'giants'. The people of Israel in those days were in comparison the size of grasshoppers. 'Annakims' were a race of people of great stature and their country was known as 'Ammon'. The King of Ammon's bed which was made of iron measured 18 ½ feet long and 8 ½ feet wide. Dakes Annotated Reference Bible also interprets as one's who came from a union of the sons of God (fallen angels) and daughters of men who had escaped from the flood. These giants who were in existence before and after the flood had six fingers and toes on their hands and feet. Their spears weighed 25 pounds (11 kg.) in weight and Goliath who stood 13 feet tall wore an armour weighing 196 pounds (89 kgs.)! It was the purpose of Satan and his fallen angels to corrupt the human race and thereby do away with pure Adamite stock through whom the seed of the women should come. Genesis 6:4 says that God had to do away with his corruption entirely in order to fulfill his eternal plan, so he destroyed all men, women and children.

Man along with unwanted animals and birds which were found unsuitable to the progess of evolution were wiped out by God or by his messengers according to many religions by way of provoking natural calamities. The Bible, Genesis 6:7 "So the Lord said, "I will wipe mankind, whom I have created, from the face of the earth – men and animals, and creatures that move along the ground, and birds of the air – for I am grieved that I have made them." 17." I am going to bring floodwaters on the earth to destroy all life under the heavens, every creature that has the breath of life in it. Everything on earth will perish." God then commanded "Noah a righteous man, blameless among the people of his time, ..." to build an ark of special specifications, duly water-proofed and take in along with him, his wife, sons and their wives along with a male and female of all living creatures to escape the waters of the flood to be caused by 40 days and 40 nights of relentless rain.

Many world religions tell us of the havoc caused by 40 days and 40 nights of continuous rainfall. The 'Matsya Purana' (History of the 'Fish-incarnation' of Lord Vishnu, the 'Sustainer' among the Holy Trinity), tells us of how the Lord asked the present Manu,'Vaivasvadha Manu', to build a huge boat to escape from the deluge to follow due to the continuous rain which was to follow for 40 days and 40 nights. Many ancient Indian texts also mention that the four 'mind-born' sons of Lord Brahma, the Creator, who were also the holy-messengers of the Holy Trinity,'Sanaka','Sananthan a','Sanathana' and 'Sanarkumara' flew along with thirty assistants in '*fiery chariots*' (*agni rathas*) from 'Sathya loka' the realm of the Creator in the 5th plane of the "7 upper worlds", landed on earth many hundreds of millions of years ago. These four holy men who were not bound by the 'time-concept' stayed on earth for 400,000 years and wiped out entire species of life-forms that were found to be a hindrance to the evolutionary-process as a whole. At that time, the present day pacific ocean was a great mountainous forest-filled land mass, and like the gigantic animals, reptiles and birds of that time, man and ape were 50 to 60 feet tall. The holy messengers speeded up the evolutionary process and drastically shortened the height of man and ape and introduced new forms of life through what seem natural processes.

'Bogar' a great '*Siddhar*' or *Perfected being* was a master of many subjects, particularly medicine and alchemy, who with the help of a 'kuligai' (a potent herbal-potion) would often fly through space and lived for many years in China also, in his 'Bogar 1700', mentions specifically in songs 14,515 and 516 that there were Siddhars who had attained tremendous psychic and supernatural powers all over the world eons ago: 514:" ... Siddhars who lived north of the Himalaya mountain-range were as tall as a fully-grown palmyra tree(70 to 80 feet) and lived for a full life-term of three thousand years." 515." ... Siddhars who lived east of the Himalayas whose height was thre-fourths of a palmyra tree(50 to 60 feet), lived for seven hundred years and had tremendous psychic powers and possessed many magical-stones and herbs." "... Siddhars who lived south of the himalayas whose height was half of that of a palmyra tree(40 feet) and lived for three hundred years, were scholars and possessed magical-herbs and stones and springs of life-sustaining nectar and great spiritual powers." 516." ... Siddhars who lived south of the Himalayas whose height was quarter that of a palmyra tree(20 to 30 feet) and lived for a hundred and twenty years, read many scriptures, lived mostly on the foothills of the 'Pothigai mountain' range(now found in the southern tip of India)...."

'Chattai Muni' another great *Siddhar* or *Perfected being* also confirms in 'Chattai Muni 1200' the information given by Bogar that men of that era were of immense stature physically, mentally and spiritually.

Erik von Daniken, the late Swiss author has in 'Chariots of the Gods','Was God an Astronaut?','According to the Evidence', among many of his books, given ample proof of alien visits, and of earth being occupied by aliens and giants and had photographed thigh-bones of people who were not less than 18 feet tall. In the South American Amazonian jungles there are gigantic caves and under-ground shelters several hundred feet deep, whose ceilings are more than 60 feet high. Daniken very strongly feels that the ingenuity needed to blast rocks and excavate passages of such immense dimensions was beyond the scope of natives and referring to ancient texts he says that extraterrestrials had used them as hiding places and protection against radio-activity for inter-galactic warfare would have meant nuclear warfare or something even more advanced than what we could even imagine. Special arrow marks that can be spotted only from a very high altitude are found in the Mayan jungles along with rock-carvings of helmet and space-suit fitted figures point out to the fact that the world was indeed a frequent visiting place of extra-terrestrials. The gigantic rock-carvings of human-like figures found on Easter Isand, the faces have nearly no foreheads, huge eyes and thick lips, point out to extra-terrestrial origin.

Lobsang Rampa an erstwhile Buddhist monk who then lived in California, in his 'Dr. From Lhasa','Third Eye','Twilight' among others has mentioned that bodies of 'Gods of bygone eras' are preserved deep inside Tibetan underground caves and some of them are 15 feet tall.

The endless cycle of Creation, Sustenance and Destruction takes place in waves but united into a whole continuum; The one who knows this with concentrated mind attains the state of infinity by the "*secret gateway between two moments*"; – Sri Shiva Rahasya:

As a painting is made of thousands of brush-strokes of colour, just so My Creation is made of innumerable pulses of Creative Intelligence (Chit Shakti).

Thus the Cycle of Creation, Maintenance and Dissolution takes place in waves constantly arising, culminating and subsiding, upon the Shining Mirror of My Eternal Self. I, the Supreme Lord, by the Power of Unity (Yoga Bala) unite all into a whole continuum.

As a River, at once ever-the-same according to its long-established banks and ever-new according to the water that freshly runs along its course, so the Stream of Creation though initiated millions of years ago yet is projected every moment anew by Myself.

He who knows this, with concentrated mind, enters My World of Uncreated Light by the secret gateway between two moments and goes to Everlasting Life. Verily, the present moment is the Door to Eternity and the Ford for crossing the River of Time. It is the only appropriate Time for Souls to meet Me, their Creator.

Some realise Me through Meditation (Dhyana), others through the Path of Spiritual Knowledge (Jnana), others through the Path of Devotion (Bhakti) and still others through the Path of Righteous Action (Dharma).

Among the devotees, he who constantly pleases Me through Spiritual Knowledge, is the most dear to Me. For, without Spiritual Knowledge neither right Meditation, nor Devotion, nor yet Righteous Action are possible.

By acquiring Spiritual Knowledge, pure Souls become devoted to Me. By being devoted to Me either in My Manifested Form or My Formless Transcendental Self, they attain to Me, the Supreme Truth. Having realised Truth, they fall no more under the spell of worldly existence.

For, this entire Universe consisting of Matter and Spirit is pervaded by Me, it exists in Me and I alone am its Ruler.

Verily, O noble ones! I rule the Universe through My Highest Power of Yoga (Yoga Bala). He who realises That, becomes immortal.

Life Span of Man's Evolutionary-cycle (Evolutionary Time Plan)

Life Span of Beings of the "Upper Worlds"
Devas who live on the 6th plane 'Bhuvar loka'

1. Day + night-time of the Devas (Angels) – 360 human-days (or one year)
2. One month of the Devas – 30 human years
3. One year of the Devas – 360 human years
4. One hundred years of the Devas – 30,000 human years
5. One thousand years of the Devas – 360,000 human years

Beings who live on 'Suvar loka' and 'Mahar loka' have a life-span of 864 crore or 8.64 billion years.

Beings who live on 'Thaba loka' and 'Sathya loka' (the 5th plane, the realm of Lord Brahma the Creator) have a total life-span of 100 x 360 x 864 crore human years.

The Mind-Body (Manomaya kosa) is The Cause For Personal Name Variations; Adi Sankara's Viveka Chudamani; slk.167:

"The Jnanendriyas (sense-organs) and the mind (jnana-indriyani sa manasa) make up the mind-body. 'Mine' and the 'I' complex is brought about by relating to the physical body (vasthu-vikalpa-haethu). It possesses extraordinary strength (baliyan) and is the cause for personal name variations (samjnadhi-bedha-kalanakalidha); That (Tat) which is proior to this – the ethereal body completely fills, permeates and extends beyond the limits of the physical body (ya purvakosa abipurya vijrumbadhae)."

Teleportaion the next mode of travel – Albert Einstein's 'relativity theory'; 'time travel', "granny paradox", "parallel universes"; Carl Sagan, John Gribbin, Gerald Feinberg – 'tachyons, tradyons and luxyons' that travel at a trillion times the speed of light,'wormholes','black holes'; The Sri Linga Purana, The Vishnu Purana – "the 'boar craft' that tunneled past the seven lower worlds"; 'Yaga' – sacrificial holy-fire in Ramayana

& Thiruvilayadal Purana; teleportation by Sadasiva Brahmendra & Ramalingam Swami; Mecca and other holy-places of the world are portals connecting the world with seven upper and seven lower worlds & sighting of Angels, Bishop Charles Leadbeater's vision of Angels in a church in Sicily; The Sri Shiva Gita; The Mother of Pondicherry, Emperor Sibi; Ashtanga Yoga & Thirumandiram

Modern man is yet to discover teleportation which would greatly reduce the time taken to travel great distances across space as well as make it possible for even flying in the skies was thought to be an impossible feat until early 20th century. Until the advent of the motor car, it was thought that travelling faster than a horse can which is about sixty kilometers an hour would cause our hearts to burst and the brains turn into jelly. Only in 1950 did modern man's supersonic jet flown by Chuck Yaegar break the sound-barrier, which is a little less than 800 miles an hour. Even though our latest fighter jets fly at mach 5 or 6 (a little above 4000 miles per hour) and our rockets at 12 to 18 miles per second, we are far from achieving anything near the speed of light which is 186,000 miles or 300,000 kilometers per second. But even travelling at the speed of light would take us 8 minutes to reach the sun,4 years to reach the next nearest star,28 years to reach the next one and hundreds, thousands, millions and billions of years to reach some stars, in fact, it would take 12 billion years to reach the furthest distance that could be seen by our most powerful telescope!

Even if we consider Albert Einstein's 'relativity theory' according to which, a person travelling at 80 percent of the speed of light would live 1.7 times more than his twin brother living here and when travelling at 99 percent of the speed of light would live 7 times more and when travelling at exactly at the speed of light, would not age at all, no one would be prepared to travel for eons (even though the traveler wouldn't realize the passage of time) so that on returning here, could or would find his family, country, humanity and possibly the world gone out of existence!

And travelling faster than light takes us to a strange phenomenon of 'time travel' where it would be possible to travel not only to the future but also into the past where some sceptics question on what if one were to kill his own grandmother, how would his own birth be possible, and have aptly named this phenomenon as the 'granny paradox'. So the only logical conclusion would be to break the dimension-barrier whereby speed wouldn't matter a lot for we could take short-cuts to hop from one universe to another which astronomers call 'parallel universes'. And a lot of research is going on in this angle and theoretically all this seems possible.

The late Carl Sagan who had been the director of NASA and SETI (search for extraterrestrial intelligence) in 'Cosmos' and 'Contact' says that there are 13 dimensions and there could be intelligent living beings in atleast 18000 planets. SETI astronomers have found two planets,'16 Cygni C' and ' 47 Utsae majoris B' in the so-called habitable zone due to the surface water available on them. Many more planets in habitable zones have been added to the list.

John Gribbin in 'On The Edge Of Time' explains that by building a 'Time Machine', it would be possible to skip over to other dimensions and come back in no time. This might seem far fetched but Gerald Feinberg has calculated particles that travel "faster than light", these particles are known as 'tachyons','tradyons' and 'luxyons'. Contrary to Albert Einstein who had said that any particle would on attaining the speed of light gain infinite energy and infinite mass, Feinberg calculated that they *'lose'* mass and energy. These particles in fact can reach a *trillion times the speed of light!*

John Gribbin further says that space ships could travel through *'worm holes'* or tunnels through space and *black holes* could be those passages which connect our universe to other universes.

Talking of passage through worm holes and tunnels brings to memory the 'Linga Purana' in which it is mentioned that in a bid to find the source and end of Lord Shiva's infinite-form, who took to the form of an infinite column or pillar of light, Lord Brahma the Creator and Lord Vishnu the Sustainer took to their vimanas (flying crafts). Lord Brahma flew his 'Swan craft' (anna vahana) and went up and flew beyond the seven "Upper worlds" and Lord Vishnu flew his 'Boar craft'(varaha vahana) and 'tunnelled or 'bored' his way going beyond the seven "Lower worlds". The 'Vishnu Purana' quotes:" the Boar-craft stood twice as tall as the sky, the distance between the legs of the craft was many miles, its sight was awesome to look at and the roaring fire amidst deafening sound which was when its tail shook (fiery exhaust) in turn shook the walls of the universe."

Many holy places of the world of various religions also prove to be portals or gateways to various dimensions including the 'Yaga-pit' where the 'Sacrifical Holy-Fire' is lit and the whole atmospheric area extending for many miles around being purified by burning various holy products mostly attained from the holy-cow and many holy twigs and barks:

According to the Ramayana, from the Sacrifical-fire rose a Deva (Angel) who offered a golden bowl filled with a divine porridge, by partaking of which by the three wives of Emperor Dasaratha, were born Lord Rama and his three brothers.

In the Thiruvilayadal Purana it is mentioned that from the Sacrifical-Fire arose The Holy Mother as Godess Meenakshi as a three year old girl, who later ruled over the Pandyan Kingdom having Madurai as its capital city.

Sadasiva Brahmendra would not only often teleport to distant lands and be back, but would ask young children playing on the banks of the river Cauvery (near Trichy) to sit down and close their eyes, he would immediately teleport them to Madurai, he would entertain them in the Temple fair, buy them sweets etc., and in a similar manner teleport them back to their native village in a jiffy.

Ramalingam Swamy would teleport grown up people from his village Vadalur to the Holy Chidambaram Nataraja Temple and teleport them back.

There have been many sightings of Angels in the Holy city of Mecca and there are two wells located in the city, one connected to heaven and the other to hell and there have been instances of people here who have conversed with their acquaintances by clapping their hands and getting connected with them whether they were in heaven or hell.

People have seen spirits of dead priests in Churches and they have even been photographed. Bishop Charles W. Leadbeater, one of the founders of the Theosophical Society in India in early 20th century, saw the Archangel Gabriel along with ten other Angels when mass was being conducted in a church in Sicily.

Utilising one's own body to perform teleportation is the safest manner possible for the Lord Himself says in the 'Sri Shiva Gita' that among all of creation, the human body is the most perfect, complex and wonderful of them all. But to once more realize our hidden perfection, we have to literally and practically 'evolve' from the physical body to the mental, scientific and causal bodies. The Siddhars or Perfected beings have further categorized the mental or mind body into two, namely the mind 'desire body' and mind 'abstract body' for they practically see or vision the material-objects that we yearn for as miniature objects floating in front of our foreheads and the abstract thing or qualities like love, compassion, generosity etc., as beautiful colorfull waves emanating from our body. In the present day world, most of mankind are still functioning in the physical and the mind desire-boy for he is ensnared in this materialstic and lustfull world where he yearns for food, bodily pleasures power and wealth. Only a very few have evolved into their mind abstract-bodies for only those who radiate love, kindness, generosity, devotion et., are capable of functioning in the abstract mind-body.

Those who evolve into their scientific bodies are the saints who practically feel empathy when other life-forms suffer, they are hungry when others are hungry, when others are satiated they too are satiated: Ramalingam swamy would say:" I would droop with sadness when ever I saw a withered crop (plant or tree)."; The holy Mother of Pondicherry could experience the cries of agony and pain a tree suffered due to people hammering nails into it; An ancient Indian king feeling empathy on seeing the suffering of a peacock which was shivering upon being drenched in cold rain, draped his own cloak over it to provide warmth; Another king got down from his personal chariot and entwined over it a fallen drying creeper; The Emperor Sibi cut off flesh from his own thigh to save a dove and at the same time compensate a hunter who insisted on having his pound of flesh!

Finally when man evolves into his Causal body, he does not differentiate himself with anything in nature, he sees God in himself and in everything. He is 'aware' to the fullest possible sense that he is just an extension of God, and one cannot differentiate himself from God just as we cannot differentiate Jesus Christ, Krishna and Buddha from God.

When man evolves, his spiritual growth is reflected in his physical body also for the physical is based on the spiritual bodies, it is the finer bodies that give'shape' to the physical and that is why they are known in Tamil as the 'Karu udal' or the 'embryonic body'.

In the Yogic-tradition, the physical body is strengthened and made light and supple through the holistic practice of the 'ashtanga' or 'eight-limbed yoga' – "yama, niyama, asana, pranayama, pratyahara, dharana, dhyana, samadhi". The first two contain a lot of do's and don't's while leading a controlled peacefull and natural way of life; asana means 'posture' and there are said to be 8400,000 postures (as many as there are life-forms on earth) that help in unfolding and receiving various energies within and without man; pranayama is the art of controlling the system that activates and regulates the flow of Prana the vibrant dynamic sum of all forces whose outward manifestation is the air that is inhaled in; prayathara is; dharana is; dhyana is meditation whereby the thoughtless-state is achieved thereby transcending time; Samadhi is attainment of the superconscious-state. The highest of the finer bodies of man, the scientific and causal bodies are the real spiritual bodies, when man evolves into and functions in them, there is no 'jiva' – soul, only 'Siva' - God remains.

The chakras which are psychic spots, vortexes of energy and 'wisdom centres' exist in the finer bodies of man and as man evolves, the Kundalini or cosmic-energy rises, activates each of the chakras and according to his grade or degree of evolvement, the chakras also expand and whirl at tremendous speeds and emanate vibrant colors and receive and emanate various energies. As the five lower chakras contain the tattvas or instruments, the concept of the five basic substances in nature, earth, water, fire, air and the sky, as well as the concept of the seven lower and seven upper 'worlds', when with full concentration and will-power man along with the help of his dynamic-breath takes along the cosmic-energy, activates each of the chakras on his upward journey and finally lets them flow into the seventh chakra at the crown of the head, goes even further beyond and crosses the 'anda kosa yellai' or 'universe body barrier' that exists about twelve inches above the head, he literally breaks all dimension-barriers, and he is able to go anywhere in his physical body; Thirumandiram 1029:

"This sacrificial pit within
Is a hexagon formed of six adharas (chakras);

In its circle are tattvas six times six
Trembling arise;
With those tattvas under your command,
You can arise into the very heavens."

Thirumandiram 648:

"In the tenth year the yogi can expand and contract into space;
In the eleventh year he can assume the form he meditates on;
In the twelfth year all eight siddhis (supernatural powers) entire
he masters;
He then gains the powers to roam the worlds seven above and seven
below,
And take one cosmic form spanning all space."

"The Seven Heavens" – The Holy Qu'ran; sura XVII.44
"The seven heavens and the earth,
And all beings therein,
Declare His glory:…."

Sura XVIII.107:

"As those who believe
And work righteous deeds,
They have, for their entertainment,
The gardens of paradise, "

Comments by A.Yusuf Ali:" <u>Firdaus </u>in Persian means an enclosed place, a park. In technical theological language the word is used for the inner circle of Heaven, or the highest Heaven, the destination of those who perfectly fulfill both requirements, viz: a Sound faith, and perfectly righteous conduct. Small faults in either respect are forgiven; the mercy of God steps in. Perhaps there is Spiritual development and progress even after death."

'Empyrean' – the highest heaven – "Kurrat un nar "– Holy Qu'ran; sura XXXVII. 6, 7, 8:

"We have indeed decked
The lower heaven with beauty
(In) the stars, -

(For beauty) and for guard
Against all obstinate
Rebellious evil spirits,
(So) they should not strain
Their ears in the direction
Of the Exalted Assembly."

A.Yusuf Ali:" That is lower than the highest heaven, the Empyrean, the sphere of fire (Kurrat un nar), the seat, we may suppose, of the Exalted Assembly (of angels). In the poetic imagery of the East as of the West,(eg., see Milton, Paradise Lost, III,6,481-3) there are the seven heavens of the planets of the solar system; above them is the sphere of the fixed stars; above them is the crystalline sphere balancing other motions; higher still is the Premum mobile ('that first moved'), the source of heavenly motions; and above all the Empyrean. The stars and planets thus come in the lower heavens. The same imagery will be found in Dante."

Man can disappear and re-appear at will – Patanjali' Yoga Sutra; Thirumandiram; "Cloak of invisisibility"; Albert Einstein's "Unified Field Thoery"; Sadasiva Brahmendra & Swami Ramalingam's "Cause-effect body" (kaarana-kaarya rupam and teleportaion); St. Appar, Goraknath, Swami Nityananda of Vadakara,'Tai Chi' Founder Chang San Feng; Charles Berlitz, John Gribbin; Lord Rama in Kamba Ramayanam, Lord Buddha, Lord Mahavira, Lord Krishna – the 'Kshetra' – the field extended to infinity in Bhagavad Gita:

The 21st sutra of Sage Patanjali states that when man turns inward while meditating, he finally comes to realize that the physical as well as the finer astral and spiritual bodies are constructed of the 'tattvas' (principles) of the five primary substances found in nature: earth (solid), water (liquid), fire (gaseous), air (etheric), sky (super-etheric). The tattva or concept of each of these five substances exist in five of the lower chakras, for example the muladhara chakra at the base of the spinal column holds the concept of the earth. When through yogic means and particulary through the practice of pranayama and by force of prana, the Kundalini or cosmic-energy that lies in slumber, is awoken, coaxed to rise and on its upward journey, activate each of the chakras, the earth-concept at first comes under the control of the person. As each chakra is transcended, the other concepts also are conquered and finally when the cosmic-energy flows into the top most chakra at the crown of the head, he attains superconsciousness, becomes a full-blown Yogi and thus all of nature comes under his control for since the concept of the five substances inside his body comes under his command, everything outside the body too comes under his control, so he is able to convert his body into the substance he desires. In fact, he can walk on air, on water, stay under water, in fire, nothing can harm him.

Sadasiva Brahmendra who lived about 350 years ago near Trichy in Tamilnadu in Southern India, was once meditating on the banks of the river Cauvery, when sudden flood-waters covered him and he was buried under slush and mud. After the flood-waters had receded and months later, when farmers were tilling their land, the plough struck something hard and when they uncovered the sand to see what it was, to their amazement saw the yogi bleeding profusely from the head. The yogi woke up as if from deep sleep and without a word, walked away. Once the yogi entered the palace bed rooms of a Nawab utterly naked, the enraged nawab promptly cut off a hand, but to his astonishment the yogi went away with a laugh. The nawab, realizing that the person would have to be of the highest order to bear such pain and smile at the incident, followed the yogi, carrying the severed hand to seek his forgiveness. The yogi walked on at such a fast pace that the nawab could approach him only by that evening. When the nawab finally asked the yogi to forgive him, the yogi smiled at him and gestured to him to place the severed hand at the bleeding stump. The yogi caressed the mutilated part, and presto, the arm was good as new!

Sadasiva Brahmendra once stood naked on a rock near a waterfalls where a British army officer was bathing along with his family and other ladies in the resort town of Courtallam known for its many naturally flowing waterfalls which proves as a spa as well as a tourist-centre now. The angered officer took out his hunting rifle and aimed it at the naked yogi who immediately projected himself as an abnormally large tiger! The officer slowly withdrew and the yogi disappeared from sight. After a couple of years the yogi repeatedly appeared before the very same officer back in England. Once when the officer was on his daily horse-back riding routine, the yogi appeared before him at several places on the road, to the surprise and amazement of the officer!

Swami Ramalingam who lived in the 1850's and 1860's, would disappear and appear often and thrice professional photographers were brought from Madras (only huge box-cameras with tripods were available in those days) to his town Vadalur to photograph the swami along with all his followers and devotees. But try as they might, the swami's image could not be captured on film even though the images of others in the group was captured successfully. Rain or fire in no way affected him. Once he drank smolten-lead to the ashtonishment of one and all for he was pestered to reveal the secret of converting lead into gold which he had done several times!

The Saivite saint Appar was put into a burning lime-kiln and he came out singing that it felt as cool as the evening river-side breeze; no amount of torture hurt him the least and when finally he was tied to a huge grinding mill-stone and cast into the deep-seas, he floated to the coast riding the very same stone as a float!

Goraknath, when challenged by a pride-filled yogi who rode a tiger and used a deadly serpent as a whip, sat on a lifeless stone wall and ordered it to move toward the yogi, which it did to everyone's amazement!

Trilinga Swami who lived for 300 years (as much as he weighed in pounds) once seized a British Governor's sword and threw it into the depths of the Ganges river. When the enraged governor demanded back his sword, the yogi dived into the fast-flowing river and came back with two identical swords and the governor himself couldn't identify and point out which was his own sword! The yogi would sit submerged in the depths of the Ganges river for six months at a time! The yogi was locked behind bars by the British for loitering about stark naked, but again and again he was found loitering on the roof-top of the prison!

Swami Nityananda, the disciple of Sankarananda and Vadakara Sivananda, once stopped a steam-driven train by his sheer will-power in the early 20th century and try as they might, the English train-drivers couldn't make the train move; when challenged by a muslim fakir in Bombay to quaff poison, the yogi did so after much reluctance he did, and to everyone's amazement it was the fakir who vomited blood and fell down dead!

Swami Ragavendra converted trays of raw-beef into sweet smelling flowers offered by an unbelieving muslim king; He turned a mute shepherd booy into a wise person in an instant; He brought a dead boy back to life; the Tungabadra river which was in spate, parted into two to give way to the swami's disciple; He appeared out of his tomb after he had entered into Samadhi and was seen only by the British Governor Sir Thomas Munroe, who recorded the event by writing that he had met a remarkable person, which is still available in the Madras Gazette records.

Chang San Feng (1270 A.D.) the founder of the Chinese Martial Art 'Tai Chi' who was also a skilled acupuncturist and who lived for over 100 years is said to have transformed himself into a pure spiritual-state and 'flew away' for he had conquered death.

Man contains three 'fires' within him, the Prana he inhales in through his left nostril is of the 'chandra kala'(Chandra – moon, kala – rays of energy-bodies) of 16 kalas, the right-nostril breath is of the 'surya kala' (surya – sun)of 12 kalas and there is a third one known only to the yogis, that runs through the centre of the spinal-column which is of the 'agni kala'(agni – fire)of 64 kalas. When the three fires are aroused by the Kundalini or cosmic-energy and merged as one in the 'chandra mandala' or moon's sphere that exists above the forehead,'Pranava kala' is achieved. When one through yogic-means reaches the crown of the head, all the tattvas or principles that make the subtle bodies as well as everything in the universe and nature is transcended, conquered; Thirumandiram:

"Sixty four, twelve and sixteen
Are kalas that appear in agni, sun and moon;

And four are kalas of the star (soul)
The fettering tattvas six and ninety too
Are kalas to count."

Agni kala 64 + surya kala 12 + Chandra kala 16 + star (soul) kala 4 = 96 tattvas. So when all the fires are merged,'Pranava kala' is achieved so that light emanated from that person which is known as 'dejas'(from which 'Devas' (angels) originated ('devas' literally mean "those who radiate light") thus this radiation of light obviously makes the person invisible.

Scientists in England have constructed a suit made of fibre-optics which refract light totally, that is unlike diamonds that reflect light totally from its many facets, this suit does not reflect light directly, it instead 'bends' and refracts or deflects light backward totally so that the person wearing the suit or cloak seem as though he has disappeared.

Charles Berlitz, author of the famous book 'The Bermuda Trialngle' has also in his 'The Philadelphia Experiment' written in detail of paranormal activities and he has written extensively on Albert Einstein's "Unified Field Theory" and how he applied that law to make the U.S. Naval ship 'Eldrige' to not only disappear but to be teleported to a distant place.

The infamous 'Philadelphia Experiment' which is denied by the U.S. Defense Department, in brief goes like this: The U.S. Naval ship the 'Eldrige' was four hundred feet long; a full-length copper rod was placed on the ship which was bound by copper wire (like generators have)and electricity was passed through them; in the electro-magnetic field that was created around the ship, the eldrige became invisible though two ships accompanying it were visible; eldrige was in a jiffy teleported to Norfolk which was 400 miles away; after a few moments, eldrige was again teleported back to Philadelphia; two or more sailors practically went 'through' walls and disappeared from view right in front of their families!; one or more sailors are said to have gone insane.

Recently the U.S.Pentagon in a controlled electro-magnetic field (magnets placed at strategic points around a person) in a radiation-proof room, have made man disappear.

The inter-relationship among the three basic universal forces: electro-magnetic, gravitational and nuclear seem to suggest that their may be a fourth 'weak' universal force which could be related to gravity in the same way that electricity is related to magnetism. Such a field could be inter-dimensional or 'time-related'. The Pyramids ('pyr' – fire in Greek;'amid' – amidst), many holy-places of the world and the human body (which contains within it the 'fiery-serpent', the cosmic-energy or fire – that is why the walls within the pyramids feature a frieze of cobras – the multiple 'Uraei' or rearing cobras with spread-hoods) apart from all the heavenly bodies which in their core contain the Kundalini or cosmic-energy (which is the Power of the Creator) in a terrible fiery-form whose outward manifestation is molten-iron and as we now know, the earth's core contains a ball of molten iron which has a radius of eight hundred miles which proves to be a huge magnet from which we derive the north and south poles, and it produces such 'fields'just as the baseof the spinal-column of man contains the Cosmic-Energy and thus produces an electro-magnetic field and these could be utilized as portals or gateways to cross the time and dimension-barriers (an ancient Egyptian proverb thus says:" *Everything fears time – but time fears the Pyramids.*")

John Gribbin in 'In Search Of The Edge Of Time' has given theoretical proof on how in future, spaceships could pass from one universe into another (parallel universes), through 'worm-holes'in space and he says that 'black holes' could be those tunnels to move into another dimension and take a 'short-cut' back into our universe and if necessary to another part of our own globe.

But without needing any hi-tech gadgetry, when man evolves into his finer spiritual bodies, he does practically function in higher dimensions for those finer bodies are constructed of atoms of inner(lower)as well as higher dimensions where the lower and upper worlds exist. It is like shifting gears, when man in deep states of meditation by his sheer will-power shifts his total focus and attention in from the physical to the vital and higher finer bodies, he does act and function in 'other' worlds of other dimensions whose field could be extended to infinity, so for man to 'go' to distant places and be back in a jiffy is very much possible. The Kundalini or cosmic-energy in man functions in a similar manner like it does in the earth and all heavenly bodies, by creating a magnetic-field around him (the two poles being the chakras at the crown of the head and the base of the spine). Russian scientists have measured this field and they say that the field is strongest and widest when man is in deep sleep. But there are many deeper-states that yogis are able to achieve and in those states the field is much much wider. Lord Rama's, Lord Buddha's and Lord Mahavira's field were said to be many miles wide and all beings, be it human, animal and the plant kingdom were affected in a positive way when they came into the field. An enraged wild elephant had sat down meekly in front of Lord Buddha while everyone ran helter skelter in fright; A deadly hooded-cobra had provided shade to Lord Mahavira; In the 'Kamba Ramayanam' it is mentioned that all the creepers, plants and trees bloomed out blossoming-flowers out of sheer delight when Lord Rama entered the forests! Lord Krishna in the Bhagavad Gita says that the field or 'Kshetra' exists in a limited-form in man, but in a 'Purna yogi' or a full-blown yogi it covers the entire universe, so time, distance and space becomes meaningless, he could be at one, two or many places at the same given moment!

Rotating 'Black Holes' Connect Multiple Universes and Different Times

John Gribbin, in 'In Search Of The Edge Of Time', page 177." *...with rotating black holes acting as hyperspace connections exactly like the wormholes developed from the notion of Einstein-Rosen bridges that I described on page 160. A rotating balck hole may connect our universe to itself, not just once but repeatedly, offering a gateway to different places and different times."*

Again in page 234:" *In fact our universe may be one of many space-time bubbles connected by wormholes."*

"The Religious leaders of the world had forgotten their common origin ... Moses, Jesus and Mohammed were equal Prophets, mirroring God's glory, messengers bearing the imprint of the great Creator". "Later on, Zoroaster, Buddha, Confucius, Krishna, Lao and Baha'u'llah, the last

great manifestation of the Divine Being…" The 'Bab' disappeared after being shot by 750 Armenian soldiers in front of thousands…:

The 'Baha'I Faith' originated in Iran in the 19th century, its founder – 'Mirza' Ali Muhammad believed himself to be a divine manifestation projected into the world of time and space as a 'Bab'(gate) leading to a new era for mankind.

According to the Baha'i faith, "the religious leaders of the world had forgotten their common origin … Moses, Jesus and Mohammed were equal Prophets, mirroring God's glory, messengers bearing the imprint of the Great Creator."

Later on, Zoroaster, Buddha, Confucius, Krishna, Lao and Baha'u'llah, the last great manifestation of the Divine Being, whose name literally means, "the glory of God". The focus of Baha'ism is often popularized as "the Oneness of god, the Oneness of religion, and the Oneness of Humanity".

As Baha'i history records it, The Bab was sentenced to death and was executed on July 8,1850, at Tabriz. In the view of thousands,750 Armenian soldiers raised their rifles and fired at the figure of the Prophet. When the smoke cleared, the Bab had not only emerged unscathed from the fussilade of bullets, but the bullets had burned through the ropes that held him, and he stood unfettered. He then disappeared from their vision, but upon returning to his cell, the guards found him lecturing his disciples. After he had finished speaking with them, he said to the guards, "I have finished my conversation, now you may fulfill your intention." He was then executed, but at *his* will.

The Self – the Soul is the 'True Man' concealed within the body, it is the Soul of the Universe, the Lord of Time, the Great Lord, the Perfect One and is a Witness to everything as he is preent everywhere; That imperishable core is part of My Eternal Self; Man is called 'man' (Manu) because he is determined by his mind, verily what he thinks he becomes, elevating himself by noble thoughts, he once again becomes

Divine; the Soul is pristinely Pure otherwise it could never become Perfect even in hundreds of lifetimes – Sri Shiva Rahasya:

I, the One Lord, through My Play of Darkness and Light bring forth everything in sight. All created things are but sparks of My Divine Light. A part of Me, of My Infinite Self, lies hidden in all things.

Therefore, know all things to have an unseen inner core, an essence and a Soul that is the true nature and the life of everything. That imperishable core, being part of My Eternal Self, has been called the Self (Atman). That very Self is the Lord of Life.

The Self is the True Man concealed within the body of blood, flesh and bones, and it is by nature Divine. It is absolute, pure, peaceful, subtle and eternal. It exists beyond the darkness of ignorance and beyond knowledge that is expressed in words.

It is the Inner Being, the Soul of the Universe, the Life-Principle, the Lord of Time, the Great Lord, the Perfect One. Though being unseen and unknown, yet He knows. For He is present everywhere and witnesses all things from within. He is the Eternal Witness of all. The Universe is born of Him and in Him alone it dissolves. He is the Master of the Magic Power whereby He assumes various forms while remaining ever-unaffected and unchanged.

The Self is not subject to the cycle of birth and death. He is not the physical World, being neither Earth, nor Water, Fire, Wind nor Sky.

The Self is neither physical objects, nor the bodily frame; neither the breath, nor the mind; neither matter nor non-matter. He is neither sound, nor touch, nor colour and form, nor taste, nor smell, nor the Ego, nor yet a limited person who thinks, feels, speaks and acts.

O holy ones! the Self is neither a sense organ, nor the foot, neither the anus, nor the genitals. He is neither inanimate Matter, nor a living Person. In truth, the Conscious Self is neither the Breath of Life, nor the Void of sleep, nor even the Cosmic Play of Magic.

For all these pass away like waves upon the Sea. But the Self is the Imperishable, Changeless, Undying, Undecaying, Self-Existing, Self-Supporting Sea of Consciousness Itself. The Changeless Witness of all that passes.

This World consists of the five senses, hearing, seeing and the rest. The One Supreme Self is different from this even as light is different from darkness. As shade and light are different from each other in this World, so indeed the material World and the Self-Luminous Self are different.

Were the Self to be in any way soiled or impure, created and changeable, it could never become Perfect even in hundreds of lifetimes. Nor would there be any escape from that which is imperfect.

The Awakened Ones perceive their Perfect Self as intrinsically free from defects or change, free from the pairs of opposites such as light and darkness, cold and heat, pleasure and pain. They realise that the Self is eternally blissful and unchanging.

Such thoughts as, I am doing this or that, I am happy or unhappy, I am slender or stout and the like, are created by the mind of incognizant folk and superimposed upon the Perfect Self.

Having created a thought, through repetition man identifies therewith and believes himself to be that, regardless of his true nature. O Sages of broad understanding! Man is called Man (Manu) because he is determined by his Mind (Manas). Verily, what Man thinks, that he becomes. Under the influence of material existence, the Self who is by birth a God, thinks himself to be a Man, and a Man he at last becomes.

Elevating himself by noble thoughts, he becomes again Divine. Remembering Me, the All-Source, he and I are Reunited. For, all things come from Me and to Me they shall return. This is the Eternal Law (Sanatana Dharma).

Man is born with different kinds of Physical bodies and minds that correspond with inner latent tendencies developed over past lives; everything is born of the mind and the mind is nothing but the light of the soul tinted by latent tendencies of past lives; The world was created not in vain but with a purpose, Truth remedy over all sorrows; wisemen regard this Universe as made of knowledge:

As a deluded king who believes himself to be a ploughman takes to ploughing a delimited field when the whole wide World is his, even so, though the ever-shining, self-luminous Self is immensely vast and all-pervading, due to the thoughtlessness and lack of discernment of the unawakened mind, man believes himself to be a limited, individual thing and lives a diminutive life.

The Sages realise that the Self is Uncreated, Unborn, Formless, Self-Existing, Changeless, Eternal and Pure, whilst Matter is Created, Born, Many-Formed, Dependent On The Self, Ever-Changing, Transient and Tainted. But the ignorant, immersed in worldly existence like a man enmeshed in a dream, sees nothing but Matter and believes that to be the Supreme. Thus, the Self, though pure, changeless and perfect, has the qualities of Matter attributed to It, by association.

Deceived by the deluded mind, the ignorant does not comprehend that his own Self is in reality the imperishable Ultimate, the Perfect One. Thus he confuses the Self with the not-Self and the not-Self with the Self. He knows not what is Real and what is only a Dream. Ignorant of what is good and what is evil, he shuns what is right and craves what is wrong. Hence he suffers like a man whose mind is overcome by delusion.

Verily from lack of Awareness, there arises Self-forgetfulness. From that springs wrong knowledge. From wrong knowledge comes greed, lust, envy, hatred and other defects of the mind. Moreover, man reaps the fruits of his own actions. And actions are done according to his knowledge. Therefore, the performance of actions that spring from wrong knowledge is the greatest defect of all.

It is due to this cause that men are invested with different kinds of physical bodies and minds. For, one is born with a body and mind that correspond to the inner latent tendencies one has developed in a previous existence. All bodies are born of mind. And the mind is nothing but the light of the Soul tinted by latent tendencies acquired in the past. Therefore, know that whatsoever corporeal form a Soul assumes in this life or the next, the same will reflect his mental state, even as the light that passes through a coloured gem (assumes that very colour).

Verily, this is a matter a million times true: whether in this World or the next, in Heaven or on Earth, whatever comes to pass in the Three Worlds, know that there is a meaning and a reason to all things. The World was not created in vain but with a purpose. And so it is with all other things: in every thing there is a sign that teaches man a hidden secret.

This is known to Me, the Wise One Who See all things from Above and to those (the Yogis) who dwell in Unity with Me but not to any others. For, the others, being as if asleep and ever immersed in vain thoughts, even if the Truth were shown them, they would see It not.

Therefore, let all those who yearn after knowledge of the Truth listen to My Word of Truth that they may see the Truth. For, only by seeing the Truth shall their Souls find Peace and never otherwise.

Truth is the remedy for all sorrows: It frees the Soul from the burdens of the World. By hearing the Truth, bound Souls remember their Self. Remembering the Self, they know that as air is present both within and without a jar, so the Self, being Omnipresent, lies both concealed within oneself, and pervades everywhere without. It is eternal, free and ever-stainless.

Although It is One, It appears as Many through Its Magic Power and not due to Its inherent nature. For this reason, the Knowers of Truth bear witness that the Truth is One (Satyam Ekam).

As the Sky does not become soiled through contact with clouds and the Sun is ever untouched by darkness, even so the various activities of the mind such as thoughts, feelings or sense perceptions, do not affect the Perfect Self. Only the mind and the body, being by nature imperfect, are affected thereby.

As a pure crystal shines by virtue of its own lustre, as the Sun shines unaided by any lamp, as the Lightning blazes across the Sky independently of man-made fire, even so does the pure Self shine independently of any conditioning cause.

Wise men regard this Universe as being made of knowledge. For it arises from the waves of thought dancing upon the surface of the Ocean of Universal Consciousness. That Great Intelligence Which is Boundless and Radiant Beyond Measure, fashions thought from Its rays of light. Thought gives rise to perceptions; and perceptions make up the objects of the World.

Thus men of Higher Vision know that the World is made of Knowledge. Yet the dim-sighted see it as nothing but physical matter and objects. Their vision being faulty and blunt, they see not beyond the surface. Verily, the Self or Spirit is by nature changeless, omnipresent Consciousness, beyond material attributes. But it is held to be insentient matter by men of wrong knowledge. For only the Perfect Ones can see what is Perfect.

As the pure crystal when in contact with a red object like the seeds of the Gunja-berry appears to be red, or a looking-glass appears to take the shape of the objects reflected therein, even so the Great Being is perceived in the form of objects though remaining distinct from, and unaffected by, the same. As sunlight shines in many colours as it passes through a shower of rain, so the Great Lord (Maheshvara) appears as this many-formed World when seen through the eyes of mortal men. Verily, the World is He and nothing else. This is the Truth and the Good Tidings that I Myself bring unto the World.

They who know this shall be safely guided to the Abode of That Which Ever Is. But the others shall abide in darkness. Verily you who have seen My Divine Self are very fortunate indeed! In My Visible Form you have a Sign from the Unseen that you may know His Glory and follow His Will. But those who have seen Me not, will be troubled by doubt and in their anguish will ask, My Lord, how may we know that the Divine Self *Is*? Now of these, there are three kinds, the stubborn and the proud that doubt My Word and seek to try you; the thoughtful that yearn for a reasoned answer; and the believers who desire to have their faith confirmed.

Say to the stubborn and proud: O you of little faith! life on Earth lasts but a moment. Before you know it, you are overcome by Death. Of this there can be no doubt. If, at the end of your life you find that there is no Afterlife and no God, then you shall have no reason for concern. For, he that no longer is, has no concerns. But if at the end of this life you find that there is an Afterlife and a God, then you shall be overcome by remorse. Thus you shall cry, Alas! would that I had not come hither unprepared. For, you will go to an unknown place unprepared, like a fool who sets off upon a long journey with no provisions and no knowledge of the land he is bound for. Therefore, beware! do not knowingly walk in the footsteps of fools. Think not that your knowledge is faultless and that there is no one above you whose knowledge is best. You have been forewarned.

When by means of Yoga man comes to perceive nothing but Consciousness everywhere, he becomes a Perfect Knower of the Self. He abides in the Self and abiding Therein he *knows* It like unto his own self. When he perceives all living beings as abiding in the Self and the Self in all living beings, he realises the Supreme.

Yoga is the Power of Unity – *the Unity between Body, Mind and Soul is of the Human kind, that which is between Man and Nature is of the Worldwide Kind, but that which is between Man and the Lord is indeed Divine*:

O noble ones! Yoga is the Power of Unity whereby Wholeness, Harmony and Happiness are established in the World. Unity is of three kinds: Human, Worldwide and Divine.

The Unity which is between Body, Mind and Soul, is of the Human kind. That which is between people and nations as well as between Mankind and Nature, is of the Worldwide kind. But the Unity which is between Man and the Lord, that, indeed, is Divine. There is nothing higher than this.

Thus the only remedy to ignorance-based disunity, disease and suffering is the Perfect Knowledge of Yoga that leads to Spiritual Illumination, to Life in Unity with the Divine. This Perfect Knowledge I now Graciously Declare unto the World for the Salvation of all Souls who are fit to be saved.

O you who have been granted Insight into My Eternal Truth! those who possess Spiritual Knowledge know that the Sense Organs are greater than the objects they perceive.

For, that which is perceived depends upon that which perceives. When the perceiver perceives not, then the object of perception vanishes like the Moon in the dark (that is, on a Moonless night).

But when the perceiver beholds an object either in direct perception, imagination, dream or recollection, then the object comes into existence and not otherwise. Therefore the Sense Organs are greater than the objects they perceive.

Likewise, the wise know that the Lower Mind (Manas) is greater than the Sense Organs. For it is the Lower Mind that puts together the diverse perceptions of the Senses and builds them into a coherent whole. Without the Lower Mind the perceptions of the Five Senses would be scattered across the Sky (of Awareness) like clouds in the wind.

The wise know further that the Thought of I and Mine (Aham-Kara, Ego Mind)) is greater than the Lower Mind. For it is the Ego Mind by its power of appropriation that brings a perceived thing into relation with the perceiver. Otherwise the two would be for ever severed like the two halves of a broken twig.

The Intellect (Buddhi) is greater than the Ego for it determines the nature of the object and the manner in which the perceiver is to relate to it. Moreover, the Intellect that is infused with the Light of Truth, can awaken the Ego to its true identity.

The Unmanifest Matter (Prakarti) is greater than the Intellect, for Matter is that whereof the Intellect is born. Therein the Intellect rests in deep sleep and from that too it derives the power to think, feel and perceive whether in dream or when awake. The Soul Proper (Purusha) is greater than Matter for he is the perceiver and the agent whilst Matter is the object perceived and acted upon. Moreover, Matter itself is nothing but the Soul's sleeping half, as it were.

Greater than the embodied Soul is the Sphere of Maya, wherein My Power of Magic (Maya) holds sway. It envelops the entire Material Universe wherein dwell all embodied Souls, who possess physical or astral bodies according as they inhabit the Earthly or Astral World. It is Maya, the Lord's Wondrous Power that envelops the Soul like unto a veil and holds him under its magic spell. Maya keeps the unawakened Soul in his embodied state. Verily, by its five Binding Powers, Maya envelops the Soul even as swaddling clothes envelop a newborn babe.

Greater than Maya, is the radiant Sphere of Shakti, Shiva's Infinite Power, inhabited by the Liberated Souls who have gone beyond the World of Maya. They are the Great Radiant Ones, endowed with bodies of Pure Spiritual Light. In the midst of that Sphere of Power stands the Threefold Stairway to Supreme Perfection. It has Three Steps, each leading to a Higher World and together leading to the Highest. Going up by the Three Mighty Steps the Soul acquires the Three Divine Powers of Shiva which are Action, Knowledge and Will, and ascends to the Highest Heaven.

The Soul enveloped in 84,000 Veils – corresponding to the 84,000 births man takes – 42,000 births as inanimate forms auch as stones, rocks and other things made of the five basic elements; 15,000 as half-sentient things like plants and trees;12,000 in sentient things like insects and worms;9,000 as land, water and airborne creatures and 6000 in Human form:

Perfection is attained by abiding in Unity with Truth. I Am that Truth. I create the Soul out of Myself by enveloping him in Six Veils (Avarana). The Sixfold Veil of Maya is what separates man's Soul from the Perfect One. Six multiplied twofold, two being the mark of Duality, gives twelve. And twelve multiplied seven thousandfold, that is, one thousand veils to each of My Seven Worlds, yields eighty-four thousand. Thus the Soul is covered in eighty-four thousand veils that separate him from My Supreme Self. And he returns to My Supreme and Perfect Self by shedding one veil in a lifetime.

Forty-two thousand veils are shed in as many a lifetime passed in inanimate form such as stones, rocks and other things that are made of earth, water, fire, air or space. Fifteen thousand are shed in the form of half-sentient things such as plants and trees. Twelve thousand are shed as a sentient thing such as insect or worm. Nine thousand as land, water or airborne creatures. And six thousand in human form. When, after eighty-four thousand lifetimes he has shed the last veil, the Soul goes beyond Maya and is born only three more times: once as a Yogi and twice as a God. me devoted to Me. By being devoted to Me either in My Manifested Form or My Formless Transcendental Self, they attain to Me, the Supreme Truth. Having realised Truth, they fall no more under the spell of worldly existence.

The Self doesn't have to be Realized for it has already been Realized; Realize with a still mind the state between sleep and wakefulness, the gap between two perceptions; the mind should be brought to the condition of a new-born baby; One should also be free from the thought of "I see", only by transcending Will, sensation or thought, only then is Perfection possible – **Tripura Rahasya:**

Though the person might be a pandit well versed and grounded in the theory and discussion of the philosophy of the Self (Soul), he cannot realize the Self for it is not realizable for it is already realized. Realization is not attained by seeking and searching for it but by cessation of thought not by force of will but in a letting go of it in a relaxed manner. Fored effort towards realization would be like the attempt to stamp one's own shadow, it would be a hindrance and make it recede. Effort would be like a child attempting to grasp its own reflection seen on a mirror, in the same manner the beginner are fooled by the mental reflections on the mirror of the Pure and Luminous Self for realization hadn't yet dawn in them.

It is like people' attention being drawn towards objects in space for though they understand space, they are not *aware* of it. The universe in space is understood but pace itself is not regarded, similarly the Self which is the screen on which everything is played is not realized.

One should relize with a still mind the state between sleep and wakefulness, the interval between the recognition of one object after another or gap between two thoughts or perceptions. The mind should be turned inward and not outward, only a little control should be there and be attentive of the Self for with the thought that the one who seeks is in reality is the greatly sought after Self the all encompassing Soul. With just a bit of control and watchfulness and with the mind in the condition of a new born-baby, all physical or gross materials are absent with only the feeling of 'I am' persisting. A state will emerge when the Self will be realized as Pure Being or Consciousness underlying all phenomena but existing as One without any divisions similar to the baby-sense of infinity. Even the sense of one perceiving and 'I am' would also vanish and the threading together of the three states of wakefulness, sleep-state and dreamless-state or deep-sleep and surpassing it into the fourth state known as 'Turiya' is the reality, the Self within which is strung together all diverse objects of the universe like a garland strung of various flowers.

Hemachuda the King did accordingly guided by his wife and gained that exalted state and thus remained in peaceful for a long time unaware of anything but the Self.

The Perfect state of Samadhi (Oneness) not experienced by merely being in that state for a couple of hours by closing on'e eyes and stilling the thought-waves, One should always be in Perfect Equlibrium (samadharshini) – Tripura Rahasya:

"Hemalekha noticed that her husband had attained supreme Peace and so did not disturb him. He awoke in an hour and a half, opened his eyes and saw his wife nearby. Eager to fall into that state once more, he closed his eyes; and immediately Hemalekha took hold of his hands and asked him sweetly: 'My Lord, tell me what you have ascertained to be your gain on closing your eyes, or your loss on opening them, my dearest. I love to hear you. Do say what happens on the eyes being closed or left open.'

"On being pressed for an answer, he looked as if he were drunk and replied reluctantly and languidly, as follows:

"'My dear, I have found pure untainted happiness. I cannot find the least satisfaction in the activities of the world as sorrow increases when they finish. Enough of them! They are tasteless to me like a sucked orange, only indulged in by wasters, or like cattle incessantly chewing the cud. What a pity that such people should be to this day unaware of the bliss of their own Self! Just as a man goes a-begging in ignorance of the treasure hidden under his floor, so did I run after sensual pleasures unaware of the boundless ocean of bliss within me. Worldly pursuits are laden with misery and pleasures are transient. Still I was so infatuated that I mistook them for enduring pleasures, was often grief-stricken, yet did not cease to pursue them over and over again. The pity of it: Men are fools, unable to discriminate pleasure from pain. They seek pleasures but gain sorrow. Enough of these activities which increase the relish for such pleasure.

"My dear, I beg you with hands clasped. Let me fall again into the peace of my blissful self. I pity you that though knowing this state, you are not in it but are ever engaged in vain."

"The wise girl gently smiled at all this, and said to him: 'My lord, you do not yet know the highest state of sanctity (which is not besmirched by duality), reaching which the wise transcend duality and are never perplexed. That state is as far from you as the sky is from the earth. Your small measure of wisdom is as good as no wisdom, because it is not unconditional, but remains conditioned by closing or opening your eyes. Perfection cannot depend on activity or the reverse, on effort or no effort. How can that state be a perfect one if mental or physical activity can influence it or if the displacement of the eyelid by the width of a barley grain makes all the difference to it? Again, how can it be perfect if located only in the interior? What shall I say of your muddled wisdom! How ridiculous to think that your eyelid one inch long, can shut up the expanse in which millions of worlds revolve in one corner alone!'

"Listen Prince! I will tell you further. As long as these knots are not cut asunder so long will bliss not be found (The knowledge acquired is thus not effective). These knots are millions in number and are created by the bond of delusion which is no other than ignorance of Self. These knots give rise to mistaken ideas, the chief of which is the identification of the body with the Self, which in its turn gives rise to the perennial stream of happiness and misery in the shape of the cycle of births and deaths. The second knot is the differentiation of the world from the Self whose being consciousness is the mirror on which the phenomena are simply reflected. Similarly with the other knots including the differentiation of beings among themselves and from the universal Self. They have originated from time immemorial and recur with unbroken ignorance. The man is not finally redeemed until he has extricated himself from these numberless knots of ignorance.

"The state which is the result of your closing the eyes, cannot be enough, for it is pure intelligence and eternal truth transcending anything else yet serving as the magnificent mirror to reflect the phenomena arising in itself. Prove, if you can, that everything is not contained in it. Whatever you admit as known to you, is in the knowledge conveyed by that consciousness. Even what may be surmised to be in another place and at a different time, is also within your consciousness. Moreover, what is not apparent and unknown to that intelligence is a figment of imagination like the son of a barren woman. There cannot be anything that is not held by consciousness, just as there cannot be reflection without a reflecting surface.

"Therefore I tell you that your conviction: 'I shall lose it by opening my eyes' or 'I know it,' is the knot awaiting to be cut, and there will be no attainment though, remember, it cannot be the perfect state if it can be attained. What you consider the happy state as accomplished by the movements of your eyelids, cannot indeed be perfect because it is certainly intermittent and not unconditional. Is any place found where the effulgence is not, my lord, of the fire blazing at the dissolution of the universe? All will resolve into that fire and no residue will be left. Similarly also the fire of realisation will burn away all your sense of duty so that there will be nothing left for you to do. Be strong, root out your thoughts and cut off the deep-rooted knots from your heart, namely, 'I will see', 'I am not this', 'This is non-Self', and such like.

"Find wherever you turn the one undivided, eternal blissful Self; also watch the whole universe reflected as it arises and subsides in the Self. See the Self both within and without you; yet do not confound the seeing Self within as the Seer of the universal Self without, for both are the same. Inhere in the peace of your true internal Self, devoid of all phenomena."

At the end of her speech, Hemachuda's confusion was cleared up, so that he gradually became well established in the perfect Self bereft of any distinction of within and without. Being always equable, he led a very happy life with Hemalekha and others, reigned over his kingdom and made it prosperous, engaged his enemies in war and conquered them, studied the scriptures and taught them to others, filled his treasury, performed the sacrifices pertaining to royalty and lived eighty-thousand years, emancipated while yet alive (Jivanmukta).

King Janaka to sage Ashtavakra on the infinite pervasiveness of the Soul and by realizing it by withdrawing the mind from objects – Tripura Rahasya

Such is the case with pure consciousness. It is the substratum of all and identical at all times since it is pervaded within us like the reflection of space in a mirror. All that is needed is to withdraw the mind from objects, i.e., free it from identifications. Now, tell me, O Astavakra! where do you not find this illuminator? When and where is it not? It is nowhere and everywhere. One needs to withdraw one's mind from the other in order to experience consciousness as such. There is no need to replace anything new, and that is why it is not recognized in any definite form or shape like that of a concrete object. It becomes knowable by a pure mind and heart being in natural harmony. Purity of mind and heart means nothing except its freedom from the other thoughts and identifications. This is the chief method of realizing the self-essence. How can one attain to right knowledge with an impure mind? And how can the pure mind but help revealing the truth? All other efforts and ways are useless in relation to it. Meritorious deeds, worship, cultivation of detachment and such other means are meant for the purification of mind and heart. That is their value. In brief, Astavakra! purity of mind is the only way to realize the highest."

The Fire of Yoga burns the fetters of ignorance and sin; The greatest form of Yoga is that of one meditating upon oneself as identical with God's Immanent Infinite Being (practiced even by gods - angels) that leads to God-Realization and Perfection in this very life and joys of heaven experienced at the very moment, on earth – Sri Shiva Rahasya

The Lord now makes known to us a Yoga Teaching that is easily understood by all. Therein every Seeker shall find a Path to his heart's desire and as taught by his Spiritual Guide. By means of this Teaching, My devotees see their Self, the Highest Lord, shining like the blazing Sun. The fire of Yoga quickly burns the fetters of ignorance and sins. Perfect Knowledge that leads to Liberation springs from this Yoga even as dawn springs from the Sun.

Verily, Knowledge arises from Yoga and Yoga functions by means of Knowledge. He, the Greatest God, is Delighted when one is devoted to both Yoga and Knowledge. Those who practise the Great Yoga of the Greatest God, either once, twice, three times a day or even constantly, are themselves to be known as Great Beings Divine.

First, let it be understood that Yoga is of three kinds. The first is called Bhava Yoga (the Yoga of Being), the second, Abhava Yoga (the Yoga of Non-Being) and the third, Maha Yoga (the Greatest Yoga), it being the greatest among all.

The Yoga whereby one's own inner Self is meditated upon as a living Soul in the midst of mind, body and worldly possessions is spoken of as Bhava Yoga (the Yoga of Being). It leads to the realisation of one's own individual Self, unencumbered by mental delusions. Being the Yoga of Phenomenal Existence, it should be practised by those who are attached to worldly life and who wish to remain in the World in this life and the next.

The Yoga, whereby one visualises oneself as infinite, eternally blissful and beyond the Physical World, is known as Abhava Yoga (the Yoga of Non-Being). It leads to the realisation of My Divine Transcendental Self and is higher than the former. Therein all manifested things are absorbed in the Original Source Whence everything comes and Whereto everything does return, even as thoughts come to rest in the emptiness of deep sleep and waves subside in the silence of the Ocean deep. It should be practised only by those who wish to leave the World behind and merge for ever in the Formless Being.

The Yoga, however, wherein one meditates upon oneself as identical at once with the Lord's own Transcendental and Immanent Being, that is regarded as the highest Yoga leading to true God-Realisation. It is called Maha Yoga because it is the Yoga of the Great Life (Maha Satta).

The Great Life is Greater than both Being and Non-Being. It is the Supreme Being (Para Bhava or Para Satta) Itself. It is Higher than, and at the same time contains within Itself, all other forms of being. Therefore the Yoga that leads Thereto is known as Maha Yoga (Greatest Yoga) and Arya Yoga (Higher Yoga). It is also called Shiva Yoga (the Yoga of Shiva) as it leads to Identity with Shiva Who is both God and the World in One. It is called in three ways because it is Three Times the Greatest among all.

This Greatest of all Yogas shall be practised by all who wish to attain Perfection in this very life. Verily, this Yoga is practised even by the Gods. For, thereby one obtains the Joys of Heaven even now.

Those Paths of Yoga one sees being followed by others or one hears about in other Teachings, are not worth as much as one-sixteenth of this Divine Yoga. The Yoga whereby Enlightened Souls directly experience everything as One with God, that Yoga alone shall be known as the greatest of all Yogas. Those who follow it, see God in each other and at the end of their earthly life go to the Supreme Abode.

But those followers of the Yogic Way (that is, of Bhava Yoga), who, even though they have brought their mind under control still consider themselves to be separate or different from the Lord, shall not perceive the Lord as One without a Second.

Thus I, the Lord, declare. pervaded by Me, it exists in Me and I alone am its Ruler.

Perfection not attained in One Life-Time; World is ruled by Radiant-Ones who are Rays of God's Own Light; Yoga is living in Unity with Truth, the Person knows neither grief nor pain; Yogis who have attained Perfection are the Jewels of God's Creation who sit in the Assembly of Holy Sages; The Yogis task is to reveal God's Will to the world;

The Land where Yogis are Honored shall be known as the Land of Righteousness (dharmabhumi) – Sri Shiva Rahasya

The Lord grants many lives to a Soul that he may steadily grow in wisdom and become wise. For, no creature that is born imperfect attains Perfection in one lifetime. To expect man to become Perfect after ne brief life would be unjust and unwise. For the Lord is Ever Just and All-Wise, and so is His Work.

In the Beginning, He created the Upper World, the World of Light wherein abide all Beings Bright. He is the Eternal Ruler of that World. He then created the Lower World wherein abide the dwellers upon Earth. That World is ruled by the Radiant Ones who are the Rays of His Own Light and who rule over the World by the Power of Yoga and in accord with His Command.

Yoga is living in Unity with Truth. He who abides in Unity with Truth shall know neither fear nor grief; nor pain, nor yet disappointment shall he know but he shall ever rejoice in Heavenly Bliss. And rejoicing Therein he shall bring Joy unto the World even as the Sun brings joy to the flowers in the field.

Verily, the Yogis who have attained Perfection and have risen above earthly life are equal to the Gods. They are the Jewels of the Lord's Creation and rule the World together with the Gods.

The Yogis' task is to make God's Will known unto the World. They shall ever work for the establishment of Righteousness on Earth. They shall live a holy life and ever be an example of Divine Perfection unto all men. They shall sit in the Assembly of Holy Sages and be a guiding light unto the King. For they are the Lord's Messengers and He is their True Sovereign. This was ordained by the Lord for the welfare of all. He is Compassionate and All-Wise.

That land shall be known as Land of Righteousness (Dharmabhumi) wherein Yogis are honoured by all. For he that honours a Yogi who is ever immersed in Unity with God, he honours none other but God. This is God's Eternal Law.

A Great Man is Ever Desirous to Know Things of the Soul, Whilst others follow their craving for things material; Knowledge is of Three Kinds – Hearsay, Reason and Direct Experience; The Un-awakened Soul shrouded in a Power called Material-Energy (Prakriti), upper part of the dark shroud is the Intellect (buddhi), lower part is the Mind (manas) – Sri Shiva Rahasya

Verily, everything is born of will. As the Soul, so the Lord too, has a Will. Only whereas the Lord Wills out of Plenty, the Soul wills out of lack thereof. Whilst the Lord creates the World, the Soul creates limited things.

It is only when the Soul is impelled by the Lord's Will, that he desires to accomplish great things. Therefore a man of Spirit is known by his will. A great man is ever desirous to know things of the Soul. Whilst the others follow their craving for material things, he seeks for a Higher Truth.

The ones who are most wise know that Knowledge is of three kinds: Lowly, Middling and High. The lowly is that knowledge acquired from others. It is called Tradition (Agama) or Hearsay (Shabda). The middling is knowledge acquired by oneself through reason. Hence, it is called Reason (Anumana). And the highest is knowledge acquired neither from others nor indirectly through reason but in direct experience. Hence it is called Direct Experience (Anubhava). As the Knowledge, so men too are of three kinds: the lowly who never reason but live their life by Tradition or Hearsay; the middling who make use of their Reason; and the highest who wish to know for themselves.

When, impelled by the Lord's Will a Soul wishes to know the Truth, he is instructed into Truth. By the Power of that Truth he lifts himself up to Higher Planes like a bird soaring in the Sky. Having attained to Higher Worlds he becomes Awakened and Wise. Therefore the Lord's Word of Truth that you may attain the Highest!

The Awakened Soul beholds the Glory of Him Who Is One. But the Sleeping Soul sees only the World which is born of his own Power, like a dream. That Power is called Material Energy (Prakarti). Oblivious to the Joys of Heaven and wishing to experience worldly life, the Sleeping Soul descends into the World of Matter. Therein he abides as if enveloped in a dark shroud. The upper part of the shroud is the Intellect or Higher Mind, called Buddhi; the lower part is the Lower Mind, called Manas.

The One who understands the Twenty-Five Life-Principles is a Free and Happy Soul, but He who understands the Greatest Secret of Maya is One with God who Knows the Thirty-Six Principles Knows Everything and All – Sri Shiva Rahasya

The one's who are Tigers amongst men understand that the Lord of His Own Free Will Envelopes Himself in Maya, even as the Sun envelopes himself in Clouds. Like the Sun behind the Clouds the Lord surrounds Himself with the Veil of Maya and hide's Himself from the World.

Divested of His Light, the whole World goes to sleep. Having put the Souls to sleep, the Lord Ever Awake, enchants them all with His Great Dream. Verily, there is no greater Work of Magic than the World wherein all Souls dream.

No Soul shall ever rouse from the Great Sleep of Maya save by the Lord's Divine Command. But by Word of Truth shall work in those who hear It and they shall stir in their sleep. The chosen ones shall be ready for the Lord's Call. And hearing the Sound of Awakening they shall rise from their sleep like deer at the call of a great stag.

The one's who are the Jewels of the World who understand that the Twenty-Five Life-Principles from Soul down to Earth, perceives himself as a free and happy Soul. But he who understands the Great Secret of Maya, he is a Knower of all Thirty-Six Principles and is One with the Great God.

The Five Material Qualities, Five Primary Perceptions, Five Powers of Knowledge and Five of Action; Lower Mind, Ego, Intelligence, Material Energy and the Soul above these: they are the Twenty-Five. He who knows this is a Wise Soul indeed. But he who knows Maya and what lies beyond, is Three Times Wise. For he knows the Five Fetters, Maya which is their Support, and the Five Powers Divine. Verily, such a one knows the Secret of the Thirty-Six which Is the Greatest Secret of all. There is naught to be known beside the Thirty-Six. He who knows these, knows everything and all.

Everyone is a Spark of Heaven; The Thirty-Six Principles are to be Ascended gradually, the Knower knows the Secret of All Numbers and Everything; Liberating himself from bondage of the Mind by means of

Yoga, he turns from finite to Infinite, from speck of stardust to Sea of Divine Radiance, from Man-God to God–Man; Yoga is therefore to be known as the Expansion of the human soul to Cosmic Dimensions; Man is born to strive for Perfection, that One is the Seeker of Truth, he who seeks Truth seeks his True Home, Home is where man finds Peace, Peace is found in Perfection, man's life is quest for Peace – Sri Shiva Rahasya

Even ordinary men can know God deep inside themselves, in their heart of hearts. For every one of them is a Spark of Heaven, a Ray of Divine Sunlight and a Dewdrop of Universal Intelligence.

Yet this Divine State cannot be reached at once, save in extra-ordinary cases. It is to be attained gradually, ascending the well-trodden Steps of the Thirty-Six Yogic Principles, guided by the Light of the Right Means of Knowledge and adding one Ray of Light after another to one's Royal Crown of Sunlight. And finally, United with the Lord, being seated upon the Effulgent Throne of Heaven.

He who knows the Thirty-Six knows the secrets of all numbers and of everything that is. Nothing is unknown to him. By means of this Secret Knowledge the Bound Soul shall awaken to his own Divinity. He shall cast off his limitations imposed upon him by the Lord for the purpose of Limited Creation.

Liberating himself from the bondage of the Mind by means of Yoga, he shall enter upon the Great Journey from finite to Infinite, from speck of stardust to Sea of Divine Radiance. From Man-God to God-Man. From Individual to Universal. Yoga, therefore, is to be known as the Expansion of the limited human Soul to Cosmic Dimensions.

By the Power of Yoga, man attains Identity with the Lord. Having attained Identity with the Lord, he becomes the Lord of Yoga, which is the Power that holds all things together and by means whereof one can know and accomplish all things. Yoga is the Union of things that stand opposed and the Power whereby two things that were divided become one again. which is a mere shadow of the True Light. and uplift the mind of men and set it upon the Path of Truth that leads to the Highest Greatness of all. It is by means of great things that man rises above other creatures.

Therefore, having perceived My Supreme Perfection in those things that outshine all other things, man shall strive to become Perfect even as God Himself is The Most Perfect. Verily, man is born to strive for Perfection. For he that seeks Perfection is a Seeker of Truth.

All things are born of Truth and shall return to Truth. He who seeks Truth seeks his True Home. No Soul shall ever find peace till he has found his True Home. Home is that Place where a man finds Peace. Therefore the life of man is a quest for Peace. And Peace is found in Perfection, there is no Peace where there is no Perfection.

It is through the Power of Unity that man is united with the body, through the Power of Unity, Enlightened Man is united with the Awakened Soul; Through The Power of Unity, all conflicts are ended and Peace is established in the World, the Power that brings a thousand things together and preserves the life of everything; By the Power of Yoga Peace is restored to a troubled mind, by the Power of Yoga man is united with the Lord, by the Power of Yoga the brotherhood of man and Unity of Life are preserved; By the Power of Yoga God's Kingdom is Established on Earth, There is nothing that cannot be achieved by the Power of Yoga – Sri Shiva Rahasya

It is by the Power of Unity that in waking, man is united with the body and the physical World. It is by the Power of Unity that in dreams, man is united with his mind. It is by the Power of Unity that in deep sleep, man is united with his sleeping Soul. It is by the Power of Unity that in Enlightenment, man is united with his Awakened Self.

It is by the Power of Unity that the Lord is United with Creation and man is united with the object of his heart's desire. It is by the Power of Unity that all conflicts are ended and Peace is established in the World. That Power which does make a thing whole, lasting and complete; which brings two, ten, or a thousand things together; and which preserves the life of everything: That is the Power of Unity. That selfsame Power is Yoga. For, Yoga is Unity and Unity is Yoga.

By the Power of Yoga, peace is restored to a troubled mind. By the Power of Yoga, thoughts are concentrated in meditation and consciousness is unified in the deep absorption of the Self. By the Power of Yoga, man is united with the Lord. By the Power of Yoga, the Brotherhood of Man and the Unity of Life are preserved. By the Power of Yoga, God's Kingdom is established upon Earth. By the Power of Yoga, this Teaching is imparted unto those who desire to hear the Truth. By the Power of Yoga, Untruth shall be vanquished and Truth shall prevail in the World. There is nothing that cannot be achieved by the Power of Yoga.

Verily One World Only exists. Its uppermost region is called Heaven, whilst the nethermost part is called Hell. Heaven is the Realm of Pure Unity with the Divine. Hell is where dis-Unity prevails. For Sin and dis-Unity are one and the same. Earth is where both Unity and dis-Unity, Virtue and Sin are found together. The heavenward Path, that which leads upwards, is the Path to the Divine. The downward Path leads down into Hell.

Those who choose Heaven go up to God's Abode of Unity. But those who choose dis-Unity, sink into Hell which is the Abode of Discord. The Accomplished Yogis, who are Masters of Unity, live both in Heaven and on Earth. They are free to roam the Universe at will like unto birds sailing over the Wide Sky. At the Lord's Behest, they spread abroad God's Word of Unity to all quarters of the World.

Those who believe in Truth should follow the Supreme Eternal Law, which the Lord teaches and proclaims for the benefit of all. By the following thereof, one goes the upward Path which is the Path of Unity with Truth and Freedom, chosen by the righteous ones. Follow the Path of Unity. For Unity is Life and dis-Unity is Death. Unity and the One (Supreme Being) are One and the Same. Of Unity you were born, in Unity you live and to Unity you shall return.

Whether in joy or in sorrow, in war or in peace, in victory or in defeat; whether in Life or in Death, in this World or in the next, the Lord's devotee should always strive to establish Unity with Him. For Sin and Separation are one and the same. He who goes the way of Separation goes the way of Sin. But he who goes the way of Unity shall be United with the Lord. The struggle for Unity (Yoga Samgharsha, also Dharma-Yuddha) is the Struggle for the Attainment of the One. This is man's first and last duty and My Supreme Command.

The Three States – The Waking, Dreaming And Dreamless are known to All, the Fourth state – 'Turiya' is known by the Yogi, the Fifth is known only by the All Knowing One; The One who Realizes the Fourth State is an Awakened One, a Buddha; But he who conquers Sleep is a Great Yogi and a Well-Awakened (Prabuddha). He is a Great Hero (Maha Vira) and a Vanquisher of Death – Sri Shiva Rahasya

The Waking-state is known to one and all and the Yogi knows Three, but there is a Fifth-state known only by the All Knowing One, the One who has attained Divine-Wisdom known as 'Para Vidya'.

In the (wrongly presumed)Waking-state the Soul perceives the outer things of the world and hence gets ensnared in the mesh of feelings and thoughts that arise, for though the Soul is awake to the world of objects, he is asleep to himself.

In the Dreaming-state the Soul perceives not the outer world but is absorbed in mind-created dreams and hence the Soul is awake to the world of dreams but is asleep to both himself and the outer world.

In the Sleeping-state the Soul neither perceives the objects of the outer world nor the inner world of dreams, nor himself as a Conscious Soul and so being unaware abides in a state of deep and blissful slumber.

In the Fourth state of Awakeing the Soul is awake to himself as a Radiant Being of Living Light who is endowed with great Wisdom and Might, who is freed from the delusions of the inner World of mind, and freed also from the dark torpor of Sleep. The Soul is Awake to himself and to the Abode of Spirit wherefrom all Souls come and unto which they all return.

In the first Four States the Soul abides in the various stages of life. But that State wherein the Soul, having overcome the Worlds of Matter, Mind and Sleep awakens to the World of Spirit; and having awakened to the World of Spirit beholds the Effulgent Lord of Life face to face and is lost in his Master's Infinite Embrace, that, is the State beyond all states. Therein Life lives in everlasting Oneness, Peace and Bliss.

What is waking in the World of men is sleep in that of the Awakened Ones (Buddhas). And what is like unto sleep to men is waking to those who are Awake. Therefore, so long as the Yogi abides in that State called Waking by men, he shall be an Unawakened (Abuddha). And when the

Yogi pierces the veil of Dreams and becomes aware of himself, then he is an Awakened One (Buddha). But he who conquers Sleep is a Great Yogi and a Well-Awakened (Prabuddha). He is a Great Hero (Maha Vira) and a Vanquisher of Death. Verily, he who conquers Sleep, conquers Death too. For what is Death but a kind of sleep? He who has conquered Death is a Fully Awakened One (Suprabuddha), a Perfect Being (Siddha Purusha) and an Immortal. He attains the Fourth State wherefrom he beholds the other three known to mortal man. But the Yogi who rises up to the Highest State is the best of all. For, in that Supreme State he is One with the Ever Awake (Sada-Buddha) and for ever watches over all states. He is the Original Waking One (Adi Buddha), the Lord of all Yogis (Yogendra) and the Greatest God (Mahadeva) Himself.

The Awakened Yogi knows that when Earth has dissolved in Water, when Water has been consumed in Fire, when Fire has been quenched in Wind, when Wind has merged into the Sky and the Sky becomes one with the Mind whereby it is perceived, all that remains is the Light of Consciousness Which has created all this out of Itself and illumines everything by Its Self-Effulgent Light. For him who knows this Secret, the World becomes the Abode of Bliss. In the Fire of his Higher Knowledge, the World dissolves in Consciousness which is Pure Intelligence and Bliss.

He who knows this, returns to the One of Whom he was originally born and becomes One with Him. Having become One with Truth, he goes beyond earthly life, beyond Karma, beyond Death. He attains Immeasurable Wisdom, Unsurpassed Perfection and Endless Peace. Such a one indeed is a Free and Perfect One.

He is free from imperfections, free from doubt, free from sorrow, free from sin. He illumines everything wherever he goes, like the Radiant Sun on his Heavenly Path. He shines like the King of Kings and is a true Ruler of the World.

He becomes an Enlightener of the unenlightened and a Vessel for crossing the Ocean of Suffering. He becomes the All-Supporting Lord of Light and One with the Supreme. Having attained the Highest Goal, he empowers others to attain the Same. He bestows all kinds of boons like the very Wish-Fulfilling Tree of Heaven.

The existence of no other Reality save the Supreme Consciousness of Shiva is the Holy Truth of Yoga. Of this Exalted Truth (Arya Satya) all other Truths are born. First, since Consciousness Alone exists, it follows that all created things, those that breathe and those that breathe not, are the creation of the Supreme Consciousness, the Unique, Self-Existing, Uncreated One.

Second, being born of Shiva, man is essentially identical with That. As a spark of fire is identical with Fire, a ray of sunlight with the Sun and a raindrop with the Sea, so man is identical with the Supreme All-Consciousness (Parasamvid), the Mind of the Great One God (Mahadeva).

Third, the Goal of life O Enlightener of the unenlightened! do grant us the delight of learning about Your Supreme Glory Divine, O Highest One!

Hearing their words the Lord, Who Bestows all kinds of wondrous powers upon Yogis who are adepts of Unity with Him, gazed with great compassion upon them and rising from His royal seat, led them deep into the Mountain through a cleft that lay hidden in the wall of rock.

Going by a secret path, they came to a Great Vault that arched overhead like the Sky wherein they were befittingly received and saluted by the Assembly of Holy Immortals and the Lord Himself showed them the Wonders of the Higher Worlds.

First He showed them the World of the Planets, the Earth, Moon, Sun and countless myriads of Stars, where mortal men live their daily lives. Next they were taken by the Lord up to the Astral World where disembodied Souls go in their dreams; whereto they go when this life comes to an end; and where they abide before they are reborn on Earth. In that World also there lived the First Woman and Man before they descended into the earthly World and there too the Souls meet their departed forefathers. It is therefore also known as the Ancestors' World (Pitar Loka) to the wise.

Thence the Sages proceeded to the World of Sleep (Nidra Loka) which is the Dark Void whereto Souls go when in their deepest rest; where they abide before descending to the Lower Worlds (Astral- and Earth-World); and through which they pass when by the Grace of Shiva (Shiva Prasada) they go up to the Higher Worlds. Having thus left behind the World of Sleeping Souls, they ascended to the Threefold World of Power where the Awakened Ones by the Command of Shiva work many a righteous deed: Souls who have attained the Plane of Pure Vision, work by the Divine Power of Action; those who have attained the Plane of Higher Vision work by the Divine Power of Knowledge; and those who have attained the Plane of Perfect Vision work by the Divine Power of Will. Thus they all carry out Shiva's Will, each according to his Spiritual Attainment.

Last, the Sages entered the Highest World of all: the Infinite, Ever-Existing World of Supreme Intelligence and Bliss which is the True Abode of Shiva, wherein Souls ever abide in Eternal Unity with Him. Having graciously granted them a Vision of the Seven Worlds, the Lord made the Sign of Ultimate Reality and spoke: O you who are endowed with Wisdom! all the Worlds and their great wonders you have just beheld have their existence within Me. They arise, endure and subside like unto waves within Me, the Great Only-Existing Ocean of Life. They who know this, know the Highest Truth.

man life is to realise this Unity and Identity, called Yoga by the Wise. For Unity is the essence of Life: Life without Unity would be just Chaos and the Universe would fall apart. Nor can any man live in disunity with God.

And Fourth, Unity is to be realised through the Practice of Yoga and by the Grace of one's Spiritual Master, human or Divine. For nothing is achieved without practice nor is any goal in life attainable without a guide. This is the Fourfold Truth of Yoga by means whereof man goes to The Supreme Abode.

The Lord leads the holy Sages through a secret cleft in the walls of the mighty mount Kailash in the Himalayas and shows them various worlds (in various planes and other dimensions) and their beings and ultimately the Ultimate Heaven – Sri Shiva Rahasya:

O Enlightener of the unenlightened!do grant us the delight of learning about Your Supreme Glory Divine, O Highest One!

Hearing their words the Lord, Who Bestows all kinds of wondrous powers upon Yogis who are adepts of Unity with Him, gazed with great compassion upon them and rising from His royal seat, led them deep into the Mountain through a cleft that lay hidden in the wall of rock.

Going by a secret path, they came to a Great Vault that arched overhead like the Sky wherein they were befittingly received and saluted by the Assembly of Holy Immortals and the Lord Himself showed them the Wonders of the Higher Worlds.

First He showed them the World of the Planets, the Earth, Moon, Sun and countless myriads of Stars, where mortal men live their daily lives. Next they were taken by the Lord up to the Astral World where disembodied Souls go in their dreams; whereto they go when this life comes to an end; and where they abide before they are reborn on Earth. In that World also there lived the First Woman and Man before they descended into the earthly World and there too the Souls meet their departed forefathers. It is therefore also known as the Ancestors' World (Pitar Loka) to the wise.

Thence the Sages proceeded to the World of Sleep (Nidra Loka) which is the Dark Void whereto Souls go when in their deepest rest; where they abide before descending to the Lower Worlds (Astral- and Earth-World); and through which they pass when by the Grace of Shiva (Shiva Prasada) they go up to the Higher Worlds. Having thus left behind the World of Sleeping Souls, they ascended to the Threefold World of Power where the Awakened Ones by the Command of Shiva work many a righteous deed: Souls who have attained the Plane of Pure Vision, work by the Divine Power of Action; those who have attained the Plane of Higher Vision work by the Divine Power of Knowledge; and those who have attained the Plane of Perfect Vision work by the Divine Power of Will. Thus they all carry out Shiva's Will, each according to his Spiritual Attainment.

Last, the Sages entered the Highest World of all: the Infinite, Ever-Existing World of Supreme Intelligence and Bliss which is the True Abode of Shiva, wherein Souls ever abide in Eternal Unity with Him. Having graciously granted them a Vision of the Seven Worlds, the Lord made the Sign of Ultimate Reality and spoke: O you who are endowed with Wisdom! all the Worlds and their great wonders you have just beheld have their existence within Me. They arise, endure and subside like unto waves within Me, the Great Only-Existing Ocean of Life. They who know this, know the Highest Truth.

The greatest Yoga according to the Lord Himself is when one meditates with the 'bhava' – feel and belief that he and the Transcendental Immanent Lord are One – Sri Shiva Rahasya

I shall now make known to you a Yoga Teaching that is easily understood by all. Therein every Seeker shall find a Path to his heart's desire and as taught by his Spiritual Guide. By means of this Teaching, My devotees see their Self, the Highest Lord, shining like the blazing Sun. The fire of Yoga quickly burns the fetters of ignorance and sins. Perfect Knowledge that leads to Liberation springs from this Yoga even as dawn springs from the Sun.

Verily, Knowledge arises from Yoga and Yoga functions by means of Knowledge. I, the Greatest God, am Delighted when one is devoted to both Yoga and Knowledge. Those who practise the Great Yoga of the Greatest God, either once, twice, three times a day or even constantly, are themselves to be known as Great Beings Divine.

First, let it be understood that Yoga is of three kinds. The first is called Bhava Yoga (the Yoga of Being), the second, Abhava Yoga (the Yoga of Non-Being) and the third, Maha Yoga (the Greatest Yoga), it being the greatest among all.

The Yoga whereby one's own inner Self is meditated upon as a living Soul in the midst of mind, body and worldly possessions is spoken of as Bhava Yoga (the Yoga of Being). It leads to the realisation of one's own individual Self, unencumbered by mental delusions. Being the Yoga of Phenomenal Existence, it should be practised by those who are attached to worldly life and who wish to remain in the World in this life and the next.

The Yoga, whereby one visualises oneself as infinite, eternally blissful and beyond the Physical World, is known as Abhava Yoga (the Yoga of Non-Being). It leads to the realisation of My Divine Transcendental Self and is higher than the former. Therein all manifested things are absorbed in the Original Source Whence everything comes and Whereto everything does return, even as thoughts come to rest in the emptiness of deep sleep and waves subside in the silence of the Ocean deep. It should be practised only by those who wish to leave the World behind and merge for ever in the Formless Being.

The Yoga, however, wherein one meditates upon oneself as identical at once with My Transcendental and Immanent Being, that I regard as the highest Yoga leading to true God-Realisation. It is called Maha Yoga because it is the Yoga of the Great Life (Maha Satta).

The Great Life is Greater than both Being and Non-Being. It is the Supreme Being (Para Bhava or Para Satta) Itself. It is Higher than, and at the same time contains within Itself, all other forms of being. Therefore the Yoga that leads Thereto is known as Maha Yoga (Greatest Yoga) and Arya

Yoga (Higher Yoga). It is also called Shiva Yoga (the Yoga of Shiva) as it leads to Identity with Shiva Who is both God and the World in One. It is called in three ways because it is Three Times the Greatest among all.

This Greatest of all Yogas shall be practised by all who wish to attain Perfection in this very life. Verily, this Yoga is practised even by the Gods. For, thereby one obtains the Joys of Heaven even now.

Those Paths of Yoga one sees being followed by others or one hears about in other Teachings, are not worth as much as one-sixteenth of this Divine Yoga. The Yoga whereby Enlightened Souls directly experience everything as One with God, that Yoga alone shall be known as the greatest of all Yogas. Those who follow it, see God in each other and at the end of their earthly life go to the Supreme Abode.

But those followers of the Yogic Way (that is, of Bhava Yoga), who, even though they have brought their mind under control still consider themselves to be separate or different from the Lord, shall not perceive Me as One without a Second. Thus I, the Lord, declare. pervaded by Me, it exists in Me and I alone am its Ruler.

The Four Goals of Life and Supreme Perfection attained in the present life for he is born of Divine Perfection – Sir Shiva Rahasya:

He who wishes to obtain the Four Goals of Life: Righteousness, Material Prosperity, Love, Spiritual Liberation) and attain Perfection in this very life shall always follow My Law. He that earnestly follows My Law is a Yogi and a True Man. He lives in Unity with Me, with the World, and with his true self. He indeed is a blessed one! Verily, there is nothing that a follower of Unity cannot obtain. This is My Eternal Law.

Supreme Perfection is attained by abiding in Unity with Truth, Goodness and Beauty. Truth is That Which is Good, Which is Above all other things and Which Ever Is. Goodness is the Constant Abiding in Truth. Beauty is the Recognition of Truth and Goodness in all things that are good.

When the Great Life, the Great Lord, Perceives Himself and nothing else beside, that, O Sages! is the Supreme Truth. When God Establishes His Law, that is the Supreme Goodness. When He Beholds Himself in all things, that is the Supreme Beauty.

Therefore, O noble ones! let man also seek Truth, do Good, and love Beauty. By discarding all things that are false, perishable and wrong, man shall attain to Truth. By striving to establish My Law (Dharma Shasana) upon Earth, man shall do works that are Good. By seeing My Glory in all things that are both true and good, man shall see the Beauty of Him Who Is the One True and Truly Good.

Man is born of My divine Perfection and unto Perfection he shall return. This is the Eternal Law. Perfection is attained by the following of My Law. He who ever strives to be Perfect is a Yogi and a True Man. Him I shall elevate above all other men and to him I shall grant entrance into My Abode of Truth.

O you who are Rays of My Own Light! My Word of Truth shall not be doubted. For he that follows It is rightly guided. But he that follows It not, goes astray. Verily, no one can find the right path (satpatha) save he who is guided by the Guiding Light. I, the Lord, am that Eternal Light.

Those who attain perfection know the greatest Joy of all; Only the one who goes with Unity with the Lord transcends the veil of Maya, he alone is a man of Unity – an Yogi, a Perfect One – a Siddha – Sri Shiva Rahasya

O you who are ever wise! man's fate is determined by his Karma. Karma brings two Souls together or asunder; it brings health, fame and possessions and also takes them away. Good Karma depends on good deeds (satkarma). But whether man abides in darkness or rises up to the Abode of the Great Light, that depends upon naught but My Own Will. Therefore, the Soul attains Perfection at the appointed time and not a moment before. When, having received My Revelation, man is moved to follow My Law and enters upon the Righteous Path of Unity, then the Great Goal is not far. It is through Unity with Me that Perfection is attained. Only he that abides in Unity with Me, goes beyond the Veil of Maya. For he alone is a Man of Unity (Yogi) and a Perfect One (Siddha). The joys of the mind are greater by far than those of the body, and the joys of the Soul are greater than those of the mind. But he who attains Perfection knows the Highest Joy of all. The Pure Ones who through righteous deeds and a pure heart deserve to be lifted up beyond Maya, go to the World of Pure Vision wherein dwell all Souls who do good works (satkarma) for the benefit of all. Being endowed with clear sight, they see the World as it really is and no longer hanker after bodily joys. They have also conquered the cravings of the Mind. Their only craving is to act in Unity with the Lord.

Microbes *converse* with human cells according to microbiologists;"*they function like our mother.... We should love them... we are in equilibrium.*":

Dr.Abigail (microbiologist at the University of Illinois also an expert on human-microbial interactions) in an interview with the 'New York Times':" Microbes and man must live in peace together, that is how we are living. We live a peaceful life, we co-exist and co-evolute, we are in equilibrium. They live because of us. We live because of them. We should love and care for them. They function like our mothers, they clean and get rid of all our wastes."

Microbes of innumerable species live on and inside man. There are more than 50 trillion cells in the body, but there are more than a hundred times more microbes than cells inside a human body.

Researchers have now eavesdropped on the bio-chemical conversations between an organism that lives in the human-gut and the cells that line the colon, says Dr.Jeffrey Gordon, microbiologist at Washington University in St.Louis.

Microbes help to protect the body from diseases, keep the body healthy, help digest the food and provide energy. When food is scarce, microbes help in extracting ten percent *more* energy from the same amount of food.

Dr.Floyd Dewhirst (molecular biologist at the Forsythe Dental Centre, Boston)

:" There are more than six hundred varieties of microbes in man's mouth and their numbers are more than the total human population on earth. Among the six hundred varieties of microbes present, the function of only three hundred has been derived at. It is yet to be determined on the ways to make them function in a more efficient manner, yet it has been found that diet and stress might play a role."

Various States of the Mind: *"The Saiva Siddhanta Philosophy of the Tamils is the most elaborate, influential and undoubtedly the most valuable of all religions..."* - **Rev.G.U.Pope of Oxford University; Modern Science; Saiva Siddhanta Philosophy:**

Apart from when we are awake, this is what happens when we go to sleep, according to modern science: All night a person drifts down and up through different levels of consciousness, as on waves. With EEG machines and other sensors that record body temperature, pulse respiration etc., researchers have charted the stages of the long night's journey. As one is on the verge of going to sleep, the brain waves which had been low, rapid and irregular, shows a new pattern: the alpha rhythm, an even rhythm of about 9 to 12 cycles per second. This is a state of serene relaxation, devoid of concentrated thought.

The alpha waves grow smaller as the subject passes through the gates of the unconscious. The person might be awakened suddenly by a moment of a sudden spasm that causes the body to jerk. This is known as the 'myoclonic jerk' which is caused by a tiny burst of activity in the brain. It is related to the epileptic seizure, yet is normal in all human sleep. It goes in a fraction of a second, descent continues as soon as the subject is truly asleep.

Here in stage I, the pattern of the sleeper's brain waves is small and pinched, irregular and rapidly changing. The sleeper may be enjoying a floating sensation or drifting with idle thoughts and dreams. His muscles are relaxing, his heart-rate is slowing down. He awakens easily, and might insist he had not been asleep.

After a few minutes the sleeper descends to another level, stage II. Now his brain waves trace out quick bur ts – a rapid crescendo and de-crescendo, resembling a wire spindle and un-mistakable on the EEG chart; the eyes roll slowly from side to side, but if the experimenter gently opens a lid, the sleeper will not see. Still the sleeper descends – to stage III. It is characterized by large slow waves that occur about once a second. The sleeper's muscles are very relaxed and he breathes evenly. His heart rate slows. His temperature is declining. His blood pressure drops.

Some 20 or 30 minutes after he first falls asleep, the sleeper reached stage IV, the deepest level. It is marked by large, slow brain waves, called delta waves, that traces a pattern resembling jagged buttes. Stage IV is a relatively dreamless oblivion. The breathing is even, heart-rate, blood pressure and body temperature slowly falling.

But after 20 minutes or so in the depths, the sleeper begins to drift back from stage IV through lighter levels. By the time he has been asleep for about 90 minutes, he will show brain waves of the lightest sleep, even resembling those of waking. Still the sleeper is not easy to awaken, lying limply, his eyes moving jerkily under closed lids as if watching something. He is in a very special variety of stage I, known as REM (for "rapid eye movement") sleep. If awakened now he could almost remember dreaming, probably in vivid detail.\

After perhaps ten minutes in the REM state, the sleeper will probably turn over in bed and begin shifting down the levels of sleep again to the depths, to return in another hour or so fpr a longer REM dream. Each night the entire cycle is repeated about four or five times.

While the entire world is under the impression that sleep, dreams and death are different states of the physical body, it is asserted by the Saiva Siddhanta Philosophy of the Tamils as acknowledged by G.U.Pope that dreams are experiences of an independent body with 14 subtle organs called 'tattvas'.

The philosophy gives details of the various experiences of the Soul which when in the woken-state predominantly fixes its centre of activity in between the eyebrows (known as the third-eye centre and the 'Ajna chakra') for all organic activities called the 'Jagra' state; when the soul lowers its activity to the throat for all activities in the dream-state known as the 'Swapna' state; when the soul descends further for activity down to the chest-region in the dreamless-state known as 'Sushupthi' state; there are two further stages known only to the Yogi and the 'full-blown' Yogi which is the navel-centre known as the 'Turiya' state and the 'Muladhara' Chakra at the base of the spinal column and inbetween the sexual and excretory organs known as the 'Turiyatita' state. (The Turiya and Turiyatita states are also realized when the soul ascends above the forehead and the cranium).

Thirumoolar the Tamil Siddhar in his Thirumandiram which in more than 3000 songs contains the deepest and mystical secrets of Yoga and the Vedas on the various states; song 2142:

"In the waking state (jagra) twenty five are the tattvass
That take their position in the eyebrow-centre;
In the dream-state (swapna) fourteen are the tattvas
That take hold in the throat-centre;
In deep-sleep state (sushupthi) the purusha (soul)
Stands alone in the heart-centre;
In the turiya-state, He (purusha) stands
In the navel-centre."

When the Soul stands bound by desires to the human body it is known as 'Purudan' or 'Purushan'; when it stands bound to the 'Nadha-Vindhu' (Nada-Bindu in Sanskrit) which are the "Eternal Sound-Light Continuum" or Sound-Light Pulses/Vibrations, it is known as 'Jiva'; when it stands by itself it is known as 'Anma' or 'Atma'. State beyond Turiya-state is Turiyatita; Thirumandiram 2159

"Turiya is in jagra experienced;
The foxes fourteen (indriyas etc.,) of themselves die;
The swift steed of Prana flees,
How that state beyond turiya (turiyatita) is
Impossible to state, indeed."

In the turiya state, the fourteen cunning foxes (five motor-ogans, five sense-organs, four parts of the mind) function no more. But the Prana (the dynamic sum of all forces the outer manifestation of which is the breath) which is faster than the steed and helps one to experience and activate those motor and sense organs is therefore functioning, so one is able to claim that he or she have had a good sleep. But when one descends or ascends even further, even prana-activity (breathing and passage of prana in the various nadis or gross and subtle-nerves) stops, so one is unable to recollect and explain that state which is none other than the 'turiyatita' state. The five states in pure Tamil are known as 'nanavu'(woken-state),'kanavu'(dream state),'urakkam' (sleep state),'perurakkam'(deep sleep-state),'uierpadangal'(soul or superconsciousness alone exists).

The Saiva Siddhanta philosophy and Vedanta alone say that the human mind is just a device, being one among the 36 tattvas (principle ingredients) that construct the human body. The mind is further divided into four sub-divisions: mind, intellect, will and ego (manam, chittam, buddhi, ahankaram).

The soul controls everything in the human body, wherever in the body it fixes its centre of activity, the mind is for sure there predominantly. In the evolutionary cycle of man (there are 18 evolutionary-cycles in total like the 'devas'(angels),'asuras'(titans),'rakshasas'(demons) etc.,)only man is able to evolve consciously and by will, by selecting the good and avoiding the bad as he has the capacity of rational thinking and can therefore discriminate.

The human body which is constructed of 36 tattvas which make the subtle and spiritual bodies (man possesses 5 body sheaths: the physical, pranic, mental, scientific and causal) (which do not die) and 60 'tattvihas' which make the physical body (which is perishable), takes birth, dies and takes to birth again in what seem to be endless cycles caused by the good and bad deeds committed by man, the fruits of which are generally known as 'Karma'.

While life exists in the human body, some of the tattvas due to karma (fruits of actions committed in present and past lives) do not function. Due to the non-functioning of certain tattvas and the varying degrees of efficiency of the tattvas only determine the physical and intellectual-level of man, this disparity is known as 'avasta'.

When the soul lowers its activity from the jagra-state where it stands inbetween the eyebrows to the neck-region the swapna-state, the chest-region the sushupthi-state, the navel-region turiya-state and the muladhara at the base of the spine the turiyatita-state, that process is known as the "lower avastas" (Keelavathai in Tamil).

When the soul again rises along with varying number of tattvas from the muladhara, stopping at the aforesaid regions and reaching the eyebrow-centre again, it is known as the "rising avastas" (melalavaithai).

When the soul fixes its activity in the eyebrow-centre and experiences the five states like 'jagra-jagra','jagra-swapna', it is known as "mid jagrat avastha" (mathya-jagraavaithai).

All these states are experienced when the soul is bound by desire to this materialistic world.

In the same manner when the soul renounces the world and binds itself to God, there are five avastas in that state which is known as "Pure avastas"(Ninmalavaithai) and all these avasta differences or variances are generally known in Tamil as 'avaithai bedham'.

Among the final 36 tattvas,25 exist in the woken-state,14 in the swapna or dream-state, one each in sushupti and turiya, and in the turiyatita-state there is absolutely no distinction between subject and object, the merge between the individual soul and the Cosmic Soul is complete; Thirumandiram 2143:

"Of the five tattvas jagra commencing
That to tattvas six and thirty pertain,
The fourth is the luminous turiya;
Passing beyond to turiyatita
The two in one inseparate merge
The jiva himself Siva becoming;
This the order to know,
The Siva that stands in the beginning
Becomes verily end of all experiences."

There are many states which man achieves in his Yogic-quest like,'jiva-jagra','jiva-swapna','jiva-sushupthi','nirmala-jagra','nirmala-swapna','para-sushupthi','guru-jagra','guru-swapna','guru-sushupthi','guru-turiya'. But there are states even higher which could be achieved only through God's Grace, they are,'guru-turiyatita','suddha Siva-jagra','suddha Siva-swapna','suddha Siva-sushupthi','suddha Siva-turiya','suddha Siva-turiyatita'. All these states were achieved by very few saints like 'Jnana Sambandhar' of presumably the 5th century A.D. and 'Ramalinga Swamy' of the 19th century.

These compassionate saints out of love and compassion and empathy brought the dead back to life like Jnanasambhandar brought back to life 'Poombhavai' who was bitten to death by a cobra four years earlier and her ashes were stored in a jar by her father 'Sivanesan Chettiar' and Ramalingam acquired all the Five Acts of God (The Power to Create, Sustain, Annihilate, Veil, Grace enacted by Five Gods: Brahma, Vishnu, Rudra, Maheshwara, Sadasiva) and thus claimed:" You The Most Compassionate-Infinite-Light gave me the Five Acts" (*"Iynthollilhum yennakallhithai Arutperumjyothi"*)

Parallels in all Religions and all Philosophies

Patanjali in his very first among the 195 'Yoga Sutras' defining Yoga:" Yoga is keeping the mind in its un-changed (thoughtless) tranquil-state"(*"yoga chitta vritti nirodhaha"*); Zen saying:" empty your cup" – which in Japanese is known as 'mushin', the greatly sought after state of 'no-mind'; Chuang Tzu the Chinese Taoist sage on fully realized human beings:" *by their stillness become sages, by their movement kings*"; Lao Tzu the 6th century B.C. originator of Taoism, to the question, what makes muddy water clean:" *leave it alone, it will clear by itself*"; Thirumoolar of indefinite age who lived for more than 3000 years, in his Thirumandiram song 2991:

> *"Like muddied water these people's minds are,*
> *Unclear in vision, they see not and say:" this is Lord",*
> *From the heart's lake within, draw a pitcherful,*
> *And keep it stillness apart, when you thus purify it,*
> *You shall become Siva".*

Lord Krishna in the Bhagavad Gita says that the person who achieves perfect mental equilibrium and harmony with nature, conquers the universe; Huai Nan, Taoist philosopher of the 2nd century B.C., explaining how a person becomes one with the tao:" *He who conforms to the course of the tao, following the natural processes of heaven and earth, finds it easy to manage the whole world".*

Karna the Mahabharata war hero of 3rd century B.C. and son of the Sun-god:" *to yield needs more heroism than to win*"; Lao Tzu:" *be bent and you will remain straight, be vacant and you will remain full, be worn and you will remain full*"; Bruce Lee the film-star and martial arts exponent after running away from a knife wielding purse-snatcher:" *winning by losing is the way of the tao*".

Lord Muruga to saint Arunagirinathar:" *sitting quietly doing nothing is the greatest form of pleasure*"; Rinzai Zen, another Zen school on evolving towards satori (enlightenment) which is seen as the actual realization of one's Buddha-nature, body and mind being fused into a harmonious unity which needs no further improvement:" *sitting quietly, doing nothing, spring comes, and the grass grows by itself*"; Thirumandiram 2319:

"*To be actionless is Siva bliss;*
They who are actionless, seek not Siva yoga;
They who are actionless will not in world merge;
Only to them who are actionless
Is the divine message to be."

An ancient India saying:" *One who knows himself knows God*"; Lao Tzu:" *Knowing others is wisdom, knowing yourself is enlightenment.*"

Lord Krishna to Arjuna the great warrior-prince who hesitates to fight with his near and dear-ones on the battlefield:" *do your duty, but do not yearn for the fruits of your labor*"; Chuang Tzu:" *non-action does not mean doing nothing and keeping silent. Let everything be allowed to do what it naturally does, so that its nature will be satisfied.*"

Heraclitus the Greek philosopher compares the world-order to, "*an ever-living fire, kindling in measures and going out in measures*"; similar Chinese idea of the tao manifesting itelf in the cyclic interplay of yin and yang. The balance of yin (female and receptive) and yang (male and creative) determines everything including the human body where distruption in the balance causes illness"; Vedanta and Siddhanta philosophies:" The sun (female, right nostril breath – pinkala) and moon (male, left nostril breath – idakala) exist in the microcosm (human body) just as it exists in the macrocosm (the universe), its balance determines the rate of metabolism, sexual-activity, physical and mental fitness."

Zen Master Po Chang on being asked about seeking for the Buddha-nature (which is Perfection, our original nature, the realization of the process of enlightenment merely becoming what we are from the beginning):" *it is much like riding an ox in search of the ox*"; Sama Veda:" *Tat tvam asi*" (*That thou art*); Thirumandiram:" *Jiva and Siva are One*"; Jesus Christ in the Holy Bible, Matt 5,48:" *be ye perfect therefore as your heavenly Father is perfect*"; Jesus again in John,10,30:" *I and the Father are one*".

The Sufi mystic Moulana Jalaluddin Rumi:" *If you conquer your heart, it would be like performing a great haj; one pious pulsating-heart is better than a thousand Kaabas*"; Thirumandiram 2550:

> "*He who is in the body-complex,*
> *He who rules the body-land,*
> *He who within the body beams,*
> *He the Nandi, Him they seek in lands all;*
> *They know not, He within the body stands.*"

Kabir:" *Make your mind the Kaaba, your body its enclosure, and your conscience the teacher, O mullah, then only call people for prayer in the mosques that has ten gates*"; Thirumandiram 2035:

> "*If the five senses you sublimate,*
> *Then all worlds are yours;*
> *That is tapas (penance) rare;*
> *That is the Lord's Feet too;*
> *That indeed is the way to Grace receive*"; Moulana Jalaluddin Rumi:"
> *Even if after you had closed your eyes, ears and mouth, you still had not*
> *realized God's secrets, laugh at me.*"

Prophet Mohammed knew enlightenment as '*il'aham*', Lord Buddha as '*Nirvana*' and J.Krishnamurti defined the state as:" *the observer being the observed*".

Patanjali and Thirumoolar have explained it beautifully when they say that when the mind is stilled, the highest state of Yoga, Samadhi or superconsciousness is achieved. Lord Krishna in the Bhagavad Gita says that in a tranquil state of mind, mental equilibrium is achieved so one realizes thae absolute oneness of the universe. Everything is centred in the control of the senses, Gita:" For the uncontrolled there is no wisdom, nor for the uncontrolled is there power of concentration; and for him without concentration there is no peace. And for the un-peacefull, how can there be happiness?"

When 'maya' the illusive-power of the Lord is removed through Yoga, absolute Truth is revealed and the person has no more body and mind and he merges totally with the Lord; Thirumandiram 2548:

"When maya veils jiva (soul),
The truth of Vedas remain hidden;
When maya leaves, the truth of himself reveals;
Those who make maya vanish, merge in God;
No more is body, no more is mind."

In the highest state, one realizes that the Cosmic mind and the presumed individual mind are one and the same, one's infinite-nature is realized for he is no more trapped within the confines of the body; Thirumandiram 129:

"Sleeping in themselves they saw Siva's world,
Sleeping in themselves they experienced Siva Yoga,
Sleeping in themselves they experienced Siva bhoga (Wisdom),
How can one explain the state of such persons?"

We are all named before birth! – Holy Bible, Saiva Siddhanta

Jesus Christ, John the Baptist as well as one and all are named before birth itself tells the Bible in Ecc.6:10. Likewise just as the Saiva Siddhanta of the Tamils says, the Bible too tells us that each person's name, livelihood, his periods of fortune, pitfalls(read Solomon's words:"everything has a time, a time to sow, a time to reap, a time to be born..., even a time to die...", it even mentions that even every country's borders, area and fortunes are pre-determind), in fact everything is 'sealed' in the lines of one's palms, Bible, job ch.37:7.

The Vedanta and Siddhanta system very clearly state that each person's entire life could be studied by studying the position of the stars at the time of birth of the concerned person and by studying a person's palm-prints, sages like Agasthya, Vashishta, Vishwamitra and others have written in Tamil in cipher-form on palm-leaf manuscripts even about person's past-lives as well as the nature of future ones and mentioned the names of upcoming wives and children.

A Roman Catholic man's name is mentioned in the matching palm-leaves like this:" the combination of the sixth letter in the series of 'sa' and the ninth letter in the same series, is his name" ("*saavil aarum saavil onbadhum ivan thun naamam*") – the sixth letter in the series of 'sa' is 'soo' and the ninth letter is 'sai', when combined 'soosai' is the outcome, which was confirmed by the truth or one should say fortune-seeker!

An Englishman's name was given like this:" half a cubit is his name" ("*mullhathill padhi ivan thun naamam*") – half a cubit in tamil is known as 'jahn', and the Englishman indeed did confirm that his name was 'John'!

All Messages are Imprinted in the Genes! Can Man be re-programmed to become a Superman? – 80 to 100 feet tall man according to Vedas, Tamil Siddhars, Hadith of Islam; 100,000 years life-span of man in 'Kreta Yuga' more than 3 million years ago; 'Deathless –state' attained by Siddhars; 'Acquired Savant Syndrome','Acquired Foreign Accent Syndrome','Total Recall' is attainment of the '64 Arts' ('Kalai Tattvas') and recollection of experiences of more than 84,000 past lives, of One's Divinity; Lord Buddha, Lord Chaitanya, Ramalingam Swami, Shirdi Sai Baba:

AIDS which is the most dreaded disease as of present and a challenge to the medical fraternity as well as all of mankind does not seem to affect prostitutes of Nigeria who were found to be immune to the HIV virus according to WHO which conducted a global survey and after prolonged tests the aforesaid people's DNA was found to be *programmed* to resist the disease just as the DNA of the mongoose is *naturally programmed* to be immune to the deadly effects of snake venom.

The lowly yeast which is a single-celled living organism itself contains 6000 genes and its 'full' DNA or genome contains 12 million units of DNA. The DNA carry the code for 6000 genes, each of varying coding sequences and fewer than half of these genes are known to biologists and their functions remain yet to be determined. Dr.Ronald W.Davis of Stanford University medical centre along with yeast geneticists undertaken by a consortium of universities in the U.S. and Europe in 96 laboratories are trying to identify the role of each gene. They hope to unveil the lowly yeast's potential in a few years time!

India's Gujarat University has claimed that they have made yeast churn-out edible oils and fats. In the future food and synthetic oils including fuel-oils could be churned by the lowly yeast to help mighty mankind!

Man has 70,000 to 100,000 genes and the human genome contains 3 billion base pairs of DNA. The messages imprinted in them if printed on our ordinary newspaper would measure more than 16,000 kilometers long! Hereditary factors are passed from the grand-father to the father and through him to the son and all these and more messages like masterminding the entire process of life is done by the genes. Genes control all functions of the cell and body growth, the two main events in the life of most cells are multiplication (by division and synthesis of proteins). Both these operations are carried out on the basis of the blue-prints coded in the genes. There are 50 trillion cells (50,000,000,000,000) in the human body and from birth each cell 'doubles' itself 50 times and then stops multiplying. What determines the number of multiplication is a gene called the control gene. The control gene also tells the cell when to stop growing and tells for example the housefly to grow eight legs and not nine! This switching on and off of genetic activities is achieved by the presence of two molecules attached to the genes known as inducers and repressors. By genetic engineering (splicing and grafting) which is now in its initial stages, could it be possible to control cell growth thereby controlling the growth of man to the size of his liking?

The timeless Vedas say that in the first of the four cyclic-yugas known as the '*Kreta yuga*' (more than 30 million years ago) man was programmed to grow to an *average* height of 32 feet and easily stood fifty to sixty feet tall ("*as tall as a full-grown palmyra tree*" according to the Tamil Siddhar Bogar and Konganavar; and according to the Hadith a Holy book of Islam containing anecdotes of the holy Prophets, Adam was 60 cubits or 100 feet tall when he first landed on mount Sarandip in Sri Lanka).

By re-arranging the genetic code which as genetic engineers say could be done in billions of ways, can man's DNA be programmed to be immune to all the 3000 or so diseases known to modern medicine? Could the 'circadian clock' and the 'clock' gene be reset? By resetting the internal clock could man's life be extended to a great deal and extended indefinitely? For the Vedas also state that man was programmed to live for a hundred thousand (100,000) years in the first yuga and there is even mention of Siddhars (Perfected beings) having attained the '*deathless-state*' (known as '*saha kalai*' in Tamil)and of 'turning' young and living in that state for eternity (Chiranjivi). Many like Kahapusandha, Chaitanya Prabhu, Markandeya, Thirumoolar, Thiruvalluvar, Pattinathar, Ramalingam had transformed their bodies into a golden radiant-form which cannot be affected or harmed by anything material, natural or by the five basic elements. The Perfectionists acquired those exalted states while living on earth itself and which is available only after death and that too only in the Premium or Ultimate-Heaven!

Hereditary traits are said to be passed along through our genes and like for example hereditry milk-consumers have the enzyme lactose that helps in digestion of milk while others don't, if by genetic splicing and grafting that could be rectified, could man be turned into a genius who would contain the brilliance of Albert Einstein, Leonardo da vinci, Mozart, Shakespeare, the beauty of Michel Angelo's statue of David? Could all of brilliance and goodness be put in a single man? Can all of mankind be turned into supermen?

Apart from 'Acquired Immune Deficiency Syndrome' or AIDS as it is infamously known, there are many other syndromes in the news presently whereby the affected persons regain or should we say 'recall' many wonderful *dormant* skills but unrelated to their present skills like speaking in new languages or acquiring skills in music, mathematics, arts etc., but on a talent-scale like of child-prodigies and great scientists. While these sudden recollections have been caused due to unexpected accidents, the Perfected Being also gains *total recall*.

A person in Russia recently was knocked into a comatose-state by a melting falling ice-block, was able to *totally* remember the Turkish-language after recovering three or four days later in a Moscow hospital, the person had never even been near Turkey, but later doctors claim that since his fore-fathers had migrated from Turkey 250 years back, the language could have been imprinted in his genes and the heavy-blow to his head could have caused the memory to flood back! This phenomenon is now known as '*Acquired Savant Syndrome*' through which dormant skills emerge that are triggered by injuries to specific parts of the brain – Jason Padgett of Tacoma USA in 2002 was brutally attacked by muggers that caused a concussion and thus a higher IQ so that he began to see mathematical formulas and patterns in his surroundings similar to economics Nobel Prize winner John Nash; Derek Amato in 2006 injured his brain while diving in a pool and in an instant became another Beethoven who could play spontaneous concerto for six straight hours!; Karen Butler from Oregon, USA developed '*Acquired Foreign Accent Syndrome*' when he had a dental implant whereby he all of a sudden spoke with a bit British and Transylvanian twang!; Orlando Serrell of Virginia transformed into a human calendar after being hit on the head by a baseball so that he could spit out the day of the week for any date since 17 august 1979, the day he was struck, which is known as the '*Hyperthymestic Syndrome*'; another American John Sarkin became an accidental artist after suffering a stroke whose ghostly paintings now sell for $ 10,000 each!; a Harvard University Professor recollected his past-life after suffering a stroke!

Lord Buddha in a flash remembered 400 of his past lives when he attained enlightenment – the life of an eagle, hare, snake, deer ...! But even that is not total recall for even the life that we led in our true home that is heaven lies ingrained in our memory! Moreover on the ascent when man transcends the 'Art' concept which itself contains the '64 Arts' or '64 branches of knowledge' that includes astronomy, astrology, physics, chemistry, engineering, dance, music, archery, wrestling, sword fencing, painting sculpting, etc., are themselves considered as 'inferior knowledge' (*Apara Vidya*'), transcending this is 'Superior' knowledge that is 'Divine-Wisdom' (*Para Vidya*') and even beyond this are the '5 Shiva Tattvas' – the Qualities of the Primal Lord which were attained by Purna Yogis like Lord Chaitanya and Swami Ramalingam.

Lord Chaitanya could cure deadly diseases like leprosy by merely touching or even glancing at a person, such was his love and compassion towards others, When two highly learned Vedic Pandits filled with pride approached Ramalingam to test his knowledge of the Vedas, the saint gave an extempore speech on the Veda-Agamas and particularly on the questions and doubts that the Pandits wished to be clarified upon! The saint explained in great detail and spoke upon the nuances of a complicated 'Raga' (musical composition) to an accomplished musician for a length of four hours and when he asked whether he wished for more, the stunned, stupefied and amazed musician bowed to him in humility and replied that it would do for it was all beyond his understanding! When Shirdi Sai Baba (who attained Samadhi in 1919) was able to quote all the 700 slokas (verses) of the Bhagavad Gita without not having read it even once, an amazed Indian Civil Service Officer questioned the saint on how it was possible to perfom such a feat, the saint in turn replied that like the cloud that veils the brilliance of moon-light, pride, arrogance and illusion veils the mind of man, and like the passing cloud reveals the moon-light, when the aforesaid impurities are removed the Divinity and Divine-Wisdom laying latent within man shines like a gem in all its brilliance!

Fifty Letters Contain All World Languages - All world languages are contained in the 50 Sanskrit Alphabets, ancient Tamil, Japanese & Chinese Vowel-Consonants – Carl Sagan, Thirumandiram, Kanchi Sankaracharya, Holy Bible:

When Carl Sagan as director of NASA and SETI (search for extra-terrestrial Intelligence) decided to send the spacecraft 'Voyager' into space for a chance meeting with aliens, a golden record was also sent with it inscribed with drawings, figures, mathematical-formulas etc., for aliens to understand us better, and he mentions that he selected the 50 alphabets of the Sanskrit language which also happen to be the 'Prime Alphabets' or Vowel-Consonants of the Japanese and Chinese languages though the Chinese language has more than 50 to 60 alphabets, for they in totality contain the entire gamut of sounds that could emanate from the throat of any person. What is surprising is that the ancient Tamil alphabets also contain 50 vowel-consonants (prior to the round-letter era – 'vatta ellhuthu') as clearly stated by Thirumoolar in his Thirumandiram:" God created me wisely to write about Him in Tamil …" ("*Yennai nandraha Iraivan padaithan thannai nandraha tamil seyyum marae*") and "The Primal Lord Siva's tattvas are in the wonderful language Tamil…" ("*Sadasivam tattvam mutthamizh vedam…*"). Thirumandiram 965:

> "Fifty letters alone contain all Vedas,
> Fifty letters alone contain all agamas,
> Fifty letters source when realized,
> Fifty letters become five letters."

All world languages and their texts including the timeless Vedas are contained in the fifty prime alphabets of vowel-consonants. The source of these fifty letters is the 'Pranava' or 'A-U-M' which is denoted by the five words A, I, U, E, O or 'life-vowels. When this is understood and realized that person becomes 'one' with the Lord who is the source of Knowledge, so everything is known to him, Thirumandiram 910:

> "One the supreme bliss, one the supreme bliss,
> Thus chant the mantra, you shall have bliss,
> Bliss has its source in letters five;
> A, I, U, E, O and AUM the life vowels they are;
> They become the five letter mantra
> And joy that is within joy;
> Bliss lies in the seed-letters five;
> Hum – Hrim – Ham – Ksham – Am, are they."

The above song gives three alternative interpretations of the 'five –letter mantra ('panchakshara'), it could be either A, I, U, E, M or 'Sivayanama', or the tantric "Hum, Hrim, Hum, Ksham, Am".

Apart from Sanskrit, Chinese, Japanese and Tamil, the Telugu language of South India also has fifty prime alphabets. Telugu is also a very ancient language for the 'Senai' or the 'war-language' used by Emperor Ravana of Sri Lanka is said to be Telugu. Other ancient languages like Greek, Hebrew, Latin, Arabic and Aramaic (the language spoken by Jesus Christ which is till spoken by a tribe of people in Syria) do not have fifty vowel-consonants nor do they have 50 alphabets in total. Though it is to be yet determined whether vowel-consonants and in their combinations in Hebrew for example contain the entire gamut of sounds like 'saa','jha', gha','zha','hum','ksham' etc.,. The personal Name of God, linked with His revelation of Himself to Israel is found in Hebrew as a four-letter sequence of two consonants (H, H0 and two semi-vowels (Y, W) that is 'YHWH', which are pronounced as 'YAHWEH'. In the middle ages, rabbinic scholars combined the consonants and semi vowels of 'YHWH' with the vowels of 'Adonai' which meansthe Lord. Reverent jews considered the divine name too sacred to pronounce, so they substituted for it with the noun 'Adonai'and thus created a new form 'JEHOVAH'- the "self-existent one", literally, "He that is who He is", therefore "the Eternal." Later Hebrew texts also refer to God as 'Jehovah Elohim', to be accurate "YHWH Elohim".

Sound has four divisions,'Paravani' which finds manifestation only in Prana (sound-vibrations in space),'Pasyanti' which manifests in the mind,'Madhyama' in the sense-organs (or indriyas) and 'Vaikhari' in articulate expression; Thirumandiram 2007:

"Vaikhari and rest of sounds,
Maya and rest of impurities,
Purusha (soul) and rest of tattvas illusory,
All these, acting on Saktis, jnana and kriya,
The Lord true from time immemorial made."

The late Kanchi Sankaracharya in,'The Vedas', "On Sound and Creation":" Modern science defines sound as vibration while atomic science and Einstein's theory have projected the conclusion that, at the level of the atom, all matter is the same. Objects appear differently to the eyes because energy produces vibrations of different frequencies at various points. Vibration creates sound, conversely stated, if sound is to result, vibrations should be created. Since vibrations of different frequencies occur in the flood-stream of energy, the scientific explanation for the creation of the world and the Vedic pronouncement that creation resulted from the life-breath of God, are mutually in agreement.

What is the base of the health and feelings in man and beast? breath and breathing. The passage of the breath through the various nadis (pulse nerve-centres) creates vibrations which are responsible for the health of beings, or lack of it. If through yogic practices, the passage of breath through these centres is controlled or regulated, wonderful health results. In such a state, even if the blood vessels are severed, blood would not flow out. Yogis are able to stop the heart-beat and pulse-beat and remain buried underground in a state of quiescence. The venom of a snake or corpion bite leaves them unaffected. All this is possible because they are able to discipline the vibrations caused by normal breathing."

"In the wind-instruments such as the harmonium, oboe and flute, air is let out through apertures on the basis of certain calculations, to produce various musical notes. The human throat has also a similar arrangement. It is not merely the throat. From the 'muladhara' which is just below the navel, the breath is made to travel upwards in various patterns which results in speech or melody. The musical instrument which god has designed for man is much superior to those produced by man, example the flute, or the harmonium. The latter ones can produce only ordinary sounds. Birds and animals can lisp some of these words but can come nowhere near man who can raise thousands of such sounds."

The fifty words exist as fifty sound-vibrations in the the six chakras or psychic-spots in the body; Thirumandiram 1704:

"Piercing the chakras that are petalled
Four, six, ten and twelve
And the six and ten still above;
Lo! Behold then the twin-petalled centre finale;
You have indeed beheld the Holy Feet
Of the timeless One."

The muladhara chakra (all the chakras resemble flowers having varying number of petals) has 4 petals which denote four important vital nadis (astral or gross nerves) and 4 letters (4 distinct sound-vibrations), the swadhistana chakra has 6 petals and hence as many letters, the manipura 10 petals and as many letters, the anahata has 12 petals and thus 12 letters, the vissudhi has 16 petals and thus 16 letters, the ajna at the eyebrow-centre has 2 pettals and hence 2 letters. When the soul or pure-consciousness along with the Kundalini or Cosmic-Energy rises through yogic-practices, activates the other chakras on its winding upward journey, flows even beyond the eyebrow-centre and flows into the thousand-petalled or 'Sahasra chakra' at the crown of the head, only light and vibrations (the 'Eternal Sound-Light Continuum') remain which are the Holy Feet of the Timeless One; Thirumandiram 1710:

"As the gross body that decays
And the subtle body that escapes
Are in union unseen,
So are the subtle letters fifty to tattvas
That are gross,
So are the centres six to the body corporeal."

The base of the physical body is the subtle or spiritual body, the quality of the spiritual body determines the quality of the physical body, the bridge or what binds the physical and spiritual bodies are the 50 words and 96 tattvas. When one goes beyond the Sahasra chakra at the crown of the head he becomes a full-blown Yogi and realizes that the 50 letters had really expanded from the five letters A, I, E, U, O which is also the mantra AUM and in a flash comes to know all languages of the world including that of the birds and beasts and even that of the hevenly and neter-worlds, Even everything and knowledge of all texts are revealed for the word AUM contains the knowledge and thoughts and words ever contemplated, thought of and uttered by man, beast, all life-forms and even God. The Holy Bible, John,1:1 "In the beginning was the word, and the word was with God, and the word was God." John,14:" The word became flesh ..." and again in Genesis 1:6:" And God said, "Let there be light, and there was light." It is understood that God had the idea of creation even before he started the process of creation. The seers and sages of the distant past by divine grace were able to realize that the word Aum was the basic word which contained the collective thoughts of God, so the person who realizes the true meaning of Aum comes to know everything, one cannot differentiate that person from God; Thirumandiram 2676:

"Aum is the one word supreme;
Aum is the Form-Formless;
Aum is the infinite diversity;
Aum is siddhi (Perfection) and Mukti (Liberation) radiant."

The word Aum is both Form (its gross form is the word Aum like our physical body) and it is also Formless (its subtle form is 'Nada Bindu' the Eternal Sound-Light Continuum like our spiritual bodies), through Aum, one could attain 'Siddhi' or Perfection and hence all possible 'natural' and what seem to be be impossible 'supernatural' Powers come of their own accord and one could attain Liberation (physical and spiritual liberation) from what seem to be the agony-filled vice-like clutches of endless cycle of death and re-birth.

'Aum' and its Significance – The Bible, Heraclitus and 'Logos', The Vedas, The Kado Upanishad, Thirumandiram.

Aum is the most sacred and mystic symbol of Hinduism and its significance is acknowledged by Christianity where it is known as 'Amen', in Islam it is known as 'Amin', Buddhism knows it as 'Hum' and the entire world as well as everyone and being on the world and the cosmos owe their existence to it. This word has been in existence from time immemorial. It represents the Supreme Spirit, the source of all knowledge. To find out the basic word for all other words the ancient seers in a meditative exalted-state, as a revelation discovered this mystic syllable 'Aum'.

More than 20 'slokas' (verses) from the Kado Upanishad of the Vedas are added in the Bhagavad Gita which all deal with the 'Pranava' mantra 'Aum':

Sloka 15: "The goal, the word of which all the Vedas speak of;
              All tapas (penance) bring out;
              To attain attain which brahmacharya-life is led;
              I will reveal to that word, it is 'Aum'."

Sloka 16: "This word is surely God,
              It is truly supreme,
              A person who understands this word;
              Attains everything he desires."

All words that we utter have meaning and those meanings refer to the ideas or thoughts. The words for a particular object in different languages may vary in sound, but they all represent the same object which exist as an idea or as a thought in the mind. 'Water' in French is known as 'eau', in German as 'vasssar', in Italian as 'aqua' and in various other languages in various other names, but they all refer to the same substance. The word is nothing but the outward manifestation of thought which is in the mind. The Biblical passage in the 4th gospel, John 1:1,2:"In the beginning was the word, the word was with God, and the word was God, he was with God in the beginning." What does the word mean? What does it refer to? And how has the word become flesh? (John 1,14) – Thirumandiram 964 also says that the 50 words (letters, vowel-consonants)and the flesh and all that which comprises the human body had expanded from the word 'Aum'. Heraclitus the Greek philosopher of the 5th century B.C. was the first of the western world to conceive that the idea of a 'logos', which means originally a word and from word it goes back to the thought, idea and reason.

In the Cosmic mind, the thoughts existed before the words emerged, or before creation. The Genesis says: "The Lord Said:" Let there be light", and there was light." So God, before he uttered these words, had in his mind the thought of light, the idea of light. In the spiritual realm, thoughts are realities, every thought has its form, as it were, the Cosmic mind contains all the ideas or concepts of the various things that have come into existence since creation. Every object be it a tree, an animal, a tree, a bird, the world everything is a manifestation of the thought of the object which existed in the cosmic mind before creation, and that is a pattern.

The pattern exists in the cosmic mind throughout eternity, and whenever an occasion arises, through the process of evolution, that concept or idea of the object becomes real on the material plane and becomes the object. Countless number of animals, birds, reptiles, trees and various species of life-forms like the dinosaurs have become extinct in countless worlds in various planes and dimensions over time, but the pattern of them exist in the cosmic mind. When the earth or any other planet is ready and ripe for life to flourish, again will be inhabited and countless hosts of life-forms through the process of natural evolution will appear even the dinosaur if, when and where necessary.

The type or pattern or idea of the dinosaur which is in the cosmic mind, is perfect. In the cosmic mind, a pattern of the perfect dinosaur, elephant, parrot, what ever it may be, a perfect image is recorded in the cosmic mind. Similarly all the planets, the stars, everything is in the cosmic mind. If all or one of the species is destroyed today, they will be resolved in their elementary conditions and from the pattern in the cosmic mind, another one will be produced out of the same matter.

It is said in the Vedas that at the beginning of creation, the first born Lord of the universe created the sun, moon, and the stars as they existed of the previous cycle according to the pattern of those planets and stars that eternally exist in the cosmic mind.

Similarly the pattern of the Perfect man also exists in the cosmic mind. That perfect man cannot be manifested in this plane on account of the limitation of time, space and causation, so there must be some imperfection. But the type or pattern of the perfect man is there in the cosmic mind, and this type of man which is in the cosmic mind, is the 'logos'.

Every human mind is trying and striving to reach and attain that perfect type consciously or un-consciously, one may call it 'Christ' ('Christos' means one who has reached the nearest approach to the ideal man),'Buddha' or 'Krishna', they and many others did represent that perfect image.

The word 'God', which we use to represent the Supreme Spirit or Cosmic mind is incomplete, it simply refers to goodness. God does not mean anything particular, it simply gives us a vague idea of a being who is always good. We would like to find out the word that would be the basic word for all other words, and this basic word came to the ancient seers of truth as a revelation, and they discovered this mystic syllable 'Aum'. It consists of three sounds,'A','U','M', the three letters when coalesced sound like two letters. The first baic sound is represented by the position of the mouth when it is wide open, the sound which can be uttered by a person is the guttural sound 'A', being the first sound. The last sound is produced when one closes the mouth completely, the 'M' sound is produced by the lips and the 'A' sound by the throat when the larynx and the palate have to be kept wide open. Between the two sounds we get the whole gamut of sounds, all sounds that can be produced by the mouth, be it that of man, bird or beast can be made within the range of these two sounds 'A' and 'M'. And naturally it includes all thoughts and ideas which are representated by all such words, this syllable is therefore used to represent the cosmic mind that has infinite thoughts and ideas.

With this realization and with faith when one utters the mystic syllable Aum, vibrations emanate spontaneously which affects the structure and attitude of body, mind and spirit of him as well as everyone and everything surrounding him. The atoms and molecules in the body vibrate in various frequencies which gradually brings to tune the body, mind and spirit with higher dimensions and their beings and the cosmic mind. The more we commune with the Infinite Spirit, the higher we rise from the finite plane and transcend into the infinite planes. We never loose our individuality, but ours become bigger, the thinking of limitation within one's physical body is lost and we think of ourselves as expanded. Then we'd be able to realize that the same Spirit that dwells in the sun, moon, stars and countless life-forms also dwells in us. We are no longer limited by any personality, we attain that freedom, or release, which is the ideal of all religions, and claim boldly like the Sufi saint Mansoor:" Iam the Truth" ("anal haq") and Jesus Christ:" I and my Father are One."

The letters A-U-M represent not only all the thoughts in the woken-state but also the other states. The letter 'A' represent everything in the 'jagra' or woken-state, the letter 'U' everything in the 'swapna' or dream-state, the letter 'M; everything in the 'sushupti' or dreamless-state.

The mantra Aum has like the human body the gross and subtle-form, the letters 'AUM' is its gross-form while the 'Nada-Bindu' the "Eternal Sound-Light Continuum" is its subtle-form. Man realizes his divinity through the mantra Aum, which forms his physical and spiritual bodies just as it forms the cosmos; Thirumandiram 2677:

"In Aum arose the elements five;
In Aum arose the entire creation;
In the atita (finite) of Aum
The three jivas merged;
Aum is the form
Of jiva, Para and Siva in union."

Mantras Which Are Sound-Vibrations 'Protects', Heals And Has A Positive-Influence In All Life-Forms

Mantras have been known to heal, cure, activate 'Chakras' that are energy-centres and psychic-spots on the human body, move and melt rocks, shatter glass and please the gods for according to the ancient Indian music tradition each 'raga' or musical-note is the manifestation of a 'Deva' or a god, they being among the higher echelons or hierarchy of the angels. Just as slow pleasant melodious music soothes and calms humans, it is also utilized in some western countries to help cows yield more milk and plants to grow faster and produce better yield. The Ninjas of Japan and the Tanjian monks of China would chant mantras sourced from the Vedas of India, create a deadly field of high energy-frequency and resonance, make it bounce against an astral-membrane known as 'Kokoro' (that means the secret inner-heart in Japanese) and hurl it at their enemies or at walls and thus kill or shatter them from a distance. Indian Sages have also brought down rain by playing the 'Amritavarshini' raga when needed and if needed fire and Adi Sankara brought forth a rain of golden-nuggets by singing the 'Kanakathara Sthothra'.

Even animals by instinct utilize the effects of sound-frequency to their advantage for not only do cats purr when they are content, but scientists have also discovered that purring is a natural healing mechanism. Wounded cats purr because the sound frequency helps their bones and organs heal and grow stronger and that exposure to the purring sounds also improves bone density in humans. Scientists from the "Fauna Communications Research Institute" in Carolina have found that the sound frequency of a house-cat is between 27 and 44 kilohertz and 20 to 50 for all wildcats. Exposure to frequencies of 20-50 HZ strengthens human bones. Dr.David

Purdie from Hulls University Centre for metabolic bone disease said that since it was difficult to devise physical exercise for old people uffering from osteoporosis, it might be possible to create a mechanism to use tapes of cat purring to help strengthen old bones.

Birds Live In a World Expanded From Ours – National Geographic

The Tennessee Warbler weighing less than 15 grams migrates some 5000 kilometres overland from nesting sites in Canada and the Northern U.S. to wintering places in Central and South America. The blackpoll warbler makes a non-stop 3700 kms.,86 hour over-water flight to South America from the North. The Artic tern fly a distance of 20,000 kms. – from the North Pole to Antartica! The ruby-throated hummingbird which weighs less than 35 decigrams fly 8oo kms, across the gulf of Mexico, a 25 hour marathon feat!

Birds can hear infrasounds, so a migrant can hear a thunder-storm above a far-distant mountain range, an aroused surf lashing a coast 1000 kms. Away, even the rhythmic pulse of the ionosphere. Cornell University, Stephen Emlen:" *Birds are not living in the same sensory world we live in, they are hearing, seeing and sensing a world expanded from ours."*

'Jonathan Livingston Seagull' By Richard Bach on "The Strive For Perfection"; on 'Teleportation'

Jonathan Livingston Seagull the bird that had just attained the Perfect-state to another of its kind in heaven:" *why aren't there more of us here? Why, where I came from, there were .... ""... thousands and thousands of gulls. I know."* Sullivan shook his head. *"The only answer I can see, Jonathan, is that you are pretty well one-in-a-million bird. Most of us came along slowly. We went from one world into another that was almost exactly like it, forgetting right away where we had come from, not caring where we were headed, living for the moment."*

"Do you have any idea how many lives we must have gone through before we even got the first idea that there is more to life than eating or fighting, or power

in the flock? *A thousand lives, Jon, ten* thousand ! *And then another hundred lives until we began to learn that there is such a thing as* <u>Perfection,</u> *and another hundred to get the idea that our purpose for living is to find that perfection and show it forth. The same rule holds for us now. We choose our next world through what we learn here. Learn nothing, and the next world is the same as this one, all the same limitations and lead weights to overcome." But you, Jon," he said, "learned so much at one time that you didn't have to go through a thousand lives to reach this one."*

"The trick, according to Chiang, was for Jonathan to stop seeing himself as trapped inside a limited body that had a 107 cm. wingspan and performance that could be plotted on a chart. The trick was to know that his true nature lived everywhere at once across space and time." ..." *Your whole body, from wingtip to wingtip, "*Jonathan would say, *"is nothing more than your thought itself, in a form you can see. Break the chain of your thoughts, and you break the chains of your body, too."*

Realizing The Entire Universe Withing Themselves And The Self As Permeating The Entire Universe – Srimad Bhagavata

Srimad Bhagavata, Bk. X, Discourse LXXIX, 'An Account Of Balarama's Pilgrimage':" Sri Suka began again:" ... 30) The almighty Balarama imparted Pure Wisdom to the sages, by virtue of which they realized the whole universe in themselves, and the Self (Soul) as permeating the whole universe."

The Humble Fruit Fly Like The Shark, Crocodile, dolphin, Seal, Penguin, Spider, Ant, Bat, Beetle, Snake, Termite, Trees & Many Others In Nature Have Attained Perfection

The humble fruit fly beats its wings 200 *times* a second which creates most complex aerodynamics in nature baffling to us. But compared to humans (100 billion neurons) fruit flies have just 500,000 neurons. The fly uses most of these neurons to gather sensory information, including light with its eyes. smells with odour-sensitive hairs, and balance with club-shaped gyroscopes behind the wings. Those signals get funneled through the nervous system, which then sends commands to the wings. Scientists at the University of California cannot explain even *half* of the 'lift' created by the flies. By keeping the wings at steep angles, air instead of gliding smoothly over the wings, the upper stream of air forms a swirling vortex along the wings leading leading edge which lowers the air pressure above the wing, providing an extra upward boost. The flies then strangely rotate their wings and flaps in the opposite direction creating a new vortex, while the previous vortex slips off harmlessly without causing a stall one of the most important phenomena causing major aircraft accidents.

The First Revelations of The Lord Were Revealed in Both Sanskrit and Tamil

The Lord is said to have first revealed to His Divine Consort, The Holy Mother (Shakthi or Sakthi)the keys to the mysteries of life during the process of creation in the sweet Tamil language and the northern-language, Sanskrit; Thirumandiram 65:

"When rain and summer and long drawn dews stay occurring,
And when the lakes are dry after destruction,
Then did He in Sanskrit and Tamil at once,
Reveal the rich treasure of His compassion to our
Mother Supreme."

Thirumandiram 66:

"Life takes its birth, stands preserved awhile,
And then its departure takes; caught
In that momentary wave of flux, Him we glimpse,
The Lord who in Tamil sweet and northern-tounge
Life's mystery revealed."

The Three Philosophies and States that Define All of Mankind – Lord Rama, Hanuman, Ramakrishna Paramahamsa

When Lord Rama was asked to explain the three philosophies that generally segregate all of mankind: 'Dwaita' – man and God are two separate entities; 'Vishitdwaita' – man is a 'replica', a mirror-image, an aspect of the Lord; 'Adwaita' – man and the Lord are one single entity, he replied that Anjaneya or Hanuman his faithful devotee was the one who was most qualified to explain the states for he had *experienced* all of them.

Hanuman replied:" As long as Iam bound by the body and traces of cravings and limitations remain, You are the Lord and Iam a loyal slave; when Knowledge of the Soul (*jivatmabodha*) dawns in me, You are the Perfect-One (*Purna*) and Iam an exact- replica, an aspect (*amsa*)of You; when the Soul's Wisdom in its entirety which is Pure Consciousness (*shuddha chaitanya bodha*) shines in me, there is absolutely no difference between You and me, You are Me and Iam You."

Ramakrishna Paramahamsa the Guru of Swami Vivekananda gives an even simpler explanation by means of an imaginary story: A salt-doll for a very long time wished to see the ocean. One fine day with firm determination it set upon the journey to find the ocean. After a great deal of effort and difficulty it finally reached the shores of the ocean. It stood transfixed and wondered with amazement at the immensity of the mighty ocean. It took a handful of the ocean-waters to taste it and realized at once that the salt in the water and itself were made of the same material. Resolving to research even further, it entered the salt-waters and by dissolving itself, it became one with the mighty infinite-ocean!

After Death, Man lives in the 'Other World' for some time with His Name, Body-shape and Sex – Holy Bible, Holy Quran, Thirukural, Thirumandiram, Bhagavad Gita, Ramayana, Mahabharata, Silapathikaram, Swami Abhedhananda, Auvviar,291st Guru Maharaj of Madurain Adheenam

Though the soul does'nt have shape, name, sex or anyother distinction, many of the people of western countries wrongly assume the subtle-bodies that leave the physical body after death to be the soul. The soul leaves along with the subtle and spiritual bodies, the finer or subtle bodies are the ethereal - 'Pranamaya kosa' (in Sanskrit) and 'Prana udal' (in Tamil); the mind-body or 'Manomaya kosa' and 'Mana udal'; the reasoning/scientific-body or 'Vijnanamaya kosa' and 'vijnana udal'; Bliss or Causal-body or 'Anandamaya kosa' and 'Kaarana udal'. The soul along with the subtle bodies goes to the 'intermediate-world' in other planes and dimensions, stays there for the stipulated period of time which could be for a couple of months to a couple of years and even in exceptional cases hundreds and thousands of years also, which would be the time to select and choose the optimum time and place for re-birth. In this 'break' or rest-period the person lives with the same shape, sex, name and identity he or she had possessed on earth.

People of different faiths address their other worlds by various different names. When a Christian dies, they say that he goes to Paradise (which is only a intermediary-world for Jesus tells one among the two robbers who are crucified along with him that he will meet him in Paradise the next day; and Adam had also descended down to earth from Paradise where "fallen Angels" also live) or Heaven being the Kingdom of God. The Muslims say that the dead had attained 'Aharam' and the Holy Quaran calls the second world as 'Parsak' and further says that man attains a bright or dark body according to his performance here. Hindus apart from the "7 upper" and "7 lower" worlds have the world of 'Yama' the Lord of death and specifically '28 Hells' and many heavens.

The soul along with the subtle-bodies goes to either the dark-worlds (of ignorance) which is hell or the Light-worlds (wisdom) which is heaven, enjoys what is its due and then after discarding the subtle-body, it along with the spiritual bodies which carry recorded within in ultra-subtle form all good and bad experiences or 'Karma', enters into a suitable and receptive womb and takes birth again just as a Yogi transmigrates (but with total awareness) into other bodies and goes into another cycle of birth and death, Thirumandiram 2133:

"Having experienced hell and heaven
Jiva leaves subtle-body;
Entering causal-body its course continues;

And like the yogi that transmigrates
Enter yet another body'
Thus entangled in cycle of birth and death."

Swami Abhedananda, a contemporary of Vivekananda in pages 75 to 78 of his book 'Life Beyond Death':" Souls wake up after the sleep of deaths and put on new garments of bodies in order to fulfill certain purposes and gain certain experiences to rep their results of their previous actions, being subject to the law of cause and effect just as in the same way we throw away our old clothes and put on new ones." Again in pages 98 and 99 he further elaborates:" Just as an oyster or crab would manufacture a shell as a dwelling-house, so this germ of life or the subtle body of the individual, whether it is human or an animal, takes form only according to its desires, according to its tendencies. The human will manufacture a human body, and if the will be of any particular animal-form, then it manufactures that form. It has no particular form but it can take any form, this subtle body contains everything, so we do not gain anything from outside, it is already there, it has infinite potentialities and infinite possibilities.

At the time of death, the individual contracts all its forces, all its powers, and all these are centralized into a nucleus, and the nucleus retains the life, the mind, the power of senses, and all the impressions and experiences that the individual had gathered. Then when in course of time when favourable conditions come, it manufactures another form. Parents are nothing but the principal channels through which these germs of life or subtle bodies find proper conditions to manufacture a humanbeing by obeying the laws of nature. Parents do not create the soul, in fact parents cannot give birth to a child according to their will, it would be an absolute impossibility. Unless the soul comes to them and nourishes the germ, it would be an absolute impossibility. So whatever desires we possess, if the desire be strong, then that desire will mould our future, create our destiny and make us accordingly. As each individual soul possesses infinite potentialities and possibilities, so it can express an infinite variety of manifestations. We are all eternal and all part of the infinite" – pages 105-106.

"And when one understands that life is eternal, he does not worry about the conditions, the failures and successes, or the diseases and sufferings of the earthly plane. This life on this plane is only for a short time, but from the stand form of eternal-life, we are never born, we are never to die. We are birthless, deathless, eternal, immortal and part and parcel of the infinite spirit (God) which is worshipped under different names among different races" – page 111.

Thirukural's 339th couplet among 1330 very simply and beautifully interprets death:

"Death is like sleep;
Birth is like waking up from sleep."

The Bhagavad Gita, ch.8,6:" *Whatsoever desire is very strong during the life-time becomes predominant at the time of death, and that desire moulds the creation of the subtle body of the individual and that determines the future of the individual.*"

In the Ramayana it is stated that Emperor Dasaratha returned fourteen years *after* his death from heaven to Sri Lanka in his Spiritual-body and appeared his son Lord Rama and his beloved wife Sita at the time of the 'Agniparikasha' (Sita took entered a fire-pit and returned unharmed to prove her chastity). Dasaratha consoled Sita and bestowed two boons as requested by Rama.

In the 19th chapter of the Tamil classic Silapathikaram it is stated that Kovalan who was beheaded after being wrongly convicted of stealing the anklet of the Pandyan King, appeared before his beloved wife kannagi, consoled her, wiped away her tears of grief and went up to heaven surrounded by many Devas or Angels. It is also mentioned that no harm was done to his spiritual body by the beheading of his physical body. Later Kannagi too after destroying the capital city of Madurai of the Pandyan Kingdom, left for heaven in a 'Pushpaka Vimana' (flying craft) surrounded by celestials like Rambha and Urvashi who are the celestial dancers in the hall of Indra the Lord of the Angels.

In the Mahabharata's 15th chapter,'Ashram Life', it is stated that Emperor Dritarashtra along with Queen Ghandari and Kunti Devi were very keen to know about the welfare of their dear dead sons and loved ones in the after-death world, and humbly requested Sage Vyasa to show them their loved ones a few days after the mighty war. Sage Vyasa taking pity on them, took them to a secluded forest near the river Ganges and brought forth the dead Prince Duryodhana, Karna, Bhisma, Dronacharya, Kadorkaja, Abhimanyu, Sakuni, Sikandi and others. All of them were overjoyed on seeing each other, they all had heart to heart talks and the victorious Pandavas were especially pacified and happy to see their cousins living a contented life in the other worlds.

Old Testament evidence that the soul has no form or sex and leaves the physical body alone at death; The Lord answers through dreams and Prophets; Spirit can be male or female and has the same after death and could be contacted through mediums in Sam.1,28:3 to 19.

New Testament evidence that the spirit exists with its sensory organsin heaven or hell, cares about its loved ones here, those in heaven can visit earthlings and there exists a 'chasm' or void between heaven and hell, Luke ch.16;19 to 31: (this proves that the dead remember their loved-ones and come and advise them to change their mode of life to ensure a good after-life)

Quotation from the Holy Quran,6,112 and123:

112." And though we should send down angels unto them and the dead should speak unto them and we should gather against them all things array they would not believe unless Allah so willed. How bait most of them are ignorant."

123." Is he who was dead and we have raised him into life and set for him a light (heaven) wherein he walketh among men, as him, whose similitude in utter darkness (hell) whence cannot merge. Thus is their conduct made, securing for the disbelievers."

The 291st Guru Maharaj of Madurai Adheenam, in his book, "Hindu Yogi's Astounding Discoveries', delves deeply into the 'after-death' world. He like many western researchers has had great experiences in the contact with 'other-worlds' and other life-forms. Spirits which are general to all life-forms have been contacted through various means like the 'ouija board' and through compatible mediums and record their speeches on tape and other similar recording-devices and and thus have been able to confirm that there are different planes with 'bright' or light-filled ones for the virtuous and 'dark' ones for the bad and wicked just as various religious texts say. The authenticity of the spirits and their claims were tested by asking them to identify the taste of various colored liquids and by asking them to identify objects and recall events and experiences committed by dead persons.

The virtuous or exalted beings living in light-planes are permitted to travel anywhere and visit their earthly kinsmen as well as beings in the dark-planes whereas the bad ones imprisoned in treacherous-conditions are not allowed to go anywhere. Those in the light-planes are able to know immediately when anyone in this world thinks of them. They can listen to our conversations and see us performing our duties. Further it is learnt that the dead persons have all the five sensory-organs – skin, tounge, nose, ears and eyes and all working-organs – hands, legs, sex-organs as well as the mind, intellect, will and assertion, the four interior mechanisms for recording, analyzing, deciding and asserting the experiences of the soul.

By talking to the head of the department in charge of death known as Lord Yama (who is the Personification of Justice and Righteousness – 'Dharma') in most Indian languages, it is learnt that officers in that department are very capable of separating the inner organic-bodies in case of normal death without any injury to the physical as well as spiritual bodies and deliver them either to the light or dark-planes in accordance to their individual merits or de-merits.

The spirits go on to say that the entire world is under the wrong impression that dreams are mere thoughts of actions, mental projections, imaginations or wish fulfillments of the physical body whereas in reality the mind and all the prime organs are in the subtle inner dreambodywhich experiences pain and pleasures in dreams, without any assistance of the physical body and its organs. The mind can only project incidents that were recorded by the soul, but in dreams we experience several unknown incidents none of which were ever recorded in the mind. Moreover, thoughts and imaginations are under the control of the soul, whereas dream-experiences are not at all under the control of the soul.

The dead who live in the light and as well as the dark-worlds live there for any number of years which are sort of 'rest' periods and after this gap, take birth again on earth or evolve to higher planes. Those in the light-filled planes say that they have the same feelings as us, and they like us have books that they can read, take walk in the fields and meet friends on the way, but the speed of locomotion is much faster than ours. They smell the same aroma of flowers as on earth but everything is tangible and in a higher degree of beauty that has nothing to compare with here on earth. There is no decay in flower and plants, they don't wither and shrivel like here on earth, they just growing and simply disappear. Death is known as 'transition' and if transits to higher planes, it is not easy to come back and this is called 'second-death'. Those who had passed through second-death and transited or evolved to higher planes can visit persons in the lower planes but not vice versa.

The spirits say that the Holy Bible has mentioned about the second-death and go on to add that one has to die, transit or evolve to higher planes and one cannot go there at will. Exalted spirits who live on very high planes are allowed to visit lower planes but not the world of our which is materialistic but can pass on messages through persons living in the lowest of the astral-planes.

Auvviar the Tamil Saint-Poetess says that it is the spirit that carries with it the merits in subtle-form and not any amount of wealth, so the miser should remember that when the spirit leaves the body, all his buried treasures would be exploited and enjoyed by someone else:

"By hard work the money that is earned, you bury;
Fools that you are! Misers listen to me
- When the body is left and spirit departs,
Other fools will enjoy the ill-gotten money."

Thirumoolar says that heaven is not the final goal, one who is in his physical body here should realize that he and God are not different for he possesses God's qualities (Saiva Siddhanta emphatically asserts that among the 36 tattvas man is made of, 5 are 'Siva Tattvas' – the Primal Lord's qualities) and hence merges into Him. Others who do not realize their divinity, in accordance to their good and bad deeds committed go either to heaven or hell in endless cycles; Thirumandiram 2134:

"The jiva that realized that 'I' and 'You' are One
Is in Tatpara-state;
Its course inherent diverting will reach Param;
The rest of jivas reaching their destined abodes;
In heaven and earth will in sorrow wallow."

Dreams and Visions – Sigmund Freud, The Kabbalah, Holy Bible, Prophet Mohammed, Kadijah, Abdul Muthalif, Lord Buddha, The Holy Kabbalah, Saiva Siddhanta, Erich von Daniken, Niels Bohr, James D.Watson, Michelangelo, Sir Arthur Findlay

Sigmund Freud who is hailed in the Western World as the greatest exponent and authority on psycho-analysis has proclaimed that dreams are mere wih-fulfillments and imaginations. Freud has left out many aspects like premonitions of future events, higher and lower-plane and divine instructions, visions and enlightenment which stalwarts like Lord Buddha, Prophet Mohammed, Virgin Mary, Lord Mahavira, Ezekiel, divine-musicians like saint Thyagaraja, Mozart, Beethoven among many others who had attained celestial messages without which the world would have ended in chaos.

What exactly are dreams? Dreams are experiences of an independent, imperishable, prime organic spiritual inner-body. Sleep according to the Oxford Dictionary means:" bodily condition normally recurring every night and lasting several hours in which the nervous system is inactive, eyes are closed, muscles are relaxed and consciousness nearly suspended." It is asserted that all the nerves excepting those that have connection with the physical brain are active. While asleep, snoring takes place, the heart-beat is there, blood circulation goes on, body temperature exists, the life-principle or Soul is there and yet the physical body and its sensory-organs are devoid of perceptions. The ears are not plugged, the body is not covered and yet we don't hear any sound or feel the touch of the body. From this we should understand that the soul is not in direct contact with the physical organism and is in direct contact with the body that experiences dreams.

While the physical body is more or less senseless, the dream body is very active, it feels pain and pleasures, all the senses are perceptive, all organs are at work, intelligence is there, it can discriminate between good and bad, all body functions carry on and important occurrences are recorded in the mind and can be recollected after waking up. These experiences are common to all, only the degree of recollection of experiences depend upon the spiritual growth of the person.

By analysing the facts that while asleep, the physical body is devoid of all sense-perceptions and the dream body is able to experience perceptions through all the five sensesand is able to record and recollect important events it can be derived that the soul has its origin of life, senses, sex and personality in the dream or finer subtle-bodies.

There are fundamental differences between mere thoughts and imaginations and dreams. In dreams one is able to observe the subtle dream-body experiencing the same organic pleasure and pains as that of the physical body in the woken-state. In the state of dreams the thoughts and imaginations are also manifested in the dream body for the mind is only the dream body or part of it. We can in dreams enjoy real life-like sexual experiences which cant be done by mere thoughts and imaginations. These experiences in the dreams have to be enjoyed through the five senses, but in the woken-state one cannot enjoy those same senses by any amount of thinking and imagination, so it can be derived that dreams are much more complicated than what we assume them to be. The dream body should therefore possess the five sensory organs and other organs together with the mind to register the events we experience in dreams.

The mind is only an instrument, a device which records important events in life in which the soul is interested. The interesting ones are recorded in bold characters while the less-interesting one are recorded in subtle-form. Not all characters, places or experiences are remembered for the soul tells the mind to record what is needed and what needs to be discarded. Mental projections of past events and recollection of past sense-perceptions are quite different from dream-experiences. Travelling in dreams to unknown places, meeting of unknon persons, witnessing unknown events, actual feelings of sense-perceptions etc., are entirely beyond the scope of imagination, mental projections or bring to memory ofpast events.

The soul can get its desires fulfilled without any restrictions only through the dream body for it free from all barriers like physical-barriers, dimension-barriers, time and distance. In the woken-state the physical body is restricted and hindered by many barriers and so is unable to experience what it desires.

The dream-world is neither ephemeral nor imaginary as Freud would have us believe. The physical sensory-organs are really actuated by the sensory-organs in the dream body, those who have been revived and brought back to life after being declared clinically dead, tell us accurately about the spiritual world, the foremost being Dr.Denton Cooly of the Sloan Kettering Centre, New York in the U.S., who had brought back to life numerous perons who had died of cardiac-failure, by utilizing the defibrillator to pass on electricity in excess of 3000 volts to 'shock' the heart to once again pump blood in the body. Those in the spiritual world, live and move in most respects as we do in this material world, but there is more. Many highly developed or evolved spirits can be met whith whom we can converse and discuss many intricate problems. Elevated people can attain this capacity in dreams, but with yogic training or psychic development, one can converse with persons of the spiritual world even in the woken conscious state.

The prime purpose of sleep apart from the physical body getting rest is for the dream-body getting rest, therefore when the soul lowers it predominant activity from the eyebrow-centre to the throat-centre in the physical as well as the dream-body, it makes its sensory-organs inactive, thereby making the corresponding sensory-organs in the physical inactive and this state is known as the dream-state or dreamful-sleep. When the soul lowers its activity further down to the chest-region, dreamless-sleep is enjoyed. In this state the dream-body revitalizes its lost energy which in turn automatically rejuvenates the physical body which is only an outer cover or shell, cell for cell of the dream-body. Generally sleep either dreamful or dreamless occurs only when the soul ceases to think consciously or intentionally and incapacitates the ears from hearing outside sounds although they are not plugged. The physical eyes which are closed voluntarily or not by us when we go to sleep, shut down automatically when its corresponding eyelids of the dream-body shuts down due to the change of centre of activity of the soul from the forehead to the throat-region. While asleep, children can consume food and even walk some distance from one place to another which they cannot recollect after waking up. In somnambulism, adults can experience for extended periods of time, walk greater distances, drive cars etc.,. Just as the soul has to descend down from the forehead to the throat-region for making the sensory-organs of the dream-body inactive, it has to ascend upward to the forehead for making the sensory-organs active and alert. When the dream-body is out of the physical-casing, there is no need for the soul to descend down to the throat and therefore all its sensory-organs will be active.

The soul is the operating entity of the finer inner-bodies, the spiritual and the physical body. The intelligence, mind or consciousness are all immaterial properties of the soul that function and record in the mind sensations and perceptions for future rememberance and reference. Other living beings in our plane cannot remember their previous experiences, and even if they do, it is distorted because of an improper or stunted growth of the mind-body. The soul when present in the physical body has four other bodies, Thirumandiram 2127:

"The body eight span measures
With eyes, legs and hands
That serve to cover it;
In that body of pores and sores
He conjoins tattvas twenty and four
In love divine;
Thus this body He fashions,
That has four more to speak of."

The other four bodies are: The etheral or vital breath-body (Pranamaya kosa); The mind-body (Manomaya kosa); The Scientific or Intelligence-body (Vijnanamaya kosa); Causal or Bliss-body (Anandamaya kosa). Intelligence, mind and consciousness are therefore the characteristics features of the human soul. The human soul is the knower of motion, the knower of all activities and the translator of molecular activities of the brain cells into perceptions, into sensual pleasures and pain into ideas, desires and thoughts. Moreover pleasure and pain, happiness and suffering, desire and hatred are experiences of an immortal soul through the human organism while no man-made nechanism can ever perceive pain and pleasure.

If we analyse the nature of the mind, it will be seen that it is only a delicate inorganic instrument bestowed by God to the soul for recording the events in life, experienced by the soul through the five sensory-organs – the skin, tounge, nose, eyes and ears. The mind may be compared to a recording-machine like a tape or cassette-player for recording of events in life by direct experiences or by hearing or reading of the experiences of others in various walks of life. A sound recording device records our speeches and erases unwanted portions and by playing back, reproduces the required matter. In the same manner, the mind also records all our sense-perceptions and among them the sensational ones are registered in bold characters then the ordinary un-important ones. Such sensational and important occurrences are predominant in our mind and are brought to our memory and consideration more often than the other minor matters. Such consideration draw our thoughts and ideas on the matter again and again and create a desire to enjoy the same often. When such an enjoyment is repeated several times, it gets firmly rooted in the mind and turns to good or bad habits according to the development of the soul. Those weak in will-power are not able to control their senses but those with a strong one are able to control and withdraw their desires and temptations brought about by the mind by bringing back to memory a vivid picture of previous indulgences and resultant miseries attained. Thus the mind is not only a sound-recording device, but also an image-recorder and a sense-recorder in combination.

The soul gives life to plants, various creatures, birds, animals and all living-beings. Anything that has a soul, will have life and a body to operate upon with the following qualifications: it must be born in this world, it must breathe, consume food and water, it must procreate and propogate its species and it must finally die. This can be easily inferred by analyzing the birth and growth of plants, trees, animals etc., all these come to life, breathe in air, take in water and nourishment, grow up to a certain age, blossom forth flowers, buds, seeds, flowers, fruits or give birth to offspring, get old and eventually die. But plants do not possess separate sensory-organs such as the tounge, nose, eyes and ears, but they possess the sense of touch which is evident as can be seen distinctly in the plant known as "touch-me-not" whose botanical name is 'pudika mimose' which shrink immediately upon being touched and a recent finding is that when herbivores like deer start eating leaves some species of trees spray into the air a pheromone-like chemical which immediately alerts other trees which immediately turn their leaves bitter and toxic to ward-off the predators! Next are species like snails and worms with two sensory-organs, with the body and tounge to perceive the sense of touch and taste. Then come ants with their three sense-organs including the nose to the other two for smelling, feeling and tasting. Crabs, wasps and beetles are the fourth group having the fourth sensory-organ of sight. It can be therefore understood that those listed above do not have ears the fifth sensory-organ to hear sounds and the mind for recording perceptions. The fifty category are birds and animals possessing five sense-organs and in addition they possess instinct through which they are able to migrate over thousands of miles and return to their exact place of birth and feeding-grounds, like many fish like the salmon and migratory-birds like ducks and the 'artic tern', spawn and lay eggs, even without parental-guidance. Some like the dog, cat, cow, horse, elephant, parrot and dolphin are able to understand and reciprocate man's love and some are even grateful and faithfull, all this is possible for they possess a mind but at an undeveloped-state.

Finally comes man having command over all creatures with his sixth sensory-organ, the mind in a developed state. It could therefore be understood that the mind like other sensory-organs is dependent on a soul for its very operation and functioning, but a soul can operate a given body with or without the mind. Moreover without the mind it will not be possible to make any inference of the unknown cause from the known effect. For example when we witness a boxing match, we see two boxers pummel each other and finally one receives a knock-out blow to the head and he falls down dead. Although the other five senses were able to experience their limited sensations, only the mind in a developed-state is able to make an inference by deduction that an inner invisible-force that powered the body earlier had left the physical body and thus made it inert and lifeless.

Souls are 'born' (they take birth through such mediums) from eggs, sweat, seed and womb, which can be classified as 1. 'Celestials' 2. Human beings 3. Animals 4. Birds 5. Those that crawl 6. Those that live in water 7. Plants. From these seven kinds emerge 84,00,000 variations and they are accounted like this: egg-born – 25,00,000; sweat-born – 10,00,000; seed-born – 19,00,000; placenta-born – 30,00,000, and from these, countless more variations.

If a soul is to avoid all other births and is born as a human being, it would be like a person crossing the ocean by swimming in turbulent-waters fighting against time and tide. After taking numerous births in the 'lower' forms of life (84,000, eighty four thousand births to be precise according to the Lord Himself as He says in the Sri Shiva Rahsya and 6000 births as human alone) birth as a human is achieved. Birth as a human being alone gives the opportunities to put an end to the sufferings by getting out of the vicious cycle of births and deaths. Though at first man takes birth among barbarians and savages, he gradually but steadily advances and evolves by slowly getting rid of his strong ego, shunning violence and dominance over not only other human beings but other forms of life. As he starts evolving, he yearns for peace and harmony and thus in the following births takes birth in such ideal conditions among people of his own pleasant soft-nature. But man has to realize that like a caged-bird, he is still a prisoner caught-up in the whirlpool of endless suffering and agony and to break-free of the shackles, he has to yearn for 'mukti' or liberation. 'Sivagra Yogin' reminds us that if we do not realize that 'release' or liberation is not sought for in this life (in this very moment), it will be rare to attain it even after.

Though birth as a human being is so rare and precious, when it does occur, we find that its duration is uncertain which could end anytime like that of soap-bubble. Death may occur while still in the womb, or soon after birth, at a young age, at any time. Only those who understand and realize the body's impermanence try to attain release even while young and healthy of mind and body. Only through the impressions imprinted in the mind and the experiences experienced through our sensory organs are we able to come to a conclusion that an invisible force guides our thoughts and movements. Animals do not have even the memory to discriminate between mother, brother or sister after a stage, whereas man is able to recognize his close ones' throughout his life and after death also.

That we take numerous births can be understood by realizing that the knowledge possessed by an individual is the result of experience, and it grows day to day, year on end and births on end and it can never ever be nullified. If this knowledge and intelligence are attributable to one's own experience, the variations in the intelligence of the children of the same mother is traceable to the differences in the experiences in previous births called 'Karma' of their souls. We see millions and millions of persons with varying grades of intelligence and physical conditions and power, therefore it is to be understood that souls are also numerable of varying characters. We find that one person is not like the other because each soul is in a different state of development or evolvement.

When a soul lives in a body and activates it, it is known as 'Jivanma', it then begins to exhibit its power and character through the given body. The Saiva Siddhanta Scriptures of the Tamils clearly state that all souls are ignorant, where as God is all Knowledge or Wisdom. It is further stated that souls are as eternal as God. This view can be understood by comparing God to (pure) gold without 'verdigris' (the green-rust in copper) and the souls to copper with varying degrees of verdigris which can be removed by various means and processes so that copper (that is man) can be turned into gold (his original self) that is God.

So far as India is concerned, Sages known as 'Rishis','Siddhas' ('Siddhars' in Tamil) or the 'Perfected -ones','Gurus','Thirthankaras' etc., attained Enlightenment and in the enlightened-state had visions through which Celestial Divine-messages were delivered which they by way of mouth or in written texts provided them to man in simple form for his upliftment. In other countries, regions and various faiths and religions these exalted personalities are known as 'Messaihs' and 'Prophets'. All religions of this world are based on revelations of Saints and Prophets ('selected' by God Himself) and it is beyond doubt that revelations are entirely due to communications by enlightened spirits or agents from 'higher' or 'purer' worlds or planes. The word 'Enlightenment' has to be stressed because there are innumerable spirits and life-forms in various degrees of evolution which all could be contacted, and it would be wise to avoid many of them. The development of the psychic-power in the receipent medium determines the purity of the spiritual message. If the psychic-power is fully developed in the medium, the message will be pure and its originality, and if it is less, the transmission will be hindered and the message forms an admixture of the knowledge of the receipent-medium and of the communicating spirit. So the quality of the message received from the other-worlds depends upon the enlightenment-status of both the sender and the receiver. The late Swiss writer 'Erich Von Daniken' says in his book 'Miracle Of The Gods'. pg.227:" *Genius is not just diligence or the intelligent use of reason. I suspect that genius is mainly ability to open a highly trained brain to extraterrestrial energies. The extraterrestrial beings know what primordial knowledge is stored in the gray cells. If they did not know it, they could not release the lightning strokes of genius."* Daniken goes on to add that people of other worlds to contact us would not do it with radio waves, light waves or radar because of the time factor for even though they might go on to live for maybe thousands of years, we earthlings have a short life span so the ideal medium would of course be through – Visions!

The few chosen people who have had visions are not necessarily only the religious personalities. The Danish physicist Niels Bohr (1885-1962) visioned (in a dream) that he was sitting on a sun of burning gas. Hissing, spitting planets rushed by him, and they all seemed to be attached to the sun they were circling by fine threads. Suddenly gas, sun and planets contracted and solidified. Bohr at this moment woke up and atonce knew what he dreamt of – the atom model. He eventually was awarded the Nobel Prize for physics in 1962. The Harvard University Professor James D. Watson related how, lightning-like and oftern phantamagoric hints at possible solutions kept on cropping up, whether he was playing tennis, flirting or spending a pleasant weekend. Signals relating to the subject of his research appeared in his brain unexpectedly in situations that were worlds apart from his university laboratory. Watson in his book,'The Double Helix', "I huddled as close to the chimney as possible and dreamed of several DNA chains folded up in attractive and scientifically productive ways ..." James D.Watson and his colleagues Francis H.C.Crick and Maurice H.F.Wilkins in 1962 as a team received the Noble Prize for medicine for research into the make-up of the DNA molecule.

Apart from scientists, every field has its share of visionaries, musicians like Mozart, Beethoven and many others, dancers and even painters and sculptors. Michel Angelo:" *I do not know from where ideas come, perhaps from God*" – from 'Agony and Ecstasy' by Irving Stone.

The Holy Kabbalah the esoteric philosophy and theosophy concerned primarily with the mysteries of the universe and all of creation. The name is derived from the Hebrew verb 'kabel' ("to receive") and imples that the Kabbalah was received in the form of special revelations, by those of the elect, who were especially chosen for the privilege, because of their saintliness. Those who received the Kabbalah doctrine in turn transmitted it likewise only to a chosen few capable of receiving and understanding the mystic lore and using it properly.

Visions in the Holy Bible that Virgin Mary had regarding the birth of Jesus Christ in Luke,1.26 to 38. And the dream of Joseph regarding the conception of the Virgin Mary in Matt.1:20,21: 20 But after he had considered this, an angel of the Lord appeared to him in a dream.

Dreams of the Wise men (Magi), Matt.2:7 to 12. Joseph's dreams for saving the infant Jesus and Matt,2:1. After the departure of the wise men,

Joseph was ordered by the angel in a dream to take infant Jesus and his mother and flee to Egypt and to remain there until further notice as Herod wanted to destroy the child. When king Herod was dead the angel appeared in a dream to Joseph in Egypt and take infant Jesus and his mother into the land of Israel as those who sought the infants life had died. When Joseph was afraid of going into Judaea, the angel again instructed him in a dream to go into the parts of Galilee and Joseph accordingly took his residence in Nazareth that fulfilling the prophecy of the Prophet that Jesus would be known as Nazarene.

Dreams of Prophet Mohammed, Abdul Muthalif and Kadijah: The writings on the life of Prophet Mohammed says that he had dreams of the creation of the universe and the coming events in human life. Prophet Mohammed's grandfather Abdul Muthalif had dream foretelling the birth of Mohammed. Prophet Mohammed's wife Kadijah who was twice married before, dreamt in advance that she would marry Mohammed although he was fifteen years younger to her and employed under her.

Prophet Mohammed's visions: Prophet Mohammed is said to have had his first revelation at Mount Hira, where when he was asleep, someone appeared to him, squeezed and woke him up and asked him to read or recite. Prophet Mohammed replied:" I cannot read." Then he felt that he was squeezed by the vision twice with the same command, "read or recite", Mohammed asked, "what shall I recite", and his visitant said, "recite with the name of the Lord who is the creator. He has made man from a clot of blood. Read, for thy Lord is most generous. He teached man what he does not know." Mohammed recited this. The words were imprinted in his mind but the vision was not there. When he came out reciting these words, the Prophet suddenly heard a voice and raising up his head, he saw in the sky the vision he had seen before in the shape of a man calling to him and which ever way he looked he saw the same spirit, vision and heard the same voice. This and subsequent spirit revelations (of Angel Gabriel) which took place for twenty three years, laid the foundations for the Holy Quran.

Dreams of the Pandya and Chola Dynasty Kings mentioned in the 'Thiruvilayadal Puranam':

'kaduvettiya Cholan' the Chola King was an ardent Siva-devotee who continuously meditated on Lord Siva's form during the day and kept on repeating silently the Holy name even while at sleep. One day Lord Siva appeared in the dream of the king and asked him to come immediately to the Madurai Meenakshi Temple which was a few hundred miles away from his own capital and was beyond the Kaveri river. The Chola king left atonce for Madurai at mid-night and without informing his ministers or guards he went all alone knowing fully well that if he was captured by his enemies, death would be certain. The Chola king crossed dense forests and jungles, traversed over mountains and the swollen river-waters of the Kaveri within 'no-time' and went into the Holy Meenakshi Temple. The following day morning when the Pandyan King who was also a Siva-devotee went to the Temple to pay his daily abdulations to the Lord, was surprised and shocked to see the Chola king's seal on the northern gateway instead of his own 'Fish' seal. The panyan kin immediately stretched out on the floor bare-bodied and vowed to fast unto death until the the reason for the change of seal was known to him. Lord Siva appeared immediately in the dream of the Pandyan king and requested him to give off the fast, for it was He who had asked the Chola king to come to Madurai and it was He who had changed the seal on the northern gateway entrance.

Lord Buddha's Vision: It is said that just before Prince Siddhartha's (who became the Buddha) renunciation, he went one night into the garden of his palace and sat under a 'jamun' tree (it was only several years later he attained 'Nirvana' or enlightenment sitting under the 'Pipal' tree) and was pondering on the problems of life and death and the miseries and sorrows of this world. When he saw a vision of a lofty, majestic, calm and dignified figure. He conversed with the celestial messenger and had many doubts cleared. The messenger in the course of their conversation said, *"go out Siddhartha and accomplish your purpose, thou art Buddha, the Buddha elect, thou art destined to enlighten the world. Perseverance is thy quest and thou shalt find what you sleekest. Struggle earnestly and thou shalt conquer, heavenly wisdom guides thy steps. Thou shalt be the Buddha, you will enlighten the world."* Having thus spoken the vision vanished, this was the turning pint in prince Siddhartha's life. This resulted in Buddha's immediate resolve, *"verily I shalt become the Buddha."* He then went into his bedroom, took a last look at his beautiful princess and beloved child, bid them silent farewell, tore himself away from them, renounced all worldly pleasures, gave up his kingdom and went out into the silent night in search after Divine Truth.

The Holy Kabbalah is the Jewish esoteric philosophy and theosophy concerned primarily with the mysteries of the universe and all of creation. The name is derived from the Hebrew verb 'Kabel' – "to receive" and implies that *the Kabbalah was received in the form of special revelations* by those of the elect, who were especially chosen for the privilege, because of their saintliness. Those who received the Kabbalah doctrine in turn transmitted it likewise only to a chosen few capable of receiving and understanding the mystic lore and using it properly.

Earth getting Contaminated by Extraterrestrial Bacteria?

J.J.Merrick the English physicist, presented a paper to the tenth biological symposium at Cold Spring Harbor, Long Island in 1962, it was entitled "Frequencies of biological contact according to speciation probabilities".

Rudoph Karp, a Hungarian born biochemist put to vigorous test, meteorites that had fallen on earth,(the meteorites to avoid contamination were washed in twelve solutions including peroxide, iodine, hypertonic saline and dilute acids). They were then exposed to ultra-violet light for two days then finally submerged ina germicidal solution and placed in a germ-free, sterile isolation chamber, further work was done within the chamber, which were then found to contain ring-shaped living organisms. These organisms were essentially similar to earthly bacteria in structure, being based upon proteins, carbohydrates and lipids. Since they had no nucleus as such, scientists wonder how reproduction was done.

Merrick further says that the earth could be more likely struck by simple organisms like uni-cellular ones than multi-cellular organisms ince they exist here and all over the cosmos in large numbers. There are billions of species of bacteria, thousands of species of insects, but only a few species of animals, four species of apes and only species of man. Although there are over three billion people on earth, a single large flask contains a hundred times that of bacteria. Issac Asimov, in his book,'Change':" *The human body is constructed of fifty trillion cells (50,000,000,000,000), each of those cells is made of the same number of atoms.*" If man contains such a large number of bacteria, imagine the numbers present in the cosmos! Merrick again, "*All available evidence on the origin of life points to an evolutionary progression from simple to complex life –forms. This is true on earth. It is probably true throughout the universe. Three percent of all earth-bacteria are capable of exertingdeleterious effect upon man. If this is so, it is disturbing to think to what extent extra-terrestrial bacteria contact would have on us!"*

Scientists also know of other planes and dimensions, in fact NASA states that there are atleast 11 dimensions. Carl Sagan in his book,'Cosmos' says that there could be living-beings as well as intelligent-beings in atleast eighteen thousand planets and stars, being the most conservative estimate taking into account the vastness of space and the countless number of stars and planets existent for countless eons.

NASA and SETI (search for Extra-terrestrial intelligence) researchers say that 16 cygni C and 47 Utsae Majoris B are two planets within the so-called habitable zone due to surface water available on them, hence there is a high probability of living beings present on them. Moreover contrary to the thought that the cosmos is a barren place, it was found in 1969 that there is inter-stellar water and consequently in '69 formaldehyde, in '72 methyl alcohol, in '74 methylamine, in'76 ketene, in '78 methane, in '80 ethylene, in '84 methyl diacetylene, in '87 methyl iso cyanide, in '90 buta trieenylidene, in '95 carbon monoxide and in '96 hydrogen cyanide presence was found which proves right the ancient Indian and Tamil claim that everything in space exists in the human body (*andathil ullathu pindathil*) and everything has 'life' in it.

Evolution

Contrary to Tim White's (University of California, Berkeley) claim:" *Darwin was right: humans evolved from an African ape*", ancient Indian scripts say that about 30 million years ago,'ape-like' man and the ape *both* stood more than 50 to 60 feet tall and that he existed in the 'Lemuria' continent which was a great mass of mountain and forest-filled land that covered what is now the pacific ocean and land below Africa and India and existed all the way south to Australia and New Zealand. But, even this was only the 'third' race of man, the first two had risen and evolved elsewhere!

The First Race of Man

Several billions of years ago when the earth was cooling and settling down from the fiery gaseous-ball it was, there were no solid substances to be found. The earth orbited the sun as a smoke smothered ball, belching out fire and smoke. After tens of millions of years the earth started to cool down and there were patches of soft-ground to be found on the surface. The earth's crust as it were was very unstable and tended to drift here and there as the major part of the earth was in liquid molten-form with molten-metals like iron and copper along with gushing out lava to be found slushing about on the surface and inbetween there were only patches of soft ground to be found.

The first human-form was introduced at that time in the northern hemisphere and the form was that of vapor. Man stood nearly 175 feet tall and drifted about like the clouds, having a hazy form and a little more dense in the centre. Propagation was performed by the vapor-form of man splitting into two, not unlike the clouds that are split apart by the wind. Like we breathe in air, nourishment was sucked-in like the spong or blotting-paper draws in water, and wastes also were discarded by squeezing them out.

As he evolved over tens of millions of years, man's height gradually reduced from 175 feet to 120 feet or so. He had the sense of touch only and his intelligence, functions and customs were on par with the plant kingdom. After several hundreds of millions of years, he took a more solid-form and was prepared to evolve into the second race.

The Second Race of Man

The second race of man evolved in a great piece of land which lay in the shape of a horse-shoe in what is now ice-land. At that time there was a type of solid land to be found on the earth's northern and southern hemisphere, yet when a hole was dug on the surface, fire and hot lava would gush out and at places shoot-ot like a fountain. Copper mostly in molten-form was found on the surface, hence the temperature must have been around 3500 centigrade.

The form of man at that period was like that of a huge gigantic earthworm measuring nearly 120 feet long. He mostly crawled and rolled his way around and at times when he would try to stand upright, he would topple over like a gigantic sack packed lightly with cotton or hay. When he came into contact with anything solid, a depression of identical dimensions would appear on his soft putty-like body and would take time to fill-up and regain its former shape. When hot or cold objects came into contact with his body, small finger-like projections telescoped out of his body like a snail or turtle would project its head out of its shell and slowly retract them.

After tens of thousands of years, his movement brought forth growths on the surface of his body which he started to use as feet and he some what resembled our present day hippopotamus, only many times bigger and longer. He now swallowed his food in what appeared to be a mouth into a huge tube-shaped organ that turned out to be his stomach. To get rid of his wastes, he coughed out them along with sand and stones along with his stomach and then swallowed back his empty stomach like we pull out the inside of a sack and push it back to its former position. Propagation was performed by small boil-like growths falling off from his body and growing into new-ones and finding food and fending for themselves (this type of reproduction we can even find now in amoeba abd some species of plants). Death occurred when he gradually shrank, shriveled and dried-up and after death his body resembled that of the dried discarded skin an enormous snake or reptile.

The Third Race of Man

The third race of man evolved in the Lemuria continent which was a great mass of land that existed below south India and extended all the way south to Australia and New Zealand in the south, Africa on the east and the American continent on the west. The land was completely filled with forest, rivers, lakes, mountains and waterfalls.

After many millions of years, man was able to stand upright at times and his form also took a more solid shape. He now stood more than 50 to 60 feet tall and resembled a huge ape. He was jet-black in color, had a huge egg-shaped head with the upper-part being pointed and conical while the lower part being his jaw was blunt and broad. He had no forehead as such and had one large eye in the centre. His limbs were long and when he stood upright, which he rarely did, his arms reached all the way to the ground. His elbows and knees were in a bent-position and for fast locomotion, he used both arms and legs to lope like the rpresent day gorilla.

Though man's bones started to grow stronger and hair sprouted all over his body, the surface of his body was still soft to the touch and the depression caused by coming into contact with anything hard, too a bit of time to fill-up. Propagation was done by sweating-out germs which grew into new ones.

In the span of ten million years, man's body took a more solid shape and the single eye he had in the front slowly travelled up and descended to the back of his head and simultaneously wo new eyes sprouted in the front. As he now possessed three eyes like a coconut has, he could look both to the front and back at the same time, and since his feet extended both to the front and back, he could also walk both forward and backward with ease.

There were no distinction in the sexes for man possessed both the male and female sexual organs, he(mankind) laid eggs and hatched them.

Slow changes in the aforesaid nature of man over a period of 5 million years or so gradually made the egg-shells of man to grow thinner so the incubation period likewise grew much less than it previously was. The newly-borns also slowly developed separate male and female sexual organs and their brain and nervous-system also began developing. Now only the female laid eggs and hatched them and this procedure continued for millions of years.

Mankind after some major changes and developments started to deliver young-ones like we presently do, that is, the foetus grew inside the womb and was delivered through the uterus. Reminiscence of the egg-laying era is the placenta now found in the present-day woman. This change to take place itself took over 5 million years and for the past 10 million years or so only humans have been delivering their offspring in this manner.

The single 'third-eye' at the back of the head gradually disappeared into the head, which presently now is the pituitary-gland, a source of extraordinary-powers.

Man who had shortened greatly was still 25 to 27 feet tall, he had a terrifying-appearance, was raven-black in color and lived the life of an animal, a savage. At that time, for the development of mankind, the evolutionary-cycle and nature as a whole, a wonderfull event took place by God's Grace. In Central Asia, in what is now the Gobi desert, was a huge sea in which were two big islands known as 'Suvaydeepam' and 'Sambalam'. These two islands had beautiful meadows, waterfalls, rivers, lakes and lovely lagoons. On the island of Suvayadeepam landed 'fiery-chariots' (Agni ratha) which flew down from the 'fifth plane' (Sathya loka) bearing the four 'mind-born' (manasa puthra) sons of Lord Brahma (one among the Holy Trinity) the Creator accompanied by 30 assistants. The four 'god-men' were 'Sanaka','Sananthana', 'Sanathana' and 'Sanatkumara' generally and jointly known as the 'Sanahathi Munivars' and widely mentioned in many Puranas and are among the foremost of the pantheon of Sages. The four sages had received direct Initiation from the Primal Lord Himself, Lord Siva (Shiva in Sanskrit) in 'Kailash' the Holy-realm. The initiation was performed in the highest manner possible, with the Lord sitting in total silent communion with His hands showing the 'chin mudra' whereby the the index-finger and thumb are folded touching each other forming a perfect circle with the other three fingers aligned straight together symbolizing that when pride, arrogance and ego are eradicated, God and man meet to become One. Among the four sages, Lord Sanatkumara is said to be sixteen years old for eternity.

The four sages stayed here on earth for 400,000 (four hundred thousand) years and greatly enhanced the rate of the growth of the evolutionary cycle. The appearance, intelligence and higher qualities of mankind as well as the entire evolutionary process as a whole took vast rapid changes. Changes which took over billions of years now took within a few years. Evolution until then had been growing at the rate of 6+6+6= 18, now took to the ratio of 6x6x6= 216. The fourth race of mankind (the world and man that we know) had started to take root.

Conclussion

Man (after innumerable births as shrubs, grass, plants, trees, insects, reptiles, birds, animals, domesticated animals etc.,) at first takes birth as a savage who kills, tortures, consumes other forms of life as well as his own. After untold suffering, pain and misery he starts to loathe and finally yearn for peace. He thus evolves, takes birth among like-minded good-natured and kind-hearted people and further ascends. But by attaining enlightenment through Yoga, he finally realizes that he, the worlds all of humanity and all forms of life are part and parcel of a single entity.

Perfection or enlightenment is within the reach of all of humanity and only ignorance is what that veils or clouds our mind. Many are the veils (otherwise known as 'Maya' – the illusive Power of God) and the Perfected one's have known that there lies a veil between each of the subtle bodies of man that prove to be a hindrance to the flow of energy that emanate and are received by the 'chakras'. The veils partially dissipiate only in dreams and when on the verge of death and that is why many people are able to see, hear, communicate and experience 'after-death' and "out of body experiences" commonly known as o.b.e.'s. But the Yogi in deep contemplation is able to remove and transcend all veils and thus transcends all planes and dimensions and therefore is beyond dream and reality, life and death.

The Zen masters have rightly said: *"the mind is nowhere in particular"* – and similarly the full-blown Yogi (Purna Yogi) can be anywhere in space at any given moment. Vivekananda on Maya:" *Maya is not a theory; it is a statement of facts. Maya is the ever-present scintillating Power of God. Due to the strength of this power, truly one substance shows itself as multiduinous forms in this cosmos. Gold which is one, manifests as many objects of jewellery, similarly God explains himself as the mayaic cosmos."* The Holy Bible too teaches that there is a veil over his mind in Cor. 2:14. And in the Holy Qur'an's introduction, c.31: *"The veil was lifted from the chosen one's eyes, And his Soul for a moment was filled with divine Ecstasy ..."* Carl Jung the psychoanalyst too explains that there are "blocked-off memories" (that has the collective memories of numerous lives starting from single-celled protozoa right up to man and that these are passed on in the DNA, and that 'Total Recall' is possible) and man can by delving deeply into his mind, transcend from the lower or 'animal-mind' to the higher mind, ascend to the state of no-mind and become the 'Knower' of all which is actually Total Recall; Thirumoolar a Tamil Siddhar or Perfected Being who lived for 3000 years in his Thirumandiram 2548:

"When maya veils jiva (the Soul),
The Truth (God) of Vedas remain hidden;
When maya leaves, The Truth of Himself reveals;
Those who can make maya vanish merge in God;
No more is body, no more is mind."

Just as the umbilical-cord connecting the baby to its mother has to be cut to become a separate individual, an astral shimmering silver-cord connects the physical and astral bodies of man gets severed at the time of death. In the dream-state the silver cord along with the astral bodies extends to any length and in fact Yogis with the sight of the third-eye can see the astral bodies (with extended silver-cords) of kind and noble-hearted persons float all over the globe and even go beyond with intentions of only the upliftment of all forms of life. The Holy Bible mentions this silver-cord in Ecc.12:6.

One need not fear death, when one realizes that he can break-free from the prison that is his body of desires and cravings, he in a moment becomes physically and spiritually liberated and like the free bird that lives in a nest and not in a cage, can soar at the place and time of his choice and liking. This victory over death alone is true victory and such a liberated Soul is no more caught in the vicious cycle of birth and death.

Yoga is the means to get over the worst-case scenario the world now faces pointed out by the following two intellectual luminaries among hosts of others - Jean Paul Satre, the French existentialist:"*There is no exit from the human dilemma*" and Sir Winston Churchill on the world's dilemma:"*Our problems are beyond us.*" Though Mahatma Gandhi was an apostle of peace, he too like Martin Luther King was felled by the bullet. One has to go beyond the mind and thinking to the heart-centre of love, compassion, sympathy and empathy radiated by persons like Rabindranath Tagore who even refused to tread the garden-lawns with Gandhi for he deeply felt empathy with the living grass.

To transform the world, the individual has to first transform himself into an ocean of love, peace and bliss and for that through Yoga one can reach his core which as the Vedas say is an ocean of bliss and bliss that is equal to the Lord's, that state is beautifully explained in the Bible in Phil.4:7. Through Yoga one attains both material and spiritual wealth, name, fame and everything is secondary, but along with peace these too are added benefits according to The Bible, Matt. 6:33. The Kingdom of God is not in a faraway place, and there are numerous 'tantras' or techniques through which the Lord's infinite-nature could be attained and experienced here and now, some are as simple as by aligning oneself with the breath or by realizing that one is nothing but pure consciousness. The 'Holy Feet' of the Lord exists as the 'Nada Bindu' – the 'Eternal Sound-Light Vibrations' or 'The Eternal Continuum' above the crown of the head and when one surrenders at the holy Feet of the Lord who is beyond the "pair of opposites" who has no likes and dislikes, what more is there to be attained? When one through yogic means transcends the invisible astral-barrier known as the 'anda kosa yellai' (universe-body barrier' literally in Tamil) he breaks the Cosmic-barrier and becomes the Source of all knowledge – Divine Wisdom.

Printed in the United States
By Bookmasters